Quality Health Care: A Guide to Developing and Using Indicators

Quality Health Care:
A Guide to Developing
and Using Indicators

Robert C. Lloyd, Ph.D.
Director, Quality Resource Services
Advocate Health Care
Oak Brook, Illinois

JONES AND BARTLETT PUBLISHERS
Sudbury, Massachusetts
BOSTON   TORONTO   LONDON   SINGAPORE

World Headquarters

Jones and Bartlett
Publishers
40 Tall Pine Drive
Sudbury, MA 01776
978-443-5000
info@jbpub.com
www.jbpub.com

Jones and Bartlett
Publishers Canada
2406 Nikanna Road
Mississauga, ON L5C 2W6
CANADA

Jones and Bartlett
Publishers International
Barb House, Barb Mews
London W6 7PA
UK

Library of Congress Cataloging-in-Publication Data
Lloyd, Robert C.
  Quality health care : a guide to developing and using indicators /
Robert Lloyd.— 1st ed.
    p. ; cm.
Includes bibliographical references and index.
  ISBN 0-7637-4805-6 (hardcover)
  1. Medical care—Quality control. 2. Medical care—Evaluation. 3.
Medical care—Quality control—Case studies. 4. Medical
care—Evaluation—Case studies. 5. Quality assurance. 6. Outcome
assessment (Medical care)—Methodology.
  [DNLM: 1. Quality of Health Care—organization & administration. 2.
Program Development. 3. Quality of Health Care—Case Report. W 84.1
L793q 2004] I. Title.
  RA399.A1L567 2004
  362.1'068'5—dc22

                                                    2003021998

Production Credits
Publisher: Michael Brown
Associate Editor: Chambers Moore
Production Manager: Amy Rose
Production Assistant: Tracey Chapman
Composition and Art: Dartmouth Publishing, Inc.
Cover Design and Art: Anne Spencer
Marketing Manager: Joy Stark-Vancs
Manufacturing Buyer: Therese Bräuer
Printing and Binding: Malloy, Inc.
Cover Printing: Malloy, Inc.

Printed in the United States of America
08 07 06 05 04   10 9 8 7 6 5 4 3 2 1

Dedication

This book is dedicated to all those who work tirelessly to overcome numerical illiteracy and improve quality. Thanks for your leadership and courage.

Table of Contents

Introduction

A previous book by Carey and Lloyd (2001) outlines the foundation for applying statistical process control (SPC) methods to health care situations. As I have used this book to teach classes and seminars on SPC, however, it soon became clear to me that a number of measurement challenges were still facing health care professionals. Specifically, I discovered that the key concepts related to SPC, such as common and special causes of variation, variables and attributes data, and proper control chart selection, were quickly being grasped and understood. What health care professionals seemed to be struggling with most often, however, was something I had taken for granted: I had assumed that people knew what they wanted to measure and how to organize data collection efforts. It is difficult to apply control chart knowledge if you have not defined appropriate indicators and collected data that accurately represent the process being measured. Control charts developed from poor data may look nice graphically but they have no utility for improving care processes. Helping health care professionals address issues related to indicator development and data collection, therefore, are the primary objectives of this book. In many ways this work is a prequel to the first book.

Chapter 1 provides a context for understanding quality measurement. This context needs to be framed within a historical perspective. Specifically, the current pressures on the health care industry are not the singular result of managed care as many people seem to believe. The current pressures we are witnessing result from a multitude of forces that had their origins in the mid 1960s when Medicare and Medicaid programs were first established and culminate with recent growing demands for the public release of provider data. This chapter provides an overview of the key political and social forces that have shaped the transformation of the health care industry in the United States. It concludes by discussing various definitions of the term quality and the three key components that form the building blocks of continuous quality improvement (CQI).

In Chapter 2 the first building block of CQI is discussed. All quality journeys should begin by listening to the voice of the customer (VOC), the point at which you can learn what your customers want, need, and expect. The growing role of the customers and methods for documenting their expectations are the central topics in this chapter. Three key listening points in the customer experience are identified (pre-service, point-of-service, and post-service), and a variety of tools designed to capture data at these critical junctures are reviewed. This chapter ends with a brief example of how VOC measurement needs to be connected with voice of the process (VOP) measurement in order to make CQI a practical reality.

Chapter 3 provides details on how to select and develop specific indicators. All too often organizations take a serious detour in their quality measurement journeys because they try to measure a broad concept (e.g., patient safety) rather than identifying specific indicators that could be used to measure actual performance (e.g., medication errors per 100 admissions or the percentage of patients appropriately placed on bed alarms). This chapter provides specific guidance in selecting indicators, developing operational definitions, and executing data collection strategies (including stratification and sampling). A template is also offered to assist the reader in working through all the issues involved with selecting and building a few good indicators.

After a number of specific indicators have been developed, there is value in organizing them into a cogent and parsimonious format that can be shared with those who do not need to know all the details involved with indicator development.

Chapter 4 begins by characterizing the similarities and differences between two popular ways of organizing indicators—report cards and dashboards. The argument is made that the dashboard concept is much more relevant to health care performance measurement than is the notion of the report card. Examples of dashboards are offered, and recommendations are made for building integrated performance measurement systems that can be used at the department or board level.

After collecting data and organizing your indicators, the next major milestone in the quality measurement journey is to tap the knowledge that hides in the data. Chapters 5 addresses four topics related to this challenge: (1) the differences between data and information, (2) the role of research for efficacy, (3) the role of research for efficiency and effectiveness, and (4) the differences between static and dynamic approaches to data.

With these distinctions established, Chapter 6 provides the technical details that will help the reader to understand the variation that is an inherent part of every process and the statistical tools of quality improvement. In particular, two tools are described in detail, the run and control charts. The foundations for using these practical statistical tools are discussed as well as the basic elements of the charts, decision criteria for selecting the appropriate chart, and rules for detecting special causes of variation. This chapter closes with recommendations on how to make the appropriate management decision when faced with common and special causes of variation.

Chapter 7 presents fourteen case studies designed to demonstrate how the various quality measurement principles and tools can be applied to health care situations. These examples span a wide range of topics, including indicator selection and development, sampling applications, and control chart analysis. The case studies address clinical as well as operational aspects of health care delivery. A majority of them are based on the actual work of CQI teams that I have had the pleasure of assisting during their quality measurement journeys. Teams that were kind enough to share their actual data and stories are recognized by name. I celebrate their successes and appreciate their willingness to share their experiences with others.

The final chapter, like the first, takes a broad perspective and focuses on three levels of transformation that need to be addressed in order to make CQI an integral part of the health care industry. I firmly believe that personal, organizational, and societal transformation is required before our health care system can truly be considered a system and function at its optimum capability. At present, it functions more like a fragmented collection of independent parts than as an integrated system. We seem to have more of a sickness system than a health care system. The system functions best when you are sick and need to be admitted to a hospital. It does not function as well, however, in keeping people healthy and out of the hospital. When you think about it, however, the present structure and functioning of the health care system is totally consistent with the incentives that have been established. The payment mechanisms provide the greatest reward when people are admitted to the hospital, not when they are kept out of the hospital. If the health care industry is to be successful in transitioning from the First Curve to the Second Curve (Merry 2003) and experience a true paradigm shift (Kuhn 1996) in the way we structure and deliver care, then we need to address redesign and transformation—not mere incremental improvement. We need to stop viewing health care as a series of specialized functions that are not connected and begin to demonstrate systems thinking. We need to understand the interrelationships among costs, quality, and access instead of viewing them as tradeoffs. We need to measure what we do, make sense out of the variation that lives in our processes, and then have the courage to change behaviors and processes when they fail to meet the expectations of those we serve.

References

Kuhn. T. *The Structure of Scientific Revolutions.* Chicago: University of Chicago Press, 1996.

Merry, M. "Healthcare's Need for Revolutionary Change." *Quality Progress* (September 2003): 31-35.

Preface

In many ways our present American health care system reminds us of the opening lines of Dickens' *A Tale of Two Cities*. Health care today represents both the best of times and the worst of times. The technological capability of today's health care system is nothing short of astonishing, even for a physician trained in the early 1970s. Transplants, microsurgery, remarkable pharmaceuticals and genomics offer patients cures that I could never have offered my patients even in the early 1980s, my final years of medical practice. But this wonderful progress also has a darker side that has been largely unrecognized until very recently. This same system that delivers miraculous cures is now correctly understood as potentially harmful to those it seeks to serve.

Many readers are familiar with the notion of the canary in the coal mine, a 19th-century practice of British coal miners taking canaries into coal mines. If the canaries died, the miners were warned of potentially lethal gases emanating from the tunnels. In this tradition, several "canaries" of the modern American health care system "coal mine" have arisen. One of the earliest prophetic voices, Ivan Illich, claimed in his 1976 book, *Medical Nemesis*, the "medical establishment has become a major threat to health." Dr. Robert Lloyd, in this major contribution to moving health care quality forward, cites others who have similarly identified health care's darker side. Modern health care's remarkable technological capability is, in fact, a double-edged sword. Along with a remarkable ability to cure, our present health care system has evolved with an unintended capability to harm, even inadvertently to kill, those it seeks to cure. It is because of this newly understood element of modern health care that Dr. Lloyd's book is both timely and important.

How could such a paradoxical situation have evolved? Dr. Lloyd has a deep understanding of this paradox and a very thoughtful concept of how health care leaders at every level of their organizations—from department chairpersons to CEOs to board members—might energize the curing side of our industry and simultaneously minimize harm.

This book is an extremely important contribution to health care quality literature. As Dr. Lloyd documents in Chapter 1, health care quality was largely assumed until the early 1980s. Prior to this time, all doctors were assumed to be first in their medical school classes, and all hospitals "simply the best". Then, in 1979, things gradually began to change. The Joint Commission on Accreditation of Hospitals (JCAH, soon to evolve into Joint Commission on Accreditation of Healthcare Organizations—JCAHO) created its Quality Assurance Standard. This event was perhaps the first "official" recognition that health care quality isn't a given—it instead varies among those delivering services. Like any other endeavor of the "real world", health care can be excellent—or "not-so-good."

In the decades since JCAHO promulgated this standard, we have learned just how variable excellent versus not-so-good health care quality can be. Dr. Lloyd documents this well in this book. In fact, he draws upon an extensive literature documenting our modern understanding of the vast variation in the quality of health care received by U.S. citizens. He also offers comprehensive references to the best of recent health-care quality literature.

How is one to make sense of this paradoxical "Tale of Two Health Care Systems"? In this book, Dr. Lloyd offers definitive answers this question. In the tradition of Paul Starr's *The Social Transformation of American Medicine* and Michael Millenson's *Demanding Medical Excellence* (which this book should accompany on any serious health care reader's bookshelf), Dr. Lloyd offers a unique contribution. This book is not simply a comprehensive compilation of virtually all that is known about the application of what I call the modern quality science (Shewhart, Deming, Juran, Six Sigma, Human Factors, etc.). It is all that these names imply, including an extensive list of references for the best-of-the-best of modern health care quality science. But further—and perhaps this is this book's greatest power—it is a personal essay of Dr. Lloyd's own journey toward Six Sigma excellence within his own health care system. In this book Dr. Lloyd offers not only excellent, in-depth knowledge of the tools and techniques of modern quality science as it applies to health care, but also his personal extensive experience with this science, particularly as he and his colleagues have applied it within his own health care system. And this is an especially important point. Dr. Lloyd writes not from an academic or ivory-tower, but instead from the perspective of one who has worked in the trenches to improve the quality of both clinical and operational processes. Especially in this context, the extensive case studies he describes (Chapter 7) are so important. He writes not from just what *should* be, but what *can* be, based upon his work in the health care system.

Yes, this book **is** about theory. But it is also about the practical application of theory to practice! For any health care leader who whines, "I'd like to give better quality, but I don't know how," this book offers a compelling and detailed response: "OK, here's how to do it—from A to Z!"

Dr. Lloyd is, in fact, much more than a canary in a coal mine. He positively affirms that our present health care system is miraculous. He also has the courage to affirm that it is also potentially dangerous to those it serves. He is thus a visionary leader, expressing in this book not only an implicit vision but also a very pragmatic set of concepts and an explicit path by which leaders might build a culture of excellence.

This book is a major contribution to the advancement of health care quality. It is also a very personal sharing by a person who is both an expert in health care quality—and a human being who cares deeply about how we might all achieve our implicit goal of "miraculous curing," even as we tenaciously pursue the ancient Hippocratic dictum to "first, do no harm." In reading this book, you will inevitably become more knowledgeable about what health care quality really is, and you will have the opportunity to become a better leader, in whatever position you hold in your organization.

Martin Merry, MD
Adjunct Association Clinical Professor
of Health Management and Policy,
University of New Hampshire
Senior Advisor for Medical Affairs,
New Hampshire Hospital Association
and Foundation for Healthy Communities
Exeter, New Hampshire
January, 2004

Acknowledgments

Any journey, whether it is large or small, contains numerous stories and a variety of encounters with many individuals. The development, writing, and production of this book has been an interesting journey that requires acknowledging several specific individuals as well as a number of groups. I was first approached to consider writing this book back in the fall of 2000 by a publisher that later decided to stop producing books on healthcare topics. To my great good fortune, however, the original publisher transferred the rights to publish this book to Jones and Bartlett Publishers. Mike Brown, publisher for healthcare books at Jones and Bartlett made sure the transition was not only smooth but virtually seamless. Mike has been a wonderful sponsor and very tolerant of my need to revise the proposed work plan when my wife was diagnosed with breast cancer. I basically needed to take the better part of a year off and attend to my wife's treatment and care. Mike was not only sensitive to this unexpected detour in the journey but always asked first about my wife's health, then about any progress on the book. Thanks for your professionalism and compassion, Mike.

I also want to thank Chambers Moore, associate editor, Tracey Chapman, production assistant, Lori Rider, copy editor, and Joy Stark-Vancs, marketing manager, at Jones and Bartlett for all they did during the production phase. Chambers provided project oversight while Tracey Chapman handled all my frequent questions about style preferences, layout, and format with patience and a high degree of customer service. Lori Rider did a wonderful job of editing the original manuscript. Her attention to detail and consistency are gratefully appreciated. Joy handled all the marketing and design aspects for this project. I have been very impressed with the professionalism and courtesy of the Jones and Bartlett team. You have made this journey very easy and quite enjoyable.

There are many individuals who have provided either examples or stories that I have used in this book or discussed ideas related to data issues or the case studies. To all of you I am grateful. Individuals who made substantive contributions to the content or case studies are recognized in chapters and footnotes.

There are several individuals, however, that I would like to acknowledge specifically. At Advocate Health Care I want to thank Lee Sacks, MD, Executive Vice President and Chief Medical Officer and Lois Elia, Vice President of Clinical Excellence for encouraging me to pursue this project. I also want to thank Bill Santulli, currently Advocate's Chief Operating Officer, for sponsoring the development of the Performance Improvement (PI) Showcase while he was Chief Executive Officer at Advocate Good Samaritan Hospital. The PI Showcase served as the testing ground for many of the ideas, concepts, and case studies presented in this book. Also at Advocate Health Care I want to thank my friend and colleague Judi Miller, Director, Decision Support Services/Chief Privacy Officer for the many years we have spent together developing tools and methods aimed at indicator development. She has taught me a great deal about coding issues, automated databases, and regulatory standards. Thanks Judi for your practical perspectives and collaboration over the years. I want to extend a special thank you to Karen Svab and Kathleen Piet who work with me in the Quality Resource Services department at Advocate Health Care. Karen carefully reviewed initial drafts of the manuscript and used her artistic talents to create several of the graphs used in Chapters 5 and 6. Kathleen, thanks for keeping me organized, reminding me of conference calls with Jones and Bartlett staff, and making sure that the faxes and mailings were handled in a timely manner.

While too numerous to mention by name, I would also like to thank all the administrators, department managers, front-line staff, and physicians who have joined me in my quality classes. In these sessions we have addressed specific issues related to operational definitions, sampling, control chart selection, and interpretation of the results. You have been the inspiration for the examples and case studies I have developed. Thanks for your ideas and willingness to share. Without you this book would never have become a reality.

Finally, I want to thank my wife Gwenn and daughter Devon for bringing quality to my life's journey. You've been tolerant of my quick retreats after dinner to work on "the book." You've been patient when I did not complete my household duties on time or asked to be excused from a weekend bike ride. You've been there when I needed a laugh and a hug. Thanks for your love and support of my work. I promise that I won't start another book for at least ...well, at least for awhile.

Chapter 1

Setting the Context

Believe it or not, there was a time when data and measurement were not at the center of the healthcare debate. For example, when a patient went to see a doctor back in the 1950s, 1960s, or even the early 1970s, he or she usually said, "Thank you very much, Doctor. How much do I owe you?" Today it is more likely that the patient will ask questions such as these: "Where did you get your medical degree? How many times have you done this procedure? What is the complication rate associated with this procedure? Do you have data to show that this procedure will improve my health? Have you had a malpractice claim filed against you in the past five years?" Then, if the patient is really actively involved in their own healthcare delivery, he or she will probably pull out a piece of paper and inform the doctor, "This is what I found on the Internet last night and here is what I think is wrong with me. . . ."

Over the past two decades the healthcare industry has moved away from being an industry based on trust and partnership between physicians and their patients to one of gentle (and at times not so gentle) tension between those who provide care, those who receive it, and those who pay for it. Whenever society begins to lose confidence in an institution, there is typically a demand for greater oversight of the institution and a related push for more data on the institution and the products or services it provides.[1] This has certainly been the case in healthcare. Increasingly healthcare professionals are being asked not only to explain why they do what they do but also to provide data that demonstrate consistent performance that does not harm patients. The move away from an absolute trust in the medical system and its providers to a perspective that demands data as proof of competency represents a fundamental shift in how this nation views the healthcare industry. Yet this shift has not occurred overnight. It has basically been developing over the past thirty years.

A Brief Review of Healthcare Reform

Understanding the growing demand for data to document the quality of healthcare services and outcomes requires a clear understanding of the forces that have brought us to this point. Contrary to some popular misconceptions, however, it is not simply the growth of managed care that has "caused" healthcare to be very different from what it was "in the old days." Managed care is merely an alternative approach to organizing the delivery and financial aspects of healthcare. While the managed care industry has certainly made some questionable decisions about the cost/quality trade-off, the wide variation we see in access, costs, outcomes, customer service, and quality cannot be laid solely at the feet of managed care.

Many factors have contributed to making our healthcare system what is today.[2] Figure 1.1 shows some of the key forces that have been affecting the healthcare industry for more than twenty years. It is difficult to point to any one of these factors and say that it is the cause of healthcare reform in this country. As with most things in life, one causal factor cannot be singled out. Our own individual lives, as well as societal events, are basically large multivariate causal models (Blalock 1971) that contain several direct effects but many indirect effects. None of the factors in Figure 1.1 have "caused" our healthcare system to change by themselves. Collectively, however, they have been able to fundamentally transform how care is financed, delivered, and perceived.

A few of the more significant events impacting the U.S. healthcare system are highlighted below. Some of these events made national headlines, but others went largely unnoticed by most of the public and even by many healthcare professionals.[3] For my purposes, I am not dealing with events that occurred prior to 1965. As fascinating as the clinical and social events prior to 1965 were, they have been covered thoroughly in other sources (Codman 1917; Peabody 1927; Starr 1982; Millenson 1999). Since my objective is to discuss the dramatic increase in the role of data and measurement in the healthcare industry, 1965 serves as a key starting point for the present discussion.

Prior to 1965, healthcare was based essentially on what is known as a cost-based retrospective reimbursement. Patients would receive care or treatment, and the fees associated with the service were paid after the fact (i.e., retrospectively). There was little concern over how much a procedure

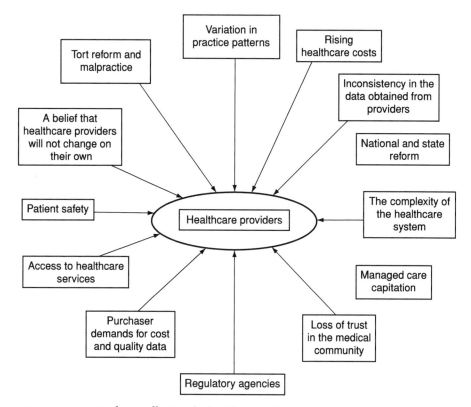

▲ FIGURE 1.1 Key forces affecting the healthcare industry

or a hospital stay would cost. Virtually no one (individual, employer, or insurance company) ever asked the physician up front, "How much will this service or procedure cost?" The basic principle was, if a procedure or test was ordered, it must be needed. The corollary to this principle was, "If we order it, someone will pay for it." This was the time in which standing orders were customary and expected even if they were not required clinically. Why? Because the test or procedure would be paid for by someone. At that time physicians, hospital administrators, and patients were all quite happy. Physicians were in total control of patient care decisions, consumer interest groups and state data commissions were not prominent, politicians did not place healthcare professionals under a microscope, and the medical profession was viewed in a very positive light (e.g., Dr. Kildare, Dr. Ben Casey, and Dr. Marcus Welby were role models on television for the medical profession). Hospital administrators were likewise happy because they reaped their success from that of the physicians. Laboratories were busy, operating rooms were at capacity, and the hospital administrators were very closely aligned with the business interests in the community.[4] Finally, the patients were happy because they could basically get whatever they wanted whenever they wanted it. Access was not an issue, and the notion of managed care was far off in the distance.

In 1965, the Johnson administration, as part of its Great Society programs, instituted Medicare and Medicaid. While cost-based reimbursement was still the primary payment methodology, new ideas and perspectives about how to organize, deliver, and pay for healthcare services were emerging. During the late 1960s the health maintenance organization (HMO) concept also started to gain momentum in California and Minnesota. Led most notably by Dr. Paul Elwood (Millenson 1999:166–168), HMOs were held up as a model of what healthcare could be. Rather than be an industry that focused on sickness and hospital admissions, why not place most of the attention on wellness and keeping people out of the hospital? The HMO, in both concept and practice (especially as it was implemented by the Kaiser Permanente Health Plan in California), was initially seen as a consumer-friendly, cost-saving approach to the delivery of healthcare services. Over the years, however, the public's attitude toward HMOs has changed rather dramatically.[5]

During the 1970s, as healthcare expenditures began to continuously increase, government officials and purchasers started to be concerned about the rapid growth in the costs of care. Several rather feeble requests by the government to have physicians freeze their fees, especially for the Medicare population, fell on deaf ears. By the end of the 1970s healthcare expenditures were increasing at double-digit levels, at a rate rapidly approaching 18% per year.

During the early 1980s the situation started to take a dramatic turn. Several events happened during this time that would fundamentally change how the United States organized and paid for healthcare. First, purchasers increased their complaints about the rising costs of healthcare and how doctors and hospitals were eroding corporate profits. They endorsed the argument that for every car produced in Detroit, more than $1000 went to pay for healthcare benefits. A view was emerging in the business and political communities that America's financial position in the world was starting to slip because of rising healthcare costs. What they failed to acknowledge was that America's position in the world economy was starting to deteriorate in general. This deterioration was not because of the healthcare system per se but rather an overall decline in leadership within the ranks of America's companies and increasingly poor quality of products and service (Deming 1992). Second, the baby boomer generation was starting to approach middle age and very quickly would be placing heavy demands on the Medicare Trust Fund. Third, TEFRA (the Tax Equity and Fiscal Responsibility Act of 1982) was enacted. This very broad omnibus reconciliation tax reform bill contained a small section (section 223) that allowed the government to place cost-per-case limits on Medicare services. Although the reform was not very successful, the fact that an attempt to limit healthcare costs was actually placed into a piece of legislation was significant. It set the tone for the next steps.

After about a year of seeking voluntary compliance with the TEFRA cost-per-case guidelines (which failed), the government decided to institute a mandatory program aimed at cost containment. In 1983–1984, the government implemented the Prospective Payment System (PPS) and decided to use diagnosis-related groups (DRGs) as the primary mechanism to reimburse hospitals for their services to the Medicare population (Grimaldi and Micheletti 1982). DRGs were initially developed at Yale University Hospital as a methodology for tracking the resources consumed by various diagnoses and related procedures. This was accomplished by first dividing all medical activity into major diagnostic categories (MDCs), which represent major body systems (respiratory, circulatory, digestive, etc.). Then the MDCs were further partitioned into medical and surgical categories followed by age breakouts of older and younger than 70 years of age. Once all of these splits were made, the Medicare program produced an initial set of 467 DRGs.[6] Each DRG was assigned prospectively a dollar value, which was fixed by the Health Care Financing Administration (HCFA), now called the Centers for Medicare and Medicaid Services (CMS). HCFA set up the initial DRGs by analyzing all the claims in the Medicare claims files to determine what the average payments were historically for each of the 467 DRGs. After eliminating outliers, they established a fixed payment for each DRG. For example, if a particular surgical procedure was determined to cost $2000 and a hospital was able to do it for $1500, the hospital made $500 per case. If, on the other hand, the hospital did the operation for $2500, it would still be paid $2000 by HCFA and would thus lose $500 per case. This was the basis of the PPS, which was established as a new approach to healthcare financing.

During the mid-1980s another new initiative came on the scene—state data commissions. State governments, pushed primarily by business coalitions concerned over the rising costs of healthcare, began to consider new ways to make the healthcare community more accountable. Both the purchaser community and state governments found a champion in the name of Walter McClure. McClure was a physicist turned healthcare reform zealot.[7] He argued that if the appropriate data were released to the public and the proper financial incentives were offered to providers, the purchasers of healthcare would "buy right" and the system would basically self-regulate. McClure's "Buy Right" strategy became a dominant factor in the healthcare reform initiatives of the mid-1980s. McClure's strategy particularly appealed to the purchasers of healthcare (especially large companies), because they believed that doctors and hospitals had very little concern over rising healthcare costs and were having a negative impact on their profits.

By the end of the 1980s a majority of the states had created data commissions. These organizations mandated by a state's legislators, required hospitals to submit data using the standard UB-82 format so that it could be analyzed and placed into comparative reports.[8] Typically, these reports were organized by DRG and further stratified by length of stay, average charges per procedure, and frequently some form of severity adjustment. The objective was to provide enough data to companies and the public so that they could become "prudent" purchasers of healthcare.[9] In Pennsylvania and then New York, the state data commissions went a step further by starting to release data on physician performance as well as hospital outcomes.[10]

As the 1980s came to a close it appeared that healthcare costs were coming under control. The percentage increase in healthcare expenditures was not as great in the late 1980s as it had been in the earlier part of the decade. Then, Senator John Heinz of Pennsylvania coined a phrase that rekindled the flames of controversy over cost–quality debate once again. He claimed that patients were being discharged "quicker and sicker" from the hospital. This claim was particularly ironic because the provider community had responded appropriately to the mandate to cut costs. Now politicians and the public started to complain that the provider community was not focused on the patient and was more concerned with money, a contention that became one of the more significant events of the late 1980s. After this point, the nature and content of the debate changed. No longer was the concern strictly on cost. The cost–quality debate was underway.

The 1990s can be characterized as the decade of managed care and public accountability. The HMO, introduced decades earlier, provided a convenient platform for insurance companies to not only control patient access to care but also start influencing how the medical profession made decisions about what patients should (and should not) receive. Initially, the HMO and the concept of managed care were not considered synonymous. Back in the 1930s when Henry J. Kaiser established the first HMO, it was viewed as a vital way to keep the workers healthy. Individuals were encouraged to see their doctors in order to practice more preventive medicine and be kept out of the hospital. As originally conceived, the HMO was seen as a positive step toward patient involvement and a prudent use of healthcare services. As the notion of managed care began to emerge and gain a foothold in the 1990s, it needed a mechanism for actually controlling how access and care would be managed. The HMO provided such a mechanism. Thus, managed care became a euphemism for controlling access and resource utilization. The HMO then became the vehicle by which this objective would be implemented.

The 1990s also witnessed the following key events:

- The rise of consumerism and a backlash against managed care and its practices
- The emergence of the Internet as a primary source of healthcare information for many Americans
- Expanded use of technology and decision support systems in medical practice
- Increased concern over the privacy of patient information
- Shortages of workers in several key healthcare disciplines, especially nurses, pharmacists, and physical therapists
- Challenges by medical residents to reform working conditions
- The public's growing concern over patient safety and medical errors
- A push to make customer service a key component of the medical process
- Concern over bioethics (e.g., stem cell research)

In short, the decade of the 1990s probably witnessed more change than any previous decade. One of the most notable changes was the growth of the consumer movement. Prior to the 1990s the consumers of healthcare were minor players in the healthcare debate. Most of the major changes between 1965 and 1990 occurred at the national and state policy levels and were driven by the agendas of large companies (i.e., purchasers of healthcare). Starting in the late 1980s, however, the consumer movement in healthcare started to gain ground.

The Growing Concern Over Service

Over the past ten years one of the most dramatic transformations in medicine has been the growing concern, on both the consumer side and the political front, that the healthcare profession not only is poor at listening but also just does not care. This is a very stark criticism for an industry that supposedly is designed to "care for people." The classic response from a nurse, for example, when asked, "Why did you get into healthcare?" was always, "Because I like people and want to make a difference." Today, however, the healthcare field seems to be in the midst of a morale crisis. Physicians, nurses, managers, insurance companies, purchasers, and patients do not seem to be very satisfied (let alone happy) with the industry and where it has been going.

In many ways it is surprising that it has taken the public so long to become concerned about the lack of listening in healthcare. A hallmark of the healthcare profession seems to be telling patients what they want, need, or can expect rather than asking them for their opinions or desires. Recent societal changes, however, have started to affect this old paradigm. Consumer organizations (e.g., the People's Medical Society) have grown in popularity and emerged as defenders of patients against the provider community. Starting in 1996 even *Consumer Reports* jumped on the bandwagon and started rating and ranking HMOs. In January of 2003 *Consumer Reports* added a new dimension to its focus on healthcare by leading with the cover page headline, "How Safe Is Your Hospital?"

While part of this clamor for more data and information on hospitals and physicians can be related to our society's increasing desire for information and knowledge, another major force seems to be the growing lack of trust in the healthcare profession. Although interest directed at gaining greater access to information on the performance of hospitals and physicians has been gradually increasing, a number of books have directly challenged the very nature and structure of our healthcare system.

One of the early leaders in this area has been Charles Inlander, M.D., president of the People's Medical Society. Inlander and his colleagues (Lowell Levin and Ed Weiner) wrote *Medicine on Trial* in 1988. This book was not merely a criticism of the status quo; it was a direct attack on the very foundations of medical training, practice, and the business of medicine. The foreword to *Medicine on Trial* states,

> This book presents a grave indictment of American medicine. It is a catalog of ineptitude, malfeasance, gross neglect, indifference, and incredible arrogance. The indictment is not ours. It is an unabridged exposé of medical mistakes taken directly from the annals of medicine and public research. . . . No one can count on reform from within the medical establishment. There are simply too many vested interests in the system trying to protect the status quo. (11–12)

The authors conclude, "It is amply clear that the medical care system is not capable of significant and sustained efforts to improve the quality of its services. It simply has too much at stake in preserving benefits to its own members. Their proposal for improvement lies with the people who are the recipients of care"(15). They write, "The people who should—and, indeed, must—alter the practice of medicine are the people it is practiced on" (19). The remainder of the book provides detailed examples of how the healthcare system has failed those it serves. Chapter 12 of this book has an intriguing title: "What Did He Say? What Did I Hear? What Did We Do?" In this chapter the authors cite case after case of how providers (especially physicians) have demonstrated a total lack of listening to patients. They cite a study at UCLA's Cancer Rehabilitation Project, for example, that concluded, "9 out of 10 physicians had never received any formal training in how to disclose a cancer diagnosis to an afflicted patient" (192). For most people listening skills do not come naturally. We are a society that is not known for listening; we would rather talk than listen. So it is no wonder that books like this one see this lack of attention to the patient's wishes as a major roadblock to healthcare reform.

In 1988 a second book was released that served as a complement to *Medicine on Trial. Taking Charge of Your Medical Fate* (Horowitz 1988) provided a roadmap to guide the patient through the healthcare maze. This book actually received more recognition than *Medicine on Trial.* Senator Edward Kennedy even claimed that "the Horowitz method can save your life—the way it saved my son's." The author, Lawrence Horowitz, M.D., was director of the U.S. Senate Subcommittee on Health and is considered a very astute observer of the healthcare industry. He meticulously lays out the steps for patients to take control of their own healthcare decisions. Despite Horowitz's efforts, consumers of the late 1980s did not take charge of their own medical fate.

It was not until the early 1990s that the consumer movement in healthcare actually started to gain serious momentum. Television talk shows, popular consumer magazines (e.g., on January 22, 1996, *Time* magazine had the following cover page: "Special Investigation—What Your Doctor Can't Tell You"), investigative reports on *60 Minutes,* and the Internet all contributed to the growing concern that healthcare providers really did not listen or pay much attention to those they serve.

The book that has made the most significant contribution to the role of consumers and measurement in healthcare is *Demanding Medical Excellence: Doctors and Accountability in the Information Age* by Michael Millenson (1999). This book picks up where the works of Starr, Inlander et al., and Horowitz left off. Millenson provides a detailed account of the major historical and political events that have shaped this country's debate over cost and quality. He then proceeds to offer a critical review of the serious flaws and fallacies in contemporary medicine. Through many examples, quotes, and case studies, Millenson traces the growing role of data and outcomes research in healthcare. He concludes that "The largest barriers to systematically measuring and improving the quality of American medicine are not technical but cultural. . . . " (xvi). He argues that the healthcare profession lacks the will to objectively measure and monitor the quality of what it produces. Chapter 2 provides additional discussion on listening to the voice of the customer and details on ways to measure customer perspectives.

Defining Continuous Quality Improvement (CQI)

There is no doubt that the healthcare industry is under tremendous pressure to demonstrate that it can transform itself. We have responded extremely well in many arenas. For example, the technological advances in medicine have been dramatic.[11] The industry has also been very creative in providing a variety of outpatient clinical and support services (e.g., mobile dental clinics, home care services for individuals with special needs, and parish nursing programs). From my perspective, however, our industry has not been equally as responsive in two key areas: (1) listening and responding to the voice of the customer (VOC), and (2) making quality measurement practices part of daily work life. These two topics provide the focal points for the remaining chapters in this book. Before diving into the details, however, let us consider the concept of quality.

Everyone is an expert in quality. We have all experienced good and bad quality. We may not be able to define it precisely, but the general opinion is that "I know it when I see it." When I teach the Introduction to CQI class within my own system, I start the class by asking everyone to take a sticky note and complete the following statement: "Quality is . . . " Figure 1.2 provides a summary of some of the definitions I have received over the past year. As you look at these comments you will notice that people attending an introductory class on quality have a fairly clear perspective on the subject.

While numerous formal definitions of quality have been offered (see Schultz [1994] for a review of these definitions), I favor the simple yet straightforward position that Deming presented. He basically said that he refused to define quality in a few words or a sentence. What he did say was that "Quality begins with intent, which is fixed by management" (Deming 1992:5) and that quality is not easy to define. Deming based his entire approach to quality improvement on the assumption that quality has no meaning without listening to the VOC. He stated that "Quality can be defined only in terms of the agent" (i.e., the customer or end user of a process). "Who is the judge of quality?" he was often heard to ask. He clarified his position with the following statement:

> The difficulty in defining quality is to translate future needs of the user into measurable characteristics, so that a product can be designed and turned out to give satisfaction at a price that the user will pay. This is not easy, and as soon as one feels fairly successful in the endeavour, he finds that the needs of the consumer have changed, competitors have moved in, there are new materials to work with, some better than the old ones, some worse; some cheaper than the old ones, some dearer. The quality of any product or service has many scales. (Deming 1992:169)

Quality is. . .

- a combination of value and outcome in the eyes of the consumer
- a process with minimal opportunities for improvement
- a product or service delivered with 100% satisfaction the first time, every time
- a product or service that provides an expected value
- a product that lasts, for the best price
- a very good product—one you would want again
- above-standard results
- accountability
- an excellent product delivered by professional, friendly, knowledgeable people in a timely manner at the appropriate time
- an unending struggle for excellence
- anticipation and fulfillment of needs
- attention to detail, timeliness, competence
- compassion
- completing a job in an accurate, efficient, and timely manner
- customer-focused service at a reasonable price
- data driven
- difficult to define
- doing the job right the first time
- going above and beyond what is expected
- listening/responding
- listening to feedback and making changes to meet customer needs, hopefully exceeding expectations
- making others feel important
- meeting and exceeding customer needs
- meeting our customer/patient needs in a cost-effective manner
- providing a product/service marketed to your customer above and beyond his or her expectations
- providing the best we can to our customer through kind and understanding dealings
- striving for excellence
- superior performance
- taking care of customers needs
- the best possible service; the most durable goods; the presence of a program for customer-focused education and service recovery when expectations fall short
- the high human motivation to perform their job at their best
- the highest form of any service with satisfaction reflected in outcome that is measurable
- timely, optimal service that provides the best outcome and satisfaction for the receiver of the service

▲ FIGURE 1.2 Definitions of quality

When you cut through all the theoretical and philosophical underpinnings offered by the recognized experts in quality (Schultz 1994), they all discuss, in one way or another, three fundamental activities that form the foundation of continuous quality improvement (CQI):

- Listening to the voice of the customer (VOC)
- Listening to the voice of the process (VOP)
- Using statistical process control (SPC) methods (i.e., using data to make decisions)

Organizations that clearly demonstrate CQI (e.g., the Baldrige winners or organizations that have won state quality awards) are able to skillfully blend all three activities together. A singular focus on one or even two of these activities is not going to achieve CQI. It is when all three activities are combined simultaneously and on a daily basis that quality, as envisioned by Deming and his contemporaries, will be realized. Figure 1.3 shows the interrelationship of these three activities.

When considering the implementation of CQI it must be remembered that it is a never-ending process of *continuous* improvement. It is not called PQI (partial quality improvement) or SQI (sometimes quality improvement) but CQI—continuous quality improvement. It is acknowledging that past success does not offer any guarantee of future success (look at what happened in 2001 to Firestone tires, for example). Quality does not happen by accident or because you want it to, wish it to, or hope and pray that things will get better. Quality results from the deliberate and intentional actions of individuals within an organization. It is not a program or a single project, nor the responsibility of one individual (e.g., the director of quality) or those assigned to the quality department. In short, quality is a way of thinking about work, approaching its improvement, and getting everyone involved. Quality is about achieving excellence—nothing less.

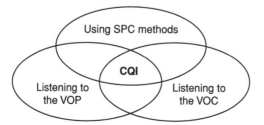

▲ FIGURE 1.3 The three key activities of continuous quality improvement (CQI)

If quality is viewed as something that has to be done, "in addition to everything else I have to do," then the organization will never understand quality or be able to achieve it.

The essential ingredients that enable an organization to achieve quality and excellence, therefore, include:

- A commitment to quality starting with the board and senior management
- A strategically defined role for quality
- A model upon which to build quality improvement strategies
- A plan for deploying CQI throughout the entire organization
- CQI education and training for all employees
- A measurement philosophy and related statistical methods
- Strategies for taking action to improve or redesign processes

These are what I refer to as the quality measurement milestones (Lloyd 2003). When these ingredients are in place and sustained over time, CQI will be part of the very fabric of the organization. Anything less will relegate quality to a nominal status within the organization.

Notes

1. Unfortunately, there are many examples of how the public has become disillusioned with various institutions and then demanded increased scrutiny of the industry, such as the TV evangelist movement (especially Jim Bakker), the Ford Pinto, Firestone tires, Enron, and the recent investigation of Catholic priests.

2. The American healthcare system has been traced most effectively by Paul Starr in his 1982 classic *The Social Transformation of American Medicine*. In this best-seller, Starr charts how medicine has gone from very humble origins in the 1700s to excessive complexity and struggles for power in the last half of the 20th century. Michael Millenson's book *Demanding Medical Excellence* (1999) picks up where Starr left off and traces the more recent developments, including the interest in patient safety. Personally, I believe that every healthcare professional should take time to read these two excellent texts. They provide a clear understanding of the forces that have shaped our industry.

3. I am constantly amazed at how many healthcare professionals have very little understanding of the social and political events that have shaped our healthcare system. I was reminded of this recently when I gave a lecture to the new residents in family practice at Advocate Christ Medical Center. When I asked the participants if they knew about the Prospective Payment System (PPS) or diagnosis-related groups (DRGs) they all had blank looks on their faces. Building a better healthcare system depends on understanding where it has been and what factors bring us to this particular moment in time. The rich history of healthcare should be a part of the training not only for clinicians but also for nonclinical managers and administrators.

4. While I am referencing the social orientation toward medicine in the late 1960s, I was reminded recently that you do not have to go back thirty or more years to feel the differences in the healthcare system. I recently had lunch with the chief executive of a medical group. We happened to be eating at a country club he had belonged to since he was hired as the chief executive back in 1985. He explained that when he was hired, membership in the local country club was a standard benefit for not only the management team but for all the physicians. The country club was where you met other business leaders, played golf, socialized, and "did business." "Now," he reflected, "I am the only one from the medical group that belongs to the country club and I have to pay my own dues."

5. Millenson's book (1999) provides a very cogent and detailed review of the role of HMOs and their history.

6. Today the PPS uses 508 valid DRGs (*DRG Expert,* 19th ed. [Igenix, Inc., 2002]). Each year this number changes slightly as the classification system is modified to accommodate changes in clinical practice and treatments.

7. McClure's contributions to the healthcare cost containment debate are well documented in Millenson's book (1999).

8. The UB-82 format is the standard format for nearly all administrative data sets, also known as minimum data sets (MDS). The development of the UB-82 format stems from the National Committee on Vital and Health Statistics (NCVHS), which in 1969 developed the first formal outline for an MDS for hospital discharge data elements. This led to

the creation of the Uniform Hospital Abstract Minimum Data Set in 1973. The Uniform Hospital Discharge Data Set (UHDDS) emerged in the early 1970s as the standard MDS referent for hospital-based services. The 14 data elements contained in the original UHDDS were then used to create the first Uniform Bill (UB) for hospital services, popularly known as UB-82 (the 82 refers to 1982, when the structure of the UB was first accepted). In the mid-1990s the UB-82 was updated and is now referred to as the UB-92. This one-page form contains 86 fields, some of which allow for multiple entries or subcategories. While the UB-92 is used primarily for processing Medicare claims, the format has been adopted by other groups (e.g., most state data commissions) to collect data on other payer groups. The elements included in the UB-92 were determined by the National Uniform Billing Committee (NUBC), which was established in 1975. Each state then has a state UBC that can recommend limited revisions to the UB-92. The NUBC's Web site is *www.nubc.org*.

9. When the Pennsylvania Health Care Cost Containment Council (HC4) issued its first report, it happened to coincide with my father's need to have a prostate operation known as a TURP (a transurethral resection of the prostate). I showed him all the data in the HC4 report on the procedure, the average length of stay, charges, and probability of complications and death (this last factor he felt was too much information for his purposes). When I asked him which hospital he would choose now that he was given all this information, he paused and said, "I think I'll just go where my doctor tells me to go." I do not think that my father's answer was quite what Walter McClure had in mind when he described how "prudent purchasers" would take all of this provider information and make healthcare choices. But I believe it was a typical response that many consumers would make when faced with a thick statistical report. This example made me realize that the primary audience for the HC4 data was not the general public but rather the benefits managers of large companies.

10. Probably the single most influential initiative to emerge during the mid-1980s was the state data commissions. Led by initiatives in Pennsylvania and New York, the state data commissions pursued a

relentless mantra—put hospital and physician data into the public arena and consumers will make prudent purchasing decisions. In other words, they would, as Walter McClure argued, "buy right." During the 1980s I worked for the Hospital Association of Pennsylvania (HAP), now known as the Hospital and Healthsystem Association of Pennsylvania, and had the opportunity to be part of a team that closely tracked the creation of the HC4. The HC4 was created by the Pennsylvania state legislature on July 8, 1986. It was a fascinating time to observe the changing structure of healthcare. On the one side were the government of Pennsylvania and purchaser groups contending that the hospitals and physicians were not disclosing enough data to the public. Walter McClure's "buy right" notion had gained a foothold in the Keystone State. In the other corner was the state medical society, which was not particularly involved with the debate because they basically could not believe that anyone would challenge the existing medical establishment. Those of us at the hospital association contended that we could support the release of outcomes data to the public as long as it took into consideration severity of outcomes and other risk adjustment considerations. The HC4 was led by several very savvy individuals. In particular, the HC4's executive director, Ernie Sessa, turned out to be not only a master at navigating the political waters but also astute enough to know when to bring in technical experts. The response to our challenge about severity and risk adjustment was to hold a competition to select a vendor that would "risk adjust" the data and thereby eliminate the challenges from the provider community. All the leading risk adjustment companies entered the competition. Intellectually, this was a wonderful opportunity to participate in a debate about which severity/risk adjusting methodology was "the best." Staging, CSI, APACHE, and MedisGroups were the leading contenders. After many long presentations that contained endless arrays of numbers and statistics, a decision was made by the HC4 to implement MedisGroups throughout the entire state as the endorsed method of severity/risk adjustment. This decision, to implement a statewide severity adjustment system, proved to be another key decision in the ongoing purchaser–provider debate. It was also seen as a good way to curtail the ever-popular complaint that "my patients are sicker than your patients."

11. For example, today a patient can have laparoscopic gall bladder surgery at an ambulatory surgery center and be back to work in a day or two. In the 1970s that same patient would have stayed in the hospital for at least a week and be off work for several more. Cataract surgery is routinely done on an outpatient basis. At Rush St. Luke's Presbyterian Hospital in Chicago they are now performing same-day hip replacement surgery and at Advocate Christ Medical Center (Oak Lawn, Illinois) they are using the da Vinci robot to repair mitral valves in the heart. We have the technology to look inside the patient without penetrating the skin. In the past it was not uncommon to do "exploratory surgery" to determine if there was a problem. Today we rely on CT scans and MRIs as primary noninvasive diagnostic tools. The application of new technology seems endless. It will continue to change not only how we think about medicine but also how it is taught and practiced.

References

Blalock, H. (ed.). *Causal Models in the Social Sciences*. Chicago: Aldine, 1971.

Codman, E. A. *A Study in Hospital Efficiency* (1917). Reprint, Oak Brook Terrace, Ill.: Joint Commission on Accreditation of Healthcare Organizations, 1996.

Deming, W. E. *Out of the Crisis*. Cambridge, Mass.: Massachusetts Institute of Technology Center for Advanced Engineering Study, 1992.

Grimaldi, P., and J. Micheletti. *Diagnosis Related Groups: A Practitioner's Guide*. Chicago: Pluribus Press, 1982.

Horowitz, L. *Taking Charge of Your Medical Fate*. New York: Random House, 1988.

Inlander, C., L. Levin, and E. Weiner. *Medicine on Trial*. New York: Prentice Hall, 1988.

Lloyd, R. "The Search for a Few Good Indicators." Ransom, Scott, M. Joshi, and D. Nash (eds.), In *The Healthcare Quality Book*. Chicago: Health Administration Press, forthcoming 2003.

Millenson, M. *Demanding Medical Excellence: Doctors and Accountability in the Information Age*. Chicago: University of Chicago Press, 1999.

Peabody, F. "The Care of the Patient." *Journal of the American Medical Association* 88 (March 19, 1927): 877–882.

Schultz, L. *Profiles in Quality*. New York: Quality Resources, 1994.

Shewhart, W. *Economic Control of Quality of Manufactured Product*. New York: D. Van Nostrand, 1931. Reprint, Milwaukee: Quality Press, 1980.

Starr, P. *The Social Transformation of American Medicine*. New York: Basic Books, 1982.

Chapter 2

Measuring the Voice of the Customer

It All Starts With Listening

"Good evening, my name is Pam and I'm calling on behalf of Acme Storm Window Company. Recently we installed new windows in your home and I was wondering if you would take a few minutes to answer several questions about our service? Yes, I realize that it is dinnertime, but I have only eight brief questions to ask you and it will take less than two minutes. No, sir, I'm not trying to sell you our service. As I said, we installed new windows in your home last week and I merely want to find out if our staff met your expectations. OK, thanks; I'll be brief. Here's the first question ..."

Sound familiar? Most of us receive one or more of this type of customer feedback calls each week. In addition, you probably also receive periodic surveys in the mail asking for your opinions on everything from how you feel about your congressman to whether or not your community should raise taxes so more trees can be planted in the parks. If you are like most people, these interruptions to your dinner hour and the added paper in your mailbox are basically irritations. But if you look at these "irritations" from the viewpoint of those making the inquiry, they are usually sincere attempts to listen to the voice of the customer (VOC).

Continuous quality improvement (CQI) begins with listening to the VOC (Scherkenbach 1991; Deming 1992; Langly 1996; Hayes 1998). Customers define quality and set the expectations for performance. So when Pam from Acme Storm Window Company calls asking for your opinions about the new windows you recently had installed, she is doing it to see if you are delighted, moderately satisfied, or totally turned off by their service. Basically, she wants to listen to the VOC. It is the first step on the road to improvement.

In healthcare it is ironic that we seem to be quite ambivalent about taking this first step and really listening to those we serve. This is even more ironic since healthcare is supposed to be a profession that "cares" about those it serves. We even list the various things we offer to patients as "services" (e.g., outpatient services, emergency services, labor and delivery services). The very name of what we provide suggests that we intend to listen to those who come to us in need. *Webster's II New Riverside University Dictionary* (1984:1066) defines service as "an act of assistance or benefit." In order to provide such benefit, however, it is essential that the provider of a service understand the type of assistance needed or the nature of the desired benefit—all of which requires listening to the recipient of the assistance or service.

Most healthcare organizations have a formal process for obtaining quantitative feedback from their patients. Although the numbers do provide a useful foundation for building improvement strategies, some of the most telling responses come from the written comments of the respondents. One comment that I recently read sticks out very clearly in my mind. It was from an elderly female patient. The handwriting was a little unstable, but the words were very clear. When asked what we could do to improve on the care and service delivered, she responded, "I wish someone would have just touched me and told me everything would be all right." We frequently forget that some of the best healing comes from a simple smile, a pat on the hand, or a few words of encouragement.

We deliver services that are much more important than installing storm windows, yet we seem to miss the basic point that Pam understood when she called us during dinner—if you ask customers for their opinions they will usually provide feedback. But it begins with a desire to listen. Once you listen (really listen) to those you serve, you will be better positioned to respond appropriately.

Creating a Service Excellence Culture

The creation of a service excellence culture does not happen by merely telling everyone to smile and be nice to people. Healthcare is not like the television show *Fantasy Island*. The host (Ricardo Montalban) would start each episode by making sure the staff were all properly aligned and polished. As the plane circled the island and made its final turn for the landing approach, Montalban would recite the opening line, "Smiles, everyone." A dazzling smile will never replace behaviors that demonstrate that the workers really care about the patients or that you have processes in place that are user friendly and exceed customer expectations. Yet many healthcare organizations think the "Smiles, everyone" approach is all they need.

Figure 2.1 depicts the organizational components that influence the creation of a VOC culture. Service excellence does not happen by chance. It also does not exist merely because your organization won a quality award two years ago. Service excellence results from a very deliberate focus on the four basic components shown in this figure. These factors will determine the culture your customers experience on a day-to-day basis.

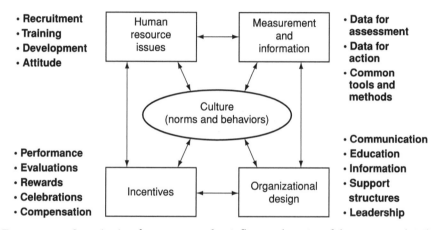

▲ FIGURE 2.1 Organizational components that influence the voice of the customer (VOC)

Human Resource Issues

It all begins with the individuals we hire, how we train them, and what we do to retain them for the long run. If the employees are our most valuable resource (which almost every organization says at one point or another), then a considerable amount of effort ought to be directed to this component. Many healthcare organizations have initiated programs to screen potential applicants to see if they are in alignment with the organization's mission, values, and philosophy. The Disney organization and Southwest Airlines are two well-known companies that use initial screenings to determine this degree of alignment. Southwest refers to their process as targeted selection. Central to the Southwest selection process are humor and the extent to which individuals seem capable of becoming part of an extended family of people who work hard and have fun at the same time (Freiberg and Freiberg 1996:67). If applicants do not meet certain criteria, they are told this up front so that they do not waste their time or the company's. Failure to achieve a particular score on the profile exam is not an indication that the applicant is a "bad" person. It merely reflects the fact that the applicant's perspectives and the organization's expectations are not aligned. It is much better to find this out at the initial stages of the recruitment process than to find it out six months or a year after the person is hired. How often do we hear comments such as these in healthcare: "How did she get her job? Who does she know?" "He offends everyone in the department but no one [in management] seems to care."

Every organization has employees who are notorious for being rude, domineering, and out of sync with what the organization claims to value. Yet they seem to remain, and sometimes they even get promoted while "good" people leave. How does this happen? I believe that several key factors create human resource (people) challenges in healthcare organizations. First, healthcare organizations all too often hire strictly for technical skill and assume that the person's people skills will somehow develop automatically over time. Herb Kelleher, CEO of Southwest Airlines, has made it very clear that he expects his People Department (they do not call it the human resources department) to "Hire for attitude, train for skill." Kelleher, who has been called the "High Priest of Ha Ha" by *Fortune* magazine, makes his hiring policy very clear: "We look for attitudes; people with a sense of humor who don't take themselves too seriously. We'll train you on whatever it is you have to do, but the one thing Southwest cannot change in people is inherent attitudes" (Freiberg and Freiberg 1996:67). Frequently, healthcare organizations miss or ignore the "inherent attitudes" component of the hiring process.

Second, individuals who have done well in one role (e.g., as a bedside nurse or a family practice physician) are often assumed to be prime candidates for promotion to managerial or administrative roles. Furthermore, if they have been with the organization long enough, then it is a foregone conclusion that they are "ready to move up." Faced with the offer of more money, status, and authority, most individuals will say, "Thank you, I am ready for a promotion!" Rarely will you hear, "No, thank you, I am perfectly content to stay where I am." So they accept the new managerial or administrative position. In many cases this is a major mistake for the individual and the organization. The individual soon becomes the living embodiment of what Peter and Hull (1970) refer to as the Peter Principle—that is, people will be raised to their level of incompetence. Many extremely competent physicians, for example, have been placed in high-level administrative roles only to discover that they are incompetent when it comes to managing people and dealing with the politics of the organization. They might have been excellent as practicing physicians, but they quickly become another example of the Peter Principle in action.

The third human resource consideration relates to retention of good staff. Most organizations have a statement that goes something like this: "Our employees are our most valuable resource!" Yet when you look at what many organizations actually do to retain, reward, and build a bond of loyalty with the employees, you start to wonder why anyone stays with the organization. Deming put it this way: "The greatest waste in America is failure to use the abilities of people" (1992:53). Why do some people love going to work each day and others hate even to get out of bed? Part of it relates to paying fair and competitive wages. This is only part of the equation, however. The other part, which is a major factor in the healthcare industry, is not related to money and perquisites. It is related to how people are treated, how they feel about their coworkers, the respect they have for their managers, and the opportunities they have for self-expression and meaningful work. It relates to leadership and how organizations create incentives for their most valuable resource.

Incentives

"What motivates healthcare workers? Why did you get into this profession?" I have asked these questions to many people in my quality classes, and the dominant response is, "I wanted to help people." Rarely do healthcare professionals say that their primary motivators are financial bonuses and stock options. While money is certainly a key part of any job, for healthcare workers (especially those in not-for-profit organizations) other factors also seem to provide major incentives. Any healthcare organization that does not give serious consideration to the factors that motivate their employees will never be able to develop and sustain a service excellence culture. Besides basic compensation and benefits, other key factors that lead to employee motivation include: (1) the performance evaluation process; (2) reward and recognition systems (Nelson 1994; Deal and Key 1998); (3) the extent to which micromanagement exists within the organization; (4) professional freedom and autonomy to make decisions; and (5) organizational hypocrisy (i.e., the extent to which the organization's leaders behave in a manner that is inconsistent with the organization's mission, values, and philosophy).

Deming was very interested in the topic of incentives and motivation. In fact, one of his four areas of profound knowledge (Schultz 1994:18–27) includes human behavior or psychology. While Deming acknowledged readily that he was not a psychologist, he pointed out constantly that if leaders did not realize that people (their employees) had differing desires, hopes, aspirations, ambitions, and learning styles, the organization would never succeed. Central to his interest in this subject was the question of whether individuals are intrinsically or extrinsically motivated. Deming believed very strongly in the value of a person's intrinsic motivation. His writings and lectures all reinforced the notion that people are born with a natural inclination to learn and be innovative. His concern was that organizations knock these intrinsic desires out of individuals and try to replace them with extrinsic motivation factors. The extrinsic motivation camp, led primarily by B. F. Skinner and his mentor Pavlov, takes a behavioral modification approach to motivation (i.e., if you perform this task as I want you to, I'll give you a reward). For organizations this translates into offering bonuses, incentives, and other inducements to the workers in order to get the workers to perform in ways that management wants them to. It assumes that the workers will do anything for the reward (just like Pavlov's dog responding in a positive way for a treat).

I believe this debate over intrinsic and extrinsic motivation is one of the more controversial dimensions of CQI and one that is central to an organization's success. Yet most healthcare leaders have never had a serious dialogue with their management team about this topic. All too often healthcare leaders believe that extrinsic motivators do in fact drive the workers. I have seen many not-for-profit healthcare organizations create elaborate incentive programs to dole out a few extra vacation days each year to the workers. For many employees (e.g., nurses) gaining an extra day or two is not of great benefit, because they are usually not able to use up their regular vacation time. A major challenge for creating bonus/incentive programs in healthcare is that the actual monetary payouts, or other rewards such as extra vacation days, are small and trivial relative to what they hear their counterparts receive in the for-profit sectors. As a result, many incentive programs in healthcare do less to motivate and more to provide fodder for employee humor and sarcasm.

Some healthcare organizations have decided to go the route of gain sharing (as opposed to pay for performance) as a way to reward the entire organization. Because operating margins are relatively small in our industry, a gain sharing approach, where everyone gets the same monetary share of the overall gain or operating margin, can receive favorable support. Gain sharing also has some inherent appeal to employees in not-for-profit industries, because true pay for performance systems, such as found in the sales industry, are more difficult to tie directly to individual performance in healthcare settings. In a service industry like healthcare it is often hard to decide which member of the team has outperformed the others. For example, the surgeon may have performed an excellent knee replacement surgery with no complications. Yet one of the floor nurses discovered that the patient was having a negative reaction to a particular medication, which could have severely compromised the patient's recovery. Does the nurse deserve a bonus for catching a potential medication error? Or has the physical therapist, who convinced the patient that it was actually better to move the new knee than to stay in bed, performed better than the others on the team? In short, given the collaborative nature of the healthcare profession, it is often very difficult to determine which individuals have outperformed the others.

If healthcare leaders are seriously interested in understanding what motivates their workers, then they need to read not only what Deming had to say about this topic but also what Alfie Kohn has concluded about extrinsic and intrinsic motivation. Kohn has written two critically acclaimed books on this subject. *No Contest* (1986) provides a review of the role that competition has played in human development. Contrary to popular opinion, Kohn demonstrates that our fascination with being "number one" makes no one number one. He reviews studies from around the world to place the intrinsic–extrinsic debate into clear (and frequently controversial) context. His second book, *Punished by Rewards* (1993) continues his analysis of intrinsic and extrinsic motivation. Kohn pulls no punches and takes a fairly controversial stance by claiming that "rewards simply do not work to promote lasting behavior change or to enhance performance." He continues:

> Gradually it began to dawn on me that our society is caught in a whopping paradox. We complain loudly about such things as the sagging productivity of workplaces, the crisis of our schools, and the warped values of our children. But the very strategy we use to solve those problems—dangling rewards like incentive plans and grades and candy bars in front of people—is partly responsible for the fix we're in. We are a society of loyal Skinnerians, unable to think our way out of the box we have reinforced ourselves into. (xii–xiii)

An organization's culture begins with the people it hires. The culture is cultivated, however, by the way in which the organization designs its incentives.

Organizational Design

"Every system is perfectly designed to get the results it gets." This phrase has been popularized by the Institute for Healthcare Improvement (IHI). Since it was first coined by Tom Nolan, Ph.D., statistical consultant to the IHI, this expression has been used by thousands of quality professionals to reflect the important contribution of organizational design. An organization's structure and design is the result of a direct and purposive set of decisions made by the leadership of the organization. Central among these decisions are the ways in which the following functions are designed and deployed:

- Education of staff and management
- Communication (including both the actual flow of information and the ways in which it is disseminated)
- Information flow (including the amount that is shared with the employees as well as the types of information shared)
- Support structures for providing patient care (e.g., the admitting and scheduling processes and the physical layout of the office space)
- Leadership structures (including the number of formal leaders, their ranges of responsibility, and their abilities to manage complex systems)

Healthcare is not known for its innovative approaches to management and change. Hierarchies are quite strong and play dominant roles in the healthcare profession. There are hierarchies within the ranks of physicians, nurses, and administrators. These hierarchies did not happen by accident; the leaders of the organization created them, and they are perpetuated because we allow them to continue. Yet nearly all of the healthcare professionals I have come in contact with complain regularly about the lack of flexibility and innovation in their organization's design. Although not explicitly stated, the goal of many healthcare organizations seems to be to maintain the status quo rather than to challenge existing ways of thinking and/or to redesign the ways in which things are done.

Jack Welsh, the ever flamboyant and outspoken former CEO of General Electric, provides a wonderful example of how the leader of an organization sets the tone for organizational design. He made it very clear that an employee who wanted to be promoted within the GE ranks had better take all their courses in quality and be able to demonstrate application of the concepts to make things better. He personally taught many of the classes on quality to the employees. How many healthcare CEOs can even say that they have attended quality classes, let alone taught them? In an interview with the *Chicago Tribune* (April 14, 2002), Welsh made the following statement about the role of education within an organization:

> A company's most sustainable competitive advantage is not a widget, not a piece of software, but it's the ability to learn and act on that learning. If you believe that, and I do believe that to my toes, then you are doing things in your company every single day to create an atmosphere where employees thrive on finding a better way. The challenge is in the organization to get the collective intellect raised every single day. People say to me as I go around the country, "Well, gee, this is a terrible time to be spending on education. We've got these problems." My God, this is the time to be spending. You can't stop educating employees.

Every system (organization) is perfectly designed to get the results it gets. I think Jack Welsh would agree with this statement. But as Deming pointed out (1992:53), "Money and time spent for training will be ineffective unless inhibitors to good work are removed."

It is very easy to overlook organizational design. For some it seems too abstract, for others too detailed and complicated. System thinking (another component of Deming's profound knowledge) lies at the very heart of CQI and at the core of organizational design. If the organization's individual parts and related processes are not aligned toward a common aim, then the organization's long-term results will always be at odds with what goes on within the organization on a day-to-day basis. What processes do you have in place for communicating your organization's aim, strategic objectives, and performance? Can the employees articulate your mission and strategic objectives? One of our hospitals, Advocate Christ Hospital Medical Center in Oak Lawn, Illinois, has taken this challenge down to the department level. In the hallways throughout the hospital are 83 frames. Each frame contains the mission statement of one department. The clinical, operational, and support employees created these statements—not management. They are there as a statement to the public that each department is committed to quality and excellence. Selected examples of these mission statements are shown in Figure 2.2.

Do you place your key indicators on an intranet or publish them in employee newsletters so that everyone can see how you are doing? I have frequently seen managers tell the employees that they need to improve the patient satisfaction scores, but they never share the detailed reports with the staff. If an organization is to become truly a "learning organization" (Garvin 1993; Watkins and Marsick 1993; Senge 1994; Wick and Leaon 1994) then it needs to have a plan for continuously communicating with, educating, and training the one resource they claim is most important—the employees.

Measurement and Information

Organizational measurement can be classified into two basic categories: (1) measurement of the VOC, and (2) measurement of the VOP. Within each of these major categories management and staff must decide how they will assess performance and how they will use the data they collect to make improvements. They must also make sure that they are using the right tools and techniques to really understand the variation that exists in their processes. Good measurement begins with having an overall philosophy and approach toward measurement and monitoring. Doing what has always been done and measuring what has always been measured will not contribute to the organization's long-term survival.

1. The mission of the Adult Medicine Center is to support, encourage, and respect excellence and a positive attitude in providing care for our patients.

2. The mission of Adult Respiratory Care is to verbalize, reform, and safeguard excellence and a positive attitude for our patients.

3. The mission of Audiology is to encourage, involve, support, and promote excellence through our service to our customers.

4. The mission of the Audit Department is to provide, promise, and promote integrity for insurance companies, department managers, patients, and their families.

5. The mission of Child Life Services is to embrace, impact, and advocate family-centered care for children and their families.

6. The mission of Emergency Department Registration is to provide, demonstrate, and communicate respect, dignity, compassion, and excellence to our patients, their families, and our co-associates.

7. The mission of Food Services is to prepare, serve, and provide excellent food and outstanding service to all of our patients, staff, and visitors.

8. The mission of Hemodialysis is to affirm, appreciate, and uphold wholeness and dignity for renal dialysis patients.

9. The mission of Human Resources is to lead, guide, and sustain work life quality for hospital associates.

10. The mission of the Pain Management Center is to alleviate pain, promote healing, and restore quality to the lives of persons suffering from chronic pain disorders.

11. The mission of the Pediatric Intensive Care Unit is to recognize, respect, and deliver the highest level of family-centered care for each family unit and the community.

12. The mission of the Radiation Oncology Department is to understand, encourage, and heal with dignity and respect for cancer patients and their families.

▲ FIGURE 2.2 Department mission statements from Advocate Christ Hospital Medical Center

The role of measurement in healthcare will only increase. Organizations that do not develop a strategy for measuring the VOC and the VOP will most likely find themselves on the outside looking in. They will be very upset when outside organizations and purchasers begin making judgments about the care that they deliver. In the end they will not be sure of their way. In fact, they will be like Alice in Wonderland when she asks the Cheshire Cat how to get out of Wonderland. The exchange goes as follows:

> "Would you tell me, please, which way I ought to go from here," asked Alice?
> "That depends a good deal on where you want to get to," said the Cat.
> "I don't much care where—" said Alice.
> "Then it doesn't matter which way you go," said the Cat.[1]

Measurement without a roadmap and a context for action is a fruitless journey.

These four components, then (human resource issues, incentives, organizational design, and measurement), form the key ingredients for creating a service excellence culture. While people often think of organizations as physical structures and tangible assets, the truth of the matter is that people and culture form the very essence of organizations. This is why Deming probably listed human behavior (or psychology) as one of his four key components of profound knowledge. People form the basis of all organizations. Individuals with hopes, wishes, aspirations, and desires form the culture of an organization. How the leaders of an organization choose to manage and build this culture will determine the organization's fate.

In the last 50 years there have been wonderful examples of how organizations have built positive and healthy cultures aimed at service excellence and examples of those that seem to have forgotten some very simple and basic principles. Service excellence does not happen by chance.

Who Are Your Customers?

It used to be quite simple. There was a caregiver and a patient—a very simple and straightforward customer/supplier relationship. Today, things are more complex. Caregivers have to deal with many individuals and organizations in order to practice their profession. Similarly, administrators and managers must also deal with a myriad of both internal and external customers.[2] For example, internal customers can include the board, management, the providers of care, and all those employees not involved directly with patient care but essential to the organization's operation. External customers, on the other hand, are probably the most rapidly growing and demanding group of customers. As was pointed out in Chapter 1, individuals, groups, and organizations (e.g., companies, business coalitions, consumer groups, insurance companies, managed care organizations, state data commissions, and the Joint Commission on Accreditation of Healthcare Organizations [JCAHO]) have become major players in the healthcare game. No longer are the providers of care totally free to make clinical and treatment decisions without some external group or organization reviewing or critiquing the diagnosis and/or treatment decisions. Many patients have also become much more involved with their treatment plans and the decisions affecting their lives.

The bottom line is that healthcare has become customer driven whether the providers of care like it or not. From a CQI perspective this is a welcomed outcome, because the first building block of CQI is listening to the VOC. It is imperative that healthcare providers start their quality journeys by listening to those they serve.

As I have discussed this topic with healthcare providers, managers, and support personnel, I have experienced a variety of reactions. The traditionalists in the group ask why all these "untrained patients and laypeople" are trying to make decisions about a specialized profession that they are not qualified to address. The new thinkers, on the other hand, constantly look for opportunities to include the customers in the analysis and delivery of care.[3]

In order to determine where you and your organization stand with respect to the VOC, consider your responses to the following questions:

- Who are our customers?

- How deeply do we really care about our customers?

- What do our customers want, need, and expect from us?

- Do our customers really know what they want, need, or expect?

- We serve patients—what's all this stuff about customers, anyway? Customers buy cars and refrigerators, not healthcare.

- Is the customer always right? Some of these people make unrealistic demands on us.

- The patients are not trained healthcare professionals—how do they know what they need?

I have had many interesting (and sometimes quite enthusiastic) conversations with healthcare providers about these questions. There seem to be three camps of thought around the question of the role of customers. The first group is the "You've got to be kidding" camp. This group basically cannot believe that they even have to listen to what the consumers of healthcare want, need, or expect. This group is primarily made up of individuals who are legends in their own minds. They maintain beliefs that are essentially grounded in the supposition that they are the vessels of all knowledge and that those who come to them for care and advice are of lesser levels of knowledge and understanding. Fortunately, this category is not as dominant as it once was.

The second group is the "This, too, shall pass" camp. Here we have a collection of folks who have been around long enough to become genuinely cynical about any new way of thinking. This group could also be classified as the "flavor of the month club." They have seen management fads come and go and believe that if you merely wait long enough, some new jargon or acronym will replace last month's quick fix. From this group's perspective, nothing really changes except the new management fad or slogan of the month. While skeptical, this group can become tremendous agents of change if they are convinced that the organization has constancy of purpose (Scherkenbach, 1990:13) and is sincere about turning jargon into action.

The third and final group is the "eternal optimist support group." These people are true believers. They will get behind new ideas and support them because they fit with the organization's mission and values and their own personal value sets. They want to help and be team players, and they will go out of their way to be nice to their coworkers and especially patients. Frequently this group irritates the first group because of their egalitarian optimism and receives quiet scorn from the second group because they are not converted cynics.

Over the years, I have found the perspectives of healthcare workers extremely interesting when it comes to those they serve. We have an ever-growing number of both internal and external customers to which we must respond. Yet recognizing these various customer groups and sincerely trying to find out what they want, need, and expect seem to create struggles for many in our field. This situation is particularly ironic when you ask a healthcare professional why they got into the healthcare field in the first place. The typical answer is "I wanted to help people." I find this very interesting in light of the fact that one of the most frequent patient complaints is related to interpersonal and communication issues rather than technical or medical issues.

Patients basically believe that the caregivers are competent and know the technical aspects of their jobs. For example, most patients do not know if they should have stitches or staples in their incisions. They do not know if they should have a pill for their pain or an injection. What they do know, however, is that they want to be treated with dignity and respect. They want their questions answered, and they do not want to wait for hours on end before they receive service or get answers to their questions. In many ways our patients and their families are asking for basic human courtesy. This point was corroborated recently by a study conducted by Dr. John Co and his associates (2003). Based on a survey of more than 6000 parents of children cared for in 38 hospitals across the country, Co and his colleagues discovered that overall parental satisfaction ratings of the care their children received was most closely associated with: (1) the communication the parents received about their child's condition and (2) the involvement they had in making decisions about their child's care (Co *et al.* 2003).

Another perspective on this issue comes from Dr. John Stone, a cardiologist and poet from Emery University School of Medicine. Dr. Stone's best-known work is *In the Country of Hearts.* In the section entitled "Listening to the Patient," he writes: "The inventor of the stethoscope, Laennec, knew that the medical history given by a patient is just as important—sometimes even more important—than the 'lup-dup' of the patient's heart. Among his advice to physicians is: 'Listen! Listen to your patient! He is giving you the diagnosis'" (1990:65).

One of our hospitals, Advocate South Suburban Hospital (Hazel Crest, Illinois), has built their service excellence program around a very basic aspect of listening and communicating—the Golden Rule. They realized that most patient encounters depend on how people treat each other. They gave the employees small lapel pins that were shaped like little golden rulers—reminders that the most important moments of truth are not technical in nature but human.

This notion of communicating with the patient and making them part of the healing process is not a new concept in healthcare. We seem to have merely lost perspective for a while. Dr. Francis Peabody articulated the need for patient involvement back in 1927. In his classic article "The Care of the Patient" (1927) he noted: "The most common criticism made at present by older practitioners is that young graduates have been taught a great deal about the mechanisms of disease, but very little about the practice of medicine—or, to put it more bluntly, they are too 'scientific' and do not know how to take care of patients" (877). He concludes his eloquent statement by saying, "One of the essential qualities of the clinician is interest in humanity, for the secret of the care of the patient is in caring for the patient."

Service excellence stems from a constant and deliberate dedication to listening to the VOC. But listening is not enough. Listening provides the context for responding. If providers of healthcare services do not listen and respond, their customers will find alternatives.

Defining Key Quality Characteristics

Having a customer service orientation is only the beginning. The next step is being able to turn this orientation into tactics and strategies for action. It begins by identifying quality characteristics (QCs). QCs represent a broad collection of things the customers care most about. For example, my wife has a floral design business. Her business has been growing (blossoming, if you will), and she decided it was time to buy a vehicle to carry all the arrangements to her customers (our 250,000-mile, 12-year-old Saab just was not meeting her needs anymore). So we set out exploring our options. She quickly developed a list of QCs. She knew right away that she did not want a sport utility vehicle (too small and boxy). She also eliminated a station wagon for the same reasons. This quickly reduced the field down to a van. As we explored the various QCs of vans, she soon got down to a list of key quality characteristics (KQCs), the things that she cared most about. Interestingly enough, she actually got down to a single KQC—sliding doors on both sides of the van. She really did not care about too many other options. She knew that she would need to be able to access the interior of the van from both sides. Some vans had only one door, which was unacceptable from her point of view.

Another example of defining a KQC comes from a good friend and coworker, Judi Miller. She decided it was time to purchase a new car. When I asked her what she was thinking of buying, she said proudly, "Anything that is less than 190 inches long." I told her that I had never heard of anyone buying a car strictly based on length. She said that it was very simple. It turns out that both she and her husband are great Harley-Davidson fans. Between the two of them they own three Harley-Davidson motorcycles, which they keep in the front part of their garage. This leaves roughly 190 inches remaining in the garage for a car—simple when you understand the VOC.

Defining KQCs enables you to start the VOC process. KQCs are the things customers care most about. They are the aspects of a process that are foremost in the minds of the customers. We all have KQCs irrespective of what the issue or process is. If we are not asked, however, our wants, needs, and expectations remain unknown. KQCs have the following characteristics:

- They reflect quality as defined or judged by the customer
- They reflect aspects of the process that the customer cares most about
- They represent to the customer the key measures of quality output
- They will vary from customer to customer
- They will create conflicts for you because you cannot meet all of your customers' needs simultaneously

Whenever you start to define the VOC, you should answer several basic questions:

- What is the process under review?
- When does the process begin and when does it end?
- Who is the primary customer? The secondary customer?
- Do we have consensus on the primary customer?
- What aspects of the process (the KQCs) are most important to the primary customer?

If you do not at least have a dialogue on these questions, you will probably assume that you know what the customer wants, needs, or expects. In healthcare we have a long history of being quick to prescribe and slow to listen. Historically, orders were given and the patients were expected to follow them. Yet the order, which seemed perfectly logical to the physician, may not have been what the patient wanted, needed, or desired. Because most patients defer to the judgment of the physician, however, orders will usually be followed even if they are far afield from the patients' KQCs.

One of the most frequently overlooked aspects of KQCs is that they will vary from customer to customer. If you cannot agree on the primary customer, then the KQC discussion will go round and round. This can also occur if you change the primary customer midway through an improvement initiative. If this happens, then you should revisit the KQC and see if it is still relevant to the new customer group.

It constantly amazes me how improvement teams cannot reach consensus on the primary customer. By way of example, let me offer a story from another service sector—education. I was working with a local school district to assist them in defining indicators. They were participating in a national demonstration project that required them to identify "quality indicators" that could be tracked over time. They were ready to start defining indicators and looking at the data. I asked them to consider a simple question before we started to peer at numbers: "Who is the primary customer of the educational system?" The team was composed of administrative staff, teachers, and community volunteers. As you can imagine, there were mixed responses to my question. The majority of the responses had something to do with the students as the primary customer. I asked if they would like to reconsider this response. If the students were the primary customers and the school really listened to their wants, needs, and expectations, school would begin at noon, have lunch as the first period, then move to free time for the next two hours before dismissal. School systems are not designed to maximize the KQCs of students. As we explored this question further, some team members concluded that the community was the primary customer. Others thought the business sector was the primary customer. Eventually, as the discussion dragged to a halt, the majority concluded that society was the primary customer of the educational system. Personally, I am not sure they ever really reached consensus on their primary customer. Periodically I run into the school superintendent and ask him if they ever resolved this question. He usually responds, "No, but they are still working on it."

Consider a healthcare example. Imagine that you are responsible for the billing process. If you define the patient as the customer, the KQCs might be an accurate bill, a timely bill, or a bill that is easily understood (i.e., no procedure codes, cryptic Latin phrases, or other medical jargon). If, on the other hand, the insurance company is the primary customer, then detailed procedure codes, insurance classification codes, and medical terminology might be more appropriate KQCs. If you change the primary customer the KQCs will also change. But if you cannot agree on who actually is the primary customer, then the team's discussion will have a lot of rhetoric but little practical value.

Listening Three Times

Healthcare providers are increasingly becoming interested in the VOC. The primary customers for a majority of healthcare providers are the patient, their family members, and/or other caregivers. There are, however, other customers, such as coworkers, the boss, suppliers, and people in other departments. In short, everyone has many customers. A key part of everyone's job, therefore, is to (1) know who their internal and external customers are and (2) take steps to actively listen to what these customers want, need, and expect (Lloyd 2003).

Figure 2.3 shows three key points at which listening to customers should occur. Note that these three listening points are not mutually exclusive. In fact, relying on only one or even two of these approaches will place tremendous limits on understanding what customers want, need, and expect. Multiple approaches to listening should be the standard for anyone who genuinely cares about their customers. Multiple approaches not only enhance the amount of information received but also increase the validity and reliability of the results (Campbell and Fiske 1970).

The first time to be listening to our customers is *before* they experience our products or services. This is what is typically known as preservice assessment. For example, if a hospital is thinking about creating a new service for women and children, they should devise methods and techniques to find out what po-

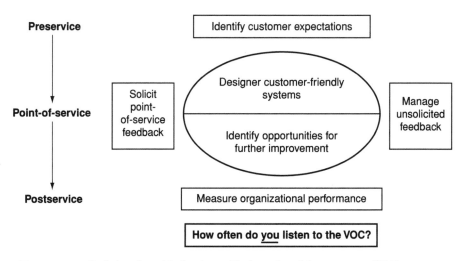

▲ FIGURE 2.3 Defining the critical points with the voice of the customer (VOC)
Reprinted with permission of Advocate Health Care.

tential patients, families, and payers expect from this service *before* it is designed and implemented. How often do we decide to open a service or program before we determine whether there is a market for the service? Healthcare is not like the classic line from the movie *Field of Dreams*—"If you build it, they will come!" Asking people how they would like something to work is the first step to a successful design. This type of listening is frequently overlooked in healthcare. Advocate Good Samaritan Hospital in Downers Grove, Illinois, successfully applied preservice listening when they redesigned their outpatient testing and therapy area. Focus groups were used to collect data from patients, families, physicians' office staff, and insurance companies. They were all asked to describe how they would like the testing and therapy process to work. Because each group had a little different perspective on the situation, the redesign team was able to gather a variety of insights that were used to design the new testing and therapy area. If they had not asked the customers *before* they designed the new service area, they would have built a facility and supporting processes that made sense to the staff but not to the customers.

The second time to listen to those we serve is while they are experiencing service or care. This is known as *point-of-service* (POS) assessment. Staff members at Advocate hospitals are actively engaged in this type of listening. Advocate Lutheran General Hospital (Park Ridge, Illinois), for example, was the first site in the system to consistently use POS feedback through rounding.[4] Managers and administrators review a very brief set of questions with patients who are well enough to be interviewed. This type of rapid-cycle feedback allows staff to implement immediate improvements. A side benefit of this type of listening (which was not anticipated at first) is that the patients find it very comforting to have someone from the management team spend a few minutes talking with them about their care and the processes they are experiencing. All Advocate sites of care (hospitals, home care, and medical groups) are now actively engaged in rounding with patients each day. This form of feedback not only enables service recovery but also the ability to start identifying patterns and opportunities for CQI teams. The major caution with this type of feedback is that it typically produces more positive results than postservice evaluations. If you rely strictly on this form of feedback, therefore, you will probably start to think that you are much better than you really are. The reason for this positive bias is simple—patients are hesitant to be totally honest with you while they are still under your care. They are concerned that you may hold something back or retaliate against them if they are honest and tell you what they really think of the care and service they are receiving. As a result, it is not uncommon to have the most frequent response from POS assessments be, "Oh, everything is just fine."

The third and most frequently used method of listening is postservice assessment. In this case, patients are asked to provide their opinions *after* they have been discharged. Most postservice assessments are obtained through either mailed or telephone surveys. Postservice assessments have three major advantages over face-to-face interviews:

- They are more reliable and valid than asking patients for opinions while they are undergoing care
- They provide patients with an opportunity to objectively reflect upon their experiences
- They allow patients to respond according to their own time frames
- They allow you to gather data from a larger segment of your total population of patients

Understanding the Tools

A comprehensive VOC measurement system should combine all three types of assessments. The first step toward building such a system is to become familiar with all the different tools and techniques that can provide VOC data. Table 2.1 summarizes some of the more popular approaches to gathering customer input. This matrix indicates at which of the three measurement points (pre, POS, and post) the tool can be used, as well as some of the advantages and disadvantages of each tool. A brief description of each method is provided below.

Surveys

Surveys are the most useful tool for gathering perspectives and attitudes from a large number of customers. If properly constructed, a survey can be extremely valuable. The problem with most surveys created by healthcare

▼ TABLE 2.1 An evaluation of customer feedback tools

Tool or approach	Service level			Cost	Advantages	Disadvantages
	Pre	POS	Post			
Surveys	✓	✓	✓	Moderate to high cost depending on the methodology used	• Generalizability • Offers continuous monitoring • Provides comparative reference data • Versatility • Reasonably quick to implement	• Requires rigorous protocols, valid and reliable instruments • May require sampling • Not highly flexible • Unwillingness of individuals to participate • Inability of respondents to recall
Focus groups	✓		✓	Moderate to high cost depending on the number conducted and who conducts them	• In-depth qualitative data • Do not require large samples • High flexibility • Can identify new issues or concerns while conducting a focus group	• Low generalizability • Requires skilled facilitators • Not anonymous
Observation		✓		Low cost	• Easy to do • Highly flexible	• Low generalizability • Low value for comparisons • Limited to publicly observable behavior • Requires considerable time and effort

Reprinted with permission of Advocate Health Care.

| Tool or Approach | Service Level | | | Cost | Advantages | Disadvantages |
	PRE	POS	POST			
Personal interviews	✓	✓	✓	High cost	• Very detailed data • Easy to probe for additional data • Effective with all socioeconomic levels	• Very labor intensive • Very time consuming • Quality of data depends on skill of interviewer • Not anonymous
Unsolicited feedback		✓	✓	Very low cost	• Identifies extreme dissatisfiers/satisfiers	• Virtually no opportunity to generalize findings
High-tech tools (TV, touchpads)		✓		Very high cost	• Provides real-time feedback • User-friendly • Flexible	• May not be appealing to certain groups of respondents • No control over sample of respondents
The experiential shopper (the "mystery shopper")		✓		High cost	• Tremendous depth of data • Can cover all aspects of a customer's experience	• Low generalizability for defining a "typical experience" • Requires the mystery shoppers to be trained and articulate

Reprinted with permission of Advocate Health Care.

workers, however, is that those constructing the surveys usually do not have sufficient knowledge of survey design and construction processes to make a valid (i.e., the survey actually measures what it purports to measure) and reliable (i.e., the survey will reproduce the same results under different administrations) survey instrument. It is not uncommon, for example, for a group of employees to sit down with a pot of coffee and develop a survey that is distributed to patients or family members by the end of the day. Although the individuals who created the survey have good intentions, most of the time these surveys are not valid or reliable, and the information received from the respondents is of a dubious value. Yet the survey development and distribution probably made the people who created it feel like they did something worthwhile. Surveys can be quite valuable, but their use requires knowledge about the issues that lead to a valid and reliable survey process. The most frequent pitfalls of survey design and use include (Carey 1999; Carey and Lloyd 2001):

- Poor questionnaire design
- Faulty and/or inadequate sampling methods
- Biased data collection
- Inadequate data analysis
- Inappropriate report formats

Hayes (1998) and Dillman (1978) also provide excellent references for developing and using surveys. Hayes not only describes how to construct a good survey but also lays out very clear steps for including surveys in a CQI program. Dillman's work is a classic in the field. He addresses all of the technical issues related to survey design and construction and then goes on to differentiate the pros and cons of mailed surveys and telephone surveys.

Surveys have become prevalent in the healthcare field. In some respects we oversurvey staff, patients, and families. Yet in this age of "We need more data," surveys seem like a quick fix for understanding customer needs. If your organization does not have an internal expert in the design, construction, and testing of surveys, then you need to consult experts who know what they are doing. Frequently some of the best resources can be found at local colleges and universities where courses in psychometrics or marketing research are taught.

To assist you in your understanding of what you know (and do not know) about survey research, I would ask that you consider the questions listed below about your organization's VOC survey system. If you cannot personally answer these questions, then find out if you have someone in your organization that can. If not, then your patient satisfaction vendor or consultant should have the answers. If no one you are currently affiliated with can answer these questions, then the surveys you are using are probably not worth the paper they are printed on. The key questions (Carey and Lloyd 2001) include:

- What is the role and function of customer surveys in our CQI efforts?
- Should we use mailed or phone surveys?
- Does it matter if we hand out the surveys to the patients?
- What is the meaning of reliability and validity? Which one is more important?
- How do we know if a survey has adequate reliability?
- Should we use factor analysis to verify the subscales in the survey?
- Should we use a yes/no response format or a Likert format?
- How do we know if we are properly sampling? Can we estimate the sampling error?
- How do we control for biased data? Interviewer bias? Respondent bias?
- Do all our employees see the results of the surveys?
- Do we have comparative reference norms? Benchmarks?
- Do we use the survey results to develop action plans?
- How do we use customer feedback to evaluate the effectiveness of improvement strategies?

If you find yourself somewhat confused by these questions, this is a good sign. It demonstrates that you are aware of what you do not know about survey research. We have all filled out numerous surveys. The mere completion of a survey, however, does not make us experts in the design, creation, and implementation of surveys.

Focus Groups

Focus groups are typically the method of choice for gathering detailed information after the patient is discharged. The major drawback of focus groups, however, is that they are generally done with small groups (10–15 people) and the results cannot be generalized to larger populations. However, focus groups do provide a wonderfully rich and detailed listening mechanism. Another pitfall with focus groups is that people frequently think that they do not have to be very rigorous in the planning and implementation of a focus group. Many of the same threats to validity and reliability of surveys apply to focus groups. If focus group facilitators are not trained in how to form and manage a focus group, they will end up with a rambling manuscript that provides little useful information. Focus groups are not informal chats with customers. All of the sites of care within the Advocate system are currently conducting two focus groups each quarter. This information is not used in isolation, however. It is combined with the results from rounding and then compared with the mailed survey results from our external vendor to gain a more complete understanding of the VOC.

Observation

Observation is the third method for gathering data on the customer. This is actually one of the most insightful methods of obtaining POS feedback. This approach is relatively low cost (compared to surveys and focus groups) since the principal costs are staff time. The observer merely selects a reasonably unobtrusive location and notes what occurs during a defined period of time. With a minimum level of training, the observer can record a fairly rich volume of information. The major drawbacks with data collected through observation are:

- The observer can be in only one place at a time.
- The observer sees events from a limited time perspective (e.g., the observer was in the emergency department for three hours on a Monday morning).
- The results have very low generalizability (i.e., can the observations made on Monday morning in the emergency department be generalized to the rest of the day, to the other days of the week, or to the other shifts?).
- The observers need to be trained in a standardized fashion so that they are all looking for the same types of events, situations, or encounters. Observation frequently suffers from not only respondent bias but also

situational bias (i.e., the very nature of the situation causes the observer to selectively focus on some events and ignore others).

Personal Interviews

Personal interviews can be used at all three measurement points. Like observation, this method can provide very rich and detailed information. Interviews have the added advantage, however, of being able to provide direct interaction with the customer. Interviews have a great deal of appeal because they seem so simple on the surface—find someone and go talk to them. The challenge comes in being a skilled interviewer who is able to probe without guiding the respondent to the answers being sought. Personal interviews are not investigative reporting sessions. They should be well thought out and conducted with consistently applied methods of inquiry. Finally, if the results are to be reflective of a larger population, then the interviews need to be of sufficient volume to capture a representative sample. This can be quite time consuming and expensive.

Unsolicited Feedback

Unsolicited feedback is one method of listening that is frequently overlooked in healthcare. This occurs most often when customers are so upset that they say, "I want to speak to someone in charge and I want to speak to them right now!" Most often this happens when customers feel the need to voice dissatisfaction with the care, service, or outcomes they are receiving. Most unsolicited feedback is negative in nature, but it does provide an opportunity to identify potential improvements. The central challenge with this type of feedback is not to overreact to single events. Ask yourself, "How many times has this happened in the past week or month?" If it is an isolated incident, engage in service recovery immediately. If it happens repeatedly, consider collecting data on the issue to see if there is a pattern and a need for improvement.

High-Tech Tools

Increasingly healthcare workers are discovering high-tech tools. These include interactive televisions, small handheld computers (PDAs), scan card devices, and interactive voice recording equipment. This approach to listening is the most expensive of all the methods, and the returns are frequently of marginal value. They are quite flexible because they can be used 24 hours a day, 7 days a week, 365 days a year. They are also very useful for rapid-cycle feedback. The major disadvantage is that they appeal to a limited segment of the population. Typically, they pique the interest of younger cohorts. Related to this issue of limited appeal is the fact that it is hard to control who uses them, how many times the same person might interact with the same touch screen, or if they provide a reliable estimate of the perspectives of the total population being served.

The Experiential Shopper

The last method to consider is the experiential shopper. This method has increased in popularity in the healthcare field. This is a classic POS method that stems primarily from the retail shopping industry (the "mystery shopper"). In this case, a consultant or staff person poses as a patient to gain firsthand knowledge of what it is like to be a patient. This method also suffers from low generalizability, but it can provide very detailed insights from the "patients" perspective. If staff pose as the mystery shopper, one of the side benefits of this method is that they typically gain a new appreciation of how patients view healthcare encounters.

Each of these methods has certain advantages and disadvantages. Healthcare providers who are serious about listening to the VOC need to: (1) become familiar with each method, (2) know the strengths and limitations of each method, and (3) be able to apply a particular method when it is needed.

Combining VOC Data With the VOP

From a CQI perspective, listening to the VOC is only a start. Listening to those we have the privilege of serving provides us with a baseline upon which we can build and improve. Once we have received customer input, however, the next thing to do is to identify the processes that influence the customers' perspectives. This is referred to as listening to the VOP. Customers can tell us what is wrong with our processes. It is up to the owners of the processes to take action and make things better. When a department or unit combines the VOC with the VOP, the probability of experiencing real improvement is greatly increased (Scherkenbach 1991).

Figure 2.4 presents a heuristic diagram that illustrates how listening to the VOC and the VOP create the foundation for improvement. It begins by conducting an enumerative study[5] to evaluate how the patients feel about their experiences in the emergency department (ED).

In Figure 2.4 an enumerative study was conducted at Time 1 to determine how satisfied ED patients were with various aspects of patient care, such as waiting time, explanation of diagnosis and treatment, comfort of the

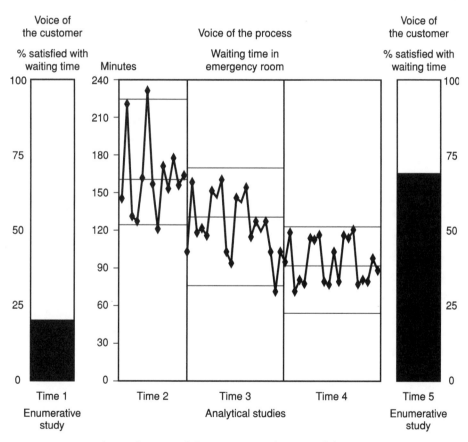

▲ FIGURE 2.4 Relating the voice of the customer to the voice of the process

Reprinted with permission of ASQ.

waiting area, and adequacy of discharge instructions. Suppose that the results of the survey showed that waiting time was the issue with which patients were least satisfied (less than 25% were satisfied) and that a majority wanted to be treated and discharged in two hours or less. As a result of this finding, a CQI team is initiated and charged with improving ED wait times. So where do they start? They should begin by realizing that the enumerative study they conducted at Time 1 captured the VOC. This is a statement of not only what the patients and their families want, need, or expect but also about the actual experiences of those going through the ED processes. This is what Gitlow *et al.* (1989) and Deming (1942) referred to as an analytic study.[6]

Figure 2.4 shows that during Time 2, the actual waiting time for 13 consecutive patients was measured and plotted on a control chart. Results show that the average wait time was about 160 minutes (a little over 2.5 hours) and that the process showed wide variation, with some waiting times both above and below the control limits.

Next, the CQI team developed and implemented an intervention (the exact details of which are unimportant for this illustration) and collected data on 20 new patients during Time 3. The average wait time during this period was reduced to a little over 2 hours, and the degree of variation was also reduced. However, the improvement was still not up to customer expectations (i.e., less than 2 hours). Therefore, another intervention was introduced, and data were collected on 20 more patients during Time 4. Results for this period demonstrated that the average wait time was reduced to approximately 90 minutes and the upper control limit was now at the 2-hour time limit voiced by patients in the enumerative study conducted during Time 1.

Finally, during Time 5, the same patient questionnaire used during Time 1 was repeated (i.e., another enumerative study was conducted). Results showed that the percentage of patients satisfied with the waiting time had increased substantially to approximately 70%. The analytic study used to measure the VOP showed that there had been two shifts in the process from Time 2 to Time 3 and from Time 3 to Time 4. The enumerative study (another patient survey) at Time 5 showed the extent to which this improvement had been perceived by patients.

While this example is only for teaching purposes, actual CQI teams use this line of thinking every day. Listening to the VOC without a plan for improving the processes of the customers' experience demonstrates listening without responding. On the other hand, listening to the VOP without connecting the process's performance to the expectations of the customers sets the stage for responding without listening. CQI requires both the VOC and the VOP, but it all begins with listening.

Notes

1. Lewis Carroll, *Alice in Wonderland* (New London: Brimax Books, 1990), 55.

2. When I use the term "customer" I am referring to anyone who receives the output of one's efforts. In a sense we are all customers and suppliers during most transactions. When I am teaching a class, for example, I am the supplier of information to the participants, but I am also a customer, because I rely on others to register participants, schedule rooms, and prepare handouts. My 9-year-old daughter, Devon, is also my customer. I want her to eat dinner, but I am not comfortable with her preparing a meal from scratch (especially lighting the gas stove). So I ask her what she would like, rice or noodles. I started doing this when she was about 3 years old. Back then she would look intently at the rice and noodle packages. For whatever reason at the time, she would pick one of the rice products and my wife or I would prepare it. Then Devon would proceed to eat it. Ever since we have always involved her in the decisions about what we will eat. She is a customer, and we should listen to her voice.

3. At the IHI's 2002 National Forum on Quality Improvement in Healthcare, Don Berwick, M.D., CEO of the IHI, provided a wonderful keynote address by having a three-way conversation with himself. He cleverly played three roles: he served as the narrator attempting to manage a debate between Dr. Oldway and Dr. Neway. Dr. Oldway was the traditionalist who pined for the way things used to be. He did not understand why the healthcare industry no longer was centered around himself, why nurses no longer seemed to respect him, why patients questioned him, and why all these outside groups were sticking their noses into his business. Dr. Neway, on the other hand, argued that by allowing patients to become more involved with their care, it actually

made life easier for the doctor. It was a very engaging and entertaining address and still available on videotape from the IHI for those who are interested.

4. This version of rounding is quite different from "clinical rounding." In fact, we have had to develop specialized training to help staff realize that patient rounding for service excellence is very different from conducting clinical rounds or grand rounds. Clinical rounding is basically a transaction. Rounding for service excellence, on the other hand, is an interaction.

5. An enumerative study (Deming 1942; Gitlow *et al.* 1989; Carey and Lloyd 2001) is done on a static population at a fixed period in time. Its purpose is merely to describe some variable of interest. Enumerative studies can be compared to taking a snapshot with a camera. It provides a limited view of events because it does not focus on how things may vary over time. An enumerative study is based on questions such as, "What was the average turnaround time last month? What was the mortality for coronary artery bypass graph (CABG) patients last year?" Enumerative studies would tell us nothing about the processes of care the patients experienced. In the most general sense of the word, enumerative studies are classic examples of data for judgment. When you look at the results of an enumerative study, you are left with only a few options: you can ask, "Does this outcome number strike me as being acceptable or not?" or "Is this outcome number different from the previous number?"

6. Analytic studies are performed on a dynamic process. They are not restricted to a single point in time and are used to predict the future rather than describe past outcomes. In this respect, an analytic study can be compared to a video recording rather than a snapshot. Analytic studies are done to determine why the outcomes were observed and how the process that produced the outcomes can be improved. An analytic study answers questions such as, "What can we predict about the length of stay for the coming year?" or "What were the causes of the observed decrease in surgical inpatients for the previous year?" A more extensive overview of the differences between enumerative and analytic studies can be found in Gitlow *et al.* (1989).

References

Campbell, D., and D. W. Fiske. "Convergent and Discriminant Validation by the Multitrait-Multimethod Matrix." In *Attitude Measurement* edited by Gene Summers. Chicago: Rand McNally & Company, 1970.

Carey, R. "How to Choose a Patient Survey System," *Journal on Quality Improvement* 25, no. 1 (January 1999): 20–25.

Carey, R., and R. Lloyd. *Measuring Quality Improvement in Healthcare: A Guide to Statistical Process Control Applications.* Milwaukee: ASQ Press, 2001.

Co, J., T. Ferris, B. Marino, C. Homer, and J. Perrin. "Are Hospital Characteristics Associated with Parental Views of Pediatric Inpatient Care Quality?" *Pediatrics* 111, no. 2 (2003): 308–314.

Connellan, T., and R. Zemke. *Sustaining Knock Your Socks Off Service.* Chicago: American Management Association, 1993.

Deal, T., and M. K. Key. *Corporate Celebration.* San Francisco: Berrett-Koehler, 1998.

Deming, W. E. "On a Classification of the Problems of Statistical Inference." *Journal of the American Statistical Association* 37, no. 218 (1942): 173–185.

_____. "On Probability as a Basis for Action." *The American Statistician.* 29, no. 4 (1975): 146–152.

_____. *Out of the Crisis.* Cambridge, Mass.: Massachusetts Institute of Technology Center for Advanced Engineering Study, 1992.

Dillman, D. A. *Mail and Telephone Surveys: The Total Design Method.* New York: Wiley, 1978.

Freiberg, K., and J. Freiberg. *NUTS! Southwest Airlines' Crazy Recipe for Business and Personal Success.* Austin: Bard Press, 1996.

Garvin, D. "Building a Learning Organization." *Harvard Business Review* (July–August, 1993).

Gitlow, H., S. Gitlow, A. Oppenheim, and R. Oppenheim. *Tools and Methods for the Improvement of Quality.* Homewood, Ill.: Irwin Press, 1989.

Hayes, B. E. *Measuring Customer Satisfaction.* Milwaukee: ASQC Press, 1998.

Kohn, A. *No Contest.* Boston: Houghton Mifflin, 1986.

_____. *Punished by Rewards: The Trouble with Gold Stars, Incentive Plans, A's, Praise, and Other Bribes.* Boston: Houghton Mifflin, 1993.

Langley, G., K. Nolan, T. Nolan, C. Norman, and L. Provost. *The Improvement Guide.* San Francisco: Jossey-Bass, 1996.

Leebov, W., G. Scott, and L. Olson. *Achieving Impressive Customer Service.* Chicago: AHA Press, 1998.

Lloyd, R. "Improving Ambulatory Care Through Better Listening." *Journal of Ambulatory Care Management* 26, no. 2 (April–June 2003): 100–109.

Nelson, B. *1001 Ways to Reward Employees.* New York: Workman, 1994.

Peabody, F. "The Care of the Patient." *Journal of the American Medical Association* 88 (March 19, 1927): 877–882.

Peter, L., and R. Hull. *The Peter Principle.* New York: Bantam Books, 1970.

Scherkenbach, W. *The Deming Route to Quality and Productivity.* Washington, D.C.: CEEPress Books, 1990.

_____. *Deming's Road to Continual Improvement.* Knoxville, Tenn.: SPC Press, 1991.

Schultz, L. *Profiles in Quality.* New York: Quality Resources, 1994.

Senge, P. *The Fifth Discipline: The Art and Practice of the Learning Organization.* New York: Currency/Doubleday, 1994.

Stone, J. *In the Country of Hearts: Journeys in the Art of Medicine.* Baton Rouge: Louisiana State University Press, 1990.

Walkins, K., and V. Marsiek. *Sculpting the Learning Organization.* San Francisco: Jossey-Bass, 1993.

Wiek, C., and L. Leaon. *The Learning Edge: How Smart Managers and Smart Companies Stay Ahead.* New York: McGraw-Hill, 1994.

Chapter 3

Indicator Selection and Development

Listening to the VOC provides the starting point. Once you understand the wants, needs, and expectations of your customers, however, it is up to you to translate these performance expectations into indicators that can be measured and tracked. Unfortunately, in healthcare it is all too often the case that indicators are selected not because the providers of a service actually have listened to the VOC, but rather because they made a priori decisions that they know what is best for the customer. In this case, the selected indicators will usually be either ones that they have "always collected" or ones that completely miss the expectations of the customers. This chapter is designed to provide a roadmap for selecting and building indicators that can be tied directly to the VOC.

As was discussed in Chapter 1, the search for a few good indicators begins by having a clear understanding of why you are engaged in measuring performance in the first place. Historically, healthcare providers have collected and analyzed data strictly for internal purposes that were directed at improving clinical and operational effectiveness and efficiency (see Chapter 5 for a more detailed discussion on this point). Over the years, however, the growing external demand for data has shifted much of the focus away from effectiveness and efficiency and more toward judgment. In other words, the business community, regulatory bodies, government officials, and consumers are all interested in answering a very simple question: "Which provider is the best?"

In an effort to answer this question, many initiatives, projects, and pieces of legislation have been developed over the years. The goal of these efforts has been to develop "report cards" on healthcare providers that can be used by large purchaser groups (e.g., companies and the government) and consumers to make informed decisions about their healthcare choices. The state data commissions, business coalitions, and consumer groups have all tried, in a variety of ways, to answer this question (see Chapter 1 for details). To date, however, there seems to be no easy answer to this simple question.

What has been the typical outcome is that external groups voluntarily ask for or mandate certain performance indicators from providers. These numbers are then combined with those from other providers; risk adjustments may be applied to the data to account for severity of the patient populations; and finally, reports are released to the public. These releases usually stimulate the following chain of events:

- Local and/or national media become interested.

- Investigative reporters are sent out to discover why *Your Hospital* has a higher coronary artery bypass graph (CABG) mortality percentage than *My Hospital* and both are higher than the average for the county in which they are located.

- The reporters present their findings in the next day's newspaper or on the six o'clock news, which usually focus on the providers at the top and bottom of the list.

- *Your Hospital* and *My Hospital* convene internal meetings to develop strategies (rationales) for countering why their numbers are higher than the average.

- Consumers become confused and/or cynical because the data do not necessarily reflect their experiences (e.g., "My father went to *Your Hospital* for his heart operation and everything was fine" or "My father went to *Your Hospital* and nearly died").

Whatever your view on the public release of data, it is quite obvious that the demand for data on provider performance will increase over the next five years. The simple question is "Are you prepared for it?" Healthcare organizations that have a measurement philosophy and a proactive plan for investigating their own results will be in a much better position to deal with external scrutiny than those that sit back and hope that the Channel 5 Action Camera van does not show up outside their hospital.

Even though there is a renewed interest in the public release of provider data, the more important reason for knowing your data better than anyone else is that it is the right thing to do and it makes business sense. The complexity of today's healthcare delivery system requires that leaders have a clear understanding of their processes and the related outcomes. In order to meet operational and financial objectives, patient safety goals, and customer service expectations, healthcare providers should consider developing what Caldwell (1995) refers to as a "strategic measurement deployment matrix." Such a matrix combines strategic vision with tactical measures. It allows an organization to determine if the things they are working on are really connected to what the organization is supposed to be achieving.

The first step, therefore, on the quality measurement journey is achieved by having some sense of why you are measuring and your approach to measurement. Is measurement a part of the organization's day-to-day functioning? Or is it something that is done periodically in order to prepare reports for board meetings? A good place to start is to develop the organization's measurement philosophy. For example, within my own system, we have developed the following measurement philosophy statement:

> ▶ **Advocate Health Care's Measurement Philosophy**
>
> *Responsible leadership demands that we know our data better than anyone else.*
>
> *It further requires that we have processes in place to accurately and consistently obtain a balanced set of measures that monitor clinical outcomes, functional status, customer satisfaction, process effectiveness, and resource utilization.*
>
> *Finally, we must use data to develop improvement strategies and then take **ACTION** to make these strategies a reality.*

I believe that every organization needs to have a serious dialogue around its measurement philosophy, the role of indicators, and how they will (and will not) be used. Without a philosophy, measurement efforts will be nothing more than a random walk through the data.

Ultimately, indicators are designed to improve quality by:

- Moving us away from anecdotes and focusing on objective data
- Enhancing our understanding of the variation that exists in a process
- Monitoring a process over time
- Seeing the effect of a change in a process
- Providing a common frame of reference
- Providing a more accurate basis for prediction

Unfortunately, many organizations run into serious roadblocks when they attempt to select indicators and use them to improve quality.

Measurement Roadblocks

Many things impede good measurement practice. In *The Measurement Mandate* (1993) JCAHO identified the following eight potential barriers to measurement:

- Concerns about disclosure of performance data and information
- Professional autonomy
- Negative attitudes developed during the quality assurance era
- Resource constraints
- Time constraints
- Peer review
- Inadequately developed and tested performance measures and misrepresentation of how performance data should be used
- Fear of numbers

Although these are useful categories, I believe they can be boiled down to five key roadblocks to good measurement:

Roadblock #1: Measurement is threatening. This is probably the largest roadblock we face with healthcare measurement. There are many examples of how data have been used both internally and externally to (figuratively) "beat people up." We often hear coworkers say that they did not want to take the monthly numbers to the boss because he or she "won't like these." Organizations have long memories when it comes to the use of data. Seasoned employees quickly tell new workers what happens when the numbers do not meet management's expectations. Quickly the new workers hear the story about how Gwenn, nurse manager of 3 East, did not get her patient satisfaction scores up by the end of the year and now Gwenn is no longer here. What the new workers don't know, however, is that Gwenn left because her husband was transferred to another city. But her leaving and the decline of her unit's patient satisfaction scores do provide the basis for a compelling story. As time passes, this story becomes legendary, gets embellished a little, and becomes part of the organization's folklore. "Remember what happened to Gwenn" becomes the standard response whenever someone's numbers are below expectations.

What I find absolutely fascinating, however, is the fact that people actually like to measure things, including their own performance. There seems to be a natural curiosity in human beings about measurement. My 9-year-old daughter, for example, loves to measure things. When I was in the garage one day doing a project she came up to me and said, "Measure me, Daddy." I took my tape measurer and proceeded to measure her height. She acknowledged the measurement and went about her business. Ten minutes later she returned and stated, "Measure me, Daddy." I said, "Devon, I don't think you have grown much in the last ten minutes." But she insisted and seemed to find the actual act of measurement not only enlightening but also entertaining. The next time I observed her in the garage she was using the tape to measure her bike, her doll, and the dog (or at least trying to measure the dog). Even adults love to measure what they do. I have a number of friends who participate in triathlons. They are very meticulous about measuring and monitoring their training regimens. I have seen similar behavior from people involved with bowling or golf.

How do we drive what seems to be an almost natural curiosity about measurement out of people when they get into work situations? The answer to me seems rather simple. Organizations frequently use data to instill a sense of fear in the employees. Once fear is established, then data become the means for intimidation and control. It is not surprising, therefore, that the workers rapidly conclude, "Why should I participate in a measurement system that will be used against me?" Several years ago I experienced this attitude when I was facilitating a team that was attempting to reduce call button response time. During a meeting that was intended to identify a measurement plan, one team member blurted out, "Why don't you go measure 4 West? I know they are worse they we are." When measurement becomes threatening, the workers will conclude that measurement should be for someone else, not for them. The truth of the matter is that the primary audience for measurement is the manager of the department or unit and the workers. These are the people who own the process and who should be responsible for its performance. If the organization does not have a philosophy of measurement and a set of related tactics for deploying measurement throughout the organization, then measurement will probably become a threat. A strategic focus on measurement as described by Caldwell (1995) will do wonders to overcome this roadblock.

Roadblock #2: The desire for precision. Believe it or not, healthcare is not a science. The federal government classifies healthcare jobs as service jobs, along with car repair, lawn service, and beauty shops. Sure, we use science and technology to accomplish what we do, but by and large healthcare is considered a service. It is interesting, therefore, that many people in our profession use the illusion of precision as a convenient excuse for not measuring. I have heard, for example, the following responses many times when I asked a team if they had finished their measurement plan:

- "We think it will take a little longer to make sure the survey is right."
- "The log sheet does not seem to capture all the elements we think we need to collect."
- "Why don't you check back with us in a couple of weeks? We might have a better plan in place at that time."

The key point is that quality measurement does not have to be as precise as measurement in controlled experiments. We are not conducting research to win the Nobel Prize. We are trying to understand the variation that lives within our processes in order to make things more effective and more efficient for those we serve. Therefore, the concept of measurement that is "good enough" needs to be our guiding mantra. The basic purpose of quality measurement is to inform the organization about its general direction and whether it is moving toward its goals and objectives. You do not need p values at the 0.01 or 0.05 level of significance to tell you this. As one CEO told me, "If it passes the sniff test, that's good enough for me." Furthermore, we are not trying to conduct research that is designed around double-blinded randomized clinical trials. We are trying to improve quality. Do not make your measurement efforts so precise and pure that you never proceed to the most important question: "How are we doing?" In short, if an organization spends its time developing academically or scientifically precise measures, it will probably never get started on its quality measurement journey. The desire for precision will be a convenient excuse for avoiding the measurement mandate. This was demonstrated very nicely by a group of physicians during an evening meeting designed to discuss their hospital's quality improvement plan. The manager of quality was doing a very good job of presenting the plan and the related indicators. Then she got to the project on deep vein thrombosis (DVT). She described the indicator (percentage of patients evaluated for DVT risk) and then showed the historic baseline and the results for the last eight months. Instead of discussing why the hospital's performance on this indicator was declining, the physicians became embroiled in a debate over the number of charts being reviewed and whether the sample of patient charts was "significant." The first mistake they made was that "significance" is not a relevant concept when it comes to sampling. Second, the sample pulled (20 charts per month through a stratified random process) was good enough for the purposes at hand (i.e., determining how well the hospital was evaluating the risk for a DVT). As I sat and watched this discussion unfold, I realized that it was a perfect example of Roadblock #2. They were questioning the method and the data instead of discussing the processes by which they evaluate a patient's potential for a DVT. Precision was creating a roadblock for improvement.

Roadblock #3: Using standards as performance objectives. Standards basically set limits on performance. Once the standard is achieved, complacency usually sets in and people say, "What more do you want from me? I met the standard." In healthcare this happens most often when the JCAHO standards are the issue. I have heard many healthcare professionals claim that they did not have to get any better because they were already at the JCAHO standard. I guess this means they believe that their performance is acceptable and in need of no further improvement. If standards serve as the goal for the quality journey, then it will be a limited journey. What worked today to satisfy customers or meet the prescribed standards will not be so tomorrow. For example, assume that you met the JCAHO standards during your last survey. What are you going to do, however, when the Centers for Medicare and Medicaid Services (CMS) start releasing hospital data (in 2004) and show that your facility is "significantly" above expected mortality percentages for the treatment of heart attack patients? Your insistence that you met the JCAHO standards will carry little weight at this point. The concepts of baseline, target, and goal provide a much better frame of reference than standards. Standards are basically used to establish minimum thresholds of performance. Compliance with standards and the desire to perform only at this level, therefore, guarantee that an organization is not really committed to CQI. CQI is a never-ending pursuit of excellence. Meeting standards is acceptance of current performance and a willingness to say, "We're good enough."

Roadblock #4: Limited knowledge of SPC. This roadblock relates to skills and competencies with quality measurement tools and techniques. Most healthcare professionals have had at least one course in statistics at some point in their careers. Yet this exposure to statistics (or sadistics, as many like to call it) is not sufficient for implementing quality initiatives. SPC is a separate and distinct body of knowledge from what many refer to as "traditional" statistical methods (see Chapter 5 for a more detailed discussion on this point). Organizations that attempt to use statistical notions (such as hypothesis testing) and methods (such as tests of significance and descriptive summary statistics) will quickly become disillusioned with their quality improvement efforts. The reason for this disillusionment is simple: they are using statistical techniques that are designed to answer questions about efficacy instead of techniques designed to answer questions about effectiveness and efficiency (Brooke, Kamberg, and McGlynn 1996). My colleague Dr. Ray Carey and I have been teaching SPC methods to healthcare professionals for more than 10 years. During this time, we have seen an increase in the level of knowledge that healthcare professionals have about SPC. Organizations like the American Society for Quality (ASQ) and the IHI have made major contributions to this growing recognition and understanding of SPC in the healthcare field. But we are still at the beginning stages of this journey when compared to the use of SPC in manufacturing and industry. Use of SPC in these arenas can be traced back to the mid-1920s when Walter Shewhart first formalized the theories and methods behind the control chart. In 1931 Shewhart published "Economic Control of Quality of Manufactured Product," which stands as the landmark reference on SPC. The good news is that healthcare professionals are becoming more aware of what SPC can do to assist them in their quality journey. The bad news is that we have a long way to go before statistical thinking is commonplace in our industry.

Roadblock #5: Numerical Illiteracy. Having skills in the use of SPC is not enough to produce world-class quality. SPC provides a wonderful foundation, but the real test comes in applying SPC knowledge to overcome the fifth and final roadblock—numerical illiteracy. Wheeler (1993:vi) describes numerical illiteracy as follows: "Numerical illiteracy is not a failure with arithmetic, but it is instead a failure to know how to use the basic tools of arithmetic to understand data. Numerical illiteracy is not addressed by traditional courses in primary or secondary schools, nor is it addressed by advanced courses in mathematics. This is why even highly educated individuals can be numerically illiterate."

What is needed to overcome numerical illiteracy is what the Statistics Division of ASQ calls "statistical thinking." The vision of the Statistics Division is that statistical thinking will be found in all aspects of organizational behavior and performance. Figure 3.1 depicts this vision. Statistical thinking encompasses five key components:

- Systems thinking
- Statistical methods
- Philosophy (of measurement)
- Analysis
- Action

The specific activities that form the actual work of statistical thinking include:

- Understanding the process being investigated
- Understanding variation (both conceptually and statistically)
- Knowing how to collect data
- Knowing how to make improvements (e.g., being skilled at applying the PDSA cycle (Plan, Do, Study, Act))

As you can see, knowledge of statistical methods is only one aspect of statistical thinking. Statistical thinking is a much broader notion that has the ability not only to overcome the numerical illiteracy roadblock but also to provide a clear road map for the entire quality journey.

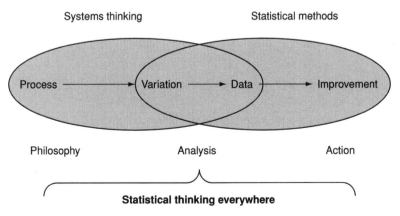

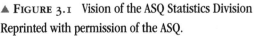

▲ FIGURE 3.1   Vision of the ASQ Statistics Division
Reprinted with permission of the ASQ.

Deming's views on the value of statistical thinking are well known and have been widely documented in his own writings (especially in *Out of the Crisis*, 1992) and those of others. Mann (1989) provides an excellent overview of how Deming and his colleagues regarded the role of statistical thinking with examples of how Deming influenced statistical thinking in this country and in Japan. In Chapter 3, entitled "Statistical Methods for Tapping into the Information Flow Generated by a Process," she uses the following quote from Deming to clarify the difference between using common sense or statistical thinking to make decisions: "There are many hazards to the use of common sense. Common sense cannot be measured. You have to be able to define and measure what is significant. Without statistical methods you don't know what the numbers mean" (Mann 1989:62).

Along this same line, Mann references the following point made by William Conway, the former CEO of the Nashua Corporation: "He pointed out [during a panel discussion] that one of the greatest handicaps of people who are trying to improve productivity and quality is that they attempt to deal with these matters in generalities. The use of statistics is a way of getting into specifics that will allow managers and workers to make decisions based on facts rather than speculation and hunches" (Mann 1989:62). In short, statistical thinking is a way to approach all aspects of work. It is a way of thinking about numbers and how they can be used to make improvements. Statistical thinking is the primary way to gain immunization over numerical illiteracy.

The five roadblocks described in this section are not insurmountable. The first step in overcoming them is merely to be aware that they exist. Once they are understood and acknowledged, then it is time to take steps to immunize yourself against their proliferation.

The Quality Measurement Road Map

Any successful journey begins with a good road map. Developing good indicators is not all that different from planning a good road trip. The road map we will use to guide our present journey is shown in Figure 3.2.

Our journey begins by identifying *types of indicators* that reflect the aspects of healthcare delivery we wish to measure. Ideally, these concepts should be capable of capturing what Donabedian (1980, 1982) refers to as the structures (S), processes (P), and outcomes (O) of medical care.

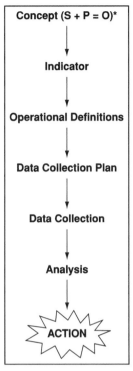

*Note: S = structures, C = processes, and O = outcomes.

▲ FIGURE 3.2 The Quality Measurement Road Map

After deciding what concepts are to be measured (e.g., patient safety), the next step in the journey is to *select a specific indicator* that allows us to measure a dimension of this concept. For example, if patient safety is the concept of interest, an indicator might be the inpatient falls rate (i.e., the number of inpatient falls per 1000 patient days). Obviously, there are many indicators that could be used to measure patient safety. The major challenge you have at this point in your journey, therefore, is to decide from all the things that you could measure which one or two indicators are vital (as opposed to merely interesting or nice to know).[1]

After selecting a specific indicator, you will come to the first potential detour in your journey. Many travelers have taken substantial detours in their quality measurement journeys because they did not take time to develop a clear *operational definition* for the indicator. Consider our example of a patient fall. Without a clear definition of what constitutes a "fall," we run the risk of including near falls, partial falls, falls with injuries, falls without injuries, and assisted falls in the same measure. Some might even include staff and visitor falls in the count if the operational definition is ambiguous.

If you successfully avoid the operational definition detour, it is time to move on to developing a *data collection plan*. This consists of two distinct steps. First, you should spend time discussing with your colleagues how you intend to actually collect the desired data. Too many people select an indicator and immediately rush off to start collecting data. This usually leads to collecting the wrong data in the wrong amounts (too little or too much). Ultimately, a rush to data can lead to poor decision making and frustration with the entire measurement act. A well-thought-out data collection plan should address issues such as the frequency of data collection, stratification issues, sampling design, and collection methods. Once these issues are resolved, the actual collection of the data usually goes very smoothly.

Data analysis does not happen by itself. All too often, however, the lack of planning for the analytic part of the journey causes a team to hit a dead end. I have seen teams put considerable effort into defining indicators and collecting data only to hit a major snag because they had not taken time to figure out how they would analyze the data and who would actually churn out the numbers. This happens frequently on nursing units, which typically do not have computers that are capable of running statistical analysis. Data are collected, then several willing nurses volunteer to use calculators and add up all the numbers. Nurses have access to the patient care data and related tools, but they usually do not have access to the statistical software needed to conduct appropriate analyses of the data. There needs to be a dialogue about this analytic step, or all the effort you put into the earlier part of your journey will leave you short of your destination.

The final leg of your measurement journey involves taking *action* with the analytic results. Data without a context for action are useless. Unfortunately, a considerable amount of healthcare data is collected, analyzed, and then not acted upon. Quality improvement requires action. Data collection should not become the ultimate goal of a CQI team; action to make things better for the customers is the ultimate goal.

These seven steps define the major milestones of the quality measurement journey. The remainder of this chapter focuses on the first five aspects of the quality measurement journey (types of indicators, selecting a specific indicator, developing operational definitions, developing a data collection plan, and collecting data). Chapters 4, 5, and 6 address the analysis of data and the appropriate management action to take once you understand the variation in your process.

Types of Indicators

An initial step toward good measurement practice begins by realizing that indicators can be classified in many different ways. A singular focus on one or even two types of indicators will give an organization an incomplete picture of its overall health and performance. Historically, the healthcare industry has not had a very balanced approach to indicator selection and analysis. Financial indicators, for example, have played a much more dominant role in our industry than quality indicators.[2] Developments over the past ten years, however, have caused healthcare providers to start thinking more broadly about what they measure. No longer are financial indicators (e.g., length of stay, average cost/charges per discharge, or variable versus fixed costs) adequate to understand the quality of an organization's outcomes and service.

Kaplan and Norton (1992, 1993, 1996) have made major contributions in this area by describing the components of what they call a "balanced scorecard." Even though their work has been directed more toward for-profit companies, the basic message they present is applicable to the healthcare industry. Specifically, they argue that "no single measure can provide a clear performance target or focus attention on the critical areas of the business" (1992:71). According to Kaplan and Norton, an organization should monitor a set of indicators that represent the key strategic areas in the organization's business plan. A well-selected and organized set of indicators should also place strategy and vision, not control, at the center of the organization (1992:79).

The key word for me when I first read the work of Kaplan and Norton was "balanced." Healthcare has a long and rich history when it comes to tracking data. What we have not done particularly well, however, is to make sure that the data we do collect is tied to our strategic objectives and represents, therefore, a balanced set of measures that cut across the full range and scope of services being delivered.

Although Florence Nightingale was keenly interested in tracking healthcare outcomes, it was Earnest A. Codman who proposed a uniform approach to performance measurement. Codman, a surgeon from Boston, was definitely a man ahead of his time. He proposed in the early 1900s that physicians should not only measure what they did in the hospital setting but also track the results of their work over time. He proposed what he called the "end result idea" as a way to find out what happened to the patients for up to a year after they received care in the hospital. He received stern criticism from his colleagues at Massachusetts General Hospital when he proposed the outlandish notion that data on physician and hospital performance should be released to the public:

> I am called eccentric for saying this in public; that hospitals, if they wish to be sure of improvement, must find out what their results are, must analyze their results, to find out their strong and weak points, must compare their results with those of other hospitals and must care for what cases they can care for well, and avoid attempting to care for cases which they are not qualified to care for well, . . . must welcome publicity not only for their successes, but for their errors. Such opinions will not be eccentric a few years hence." (Codman 1917:183).[3]

Avedis Donabedian is another physician who contributed significantly to the field of quality measurement. Donabedian provided the first framework for developing what I would consider to be a balanced set of indicators related to the delivery of medical care. In his classic two-volume work *Explorations in Quality Assessment and Monitoring* (1980, 1982), Donabedian described, in considerable detail, three key points in the delivery of medical services:

- Structures (the tools, resources, and organizational components)
- Processes (activities that connect patients, physicians, and staff)
- Outcomes (results)

He then suggested that measures should be developed to capture these three dimensions of medical service. Even though Donabedian provided a simple model for organizing indicators, like Codman, he, too, was a little ahead of the curve. Most healthcare professionals during the early 1980s did not readily embrace Donabedian's model for evaluating medical quality or his suggestions for building indicators that represent structures, processes, and outcomes.

In more recent times, JCAHO (1996) has identified nine dimensions of clinical performance that could be used to categorize indicators:

- Appropriateness
- Availability
- Continuity
- Effectiveness
- Efficacy
- Efficiency
- Respect and caring
- Safety
- Time lines

In the Institute of Medicine's (IOM) report *Crossing the Quality Chasm* (2001), six aims for improvement are identified that could also serve to categorize indicators:

- Safety
- Effectiveness
- Patient-centeredness
- Time lines
- Efficiency
- Equity

In my work, I have used the following six types of indicators to help managers and staff decide if they are taking a balanced approach to measurement:

- Clinical outcomes
- Functional status/activities of daily living
- Safety
- Customer satisfaction (patient/family, employee, and physician)
- Process efficiency/effectiveness
- Resource utilization

Irrespective of the number of categories used to identify indicators, the key point is that a balanced approach to indicator selection and development is far superior to a narrow focus. A singular or narrow focus on one or even two types of indicators will lead to shallow knowledge and ultimately suboptimal performance. A balanced approach to indicator development does not mean, however, that you have to measure 30 or 40 indicators. Focusing on the vital few (with emphasis placed on the word "few") is preferable to assembling an unmanageable array of indicators that require a small army to collect, analyze, and interpret.

Selecting a Specific Indicator

Once you have decided which types of indicators are most appropriate, the next step is to select the specific indicators that can be measured. Although this seems like a straightforward activity, I have found it surprising how many teams struggle with this task. *An indicator is a specific aspect of a process.* Yet all too often teams confuse themselves by selecting an indicator that is actually a process that could have many different indicators. For example, I asked a patient safety team what they intended to measure. They responded proudly, "patient falls prevention." This, they thought, was their indicator. What they missed was the fact that patient falls prevention is not an indicator. It is a dimension of patient safety. It is a concept, a process name, or possibly a desired end state. You cannot measure patient falls prevention. What you can measure, however, are the following specific indicators of the patient falls prevention process:

- The number of patient falls
- The percentage of patients who fall
- The falls rate

Each of these indicators identifies a specific way to look at the falls prevention process. Each indicator measures a different component and tells you something different about the falls prevention process. Using Donabedian's classification model, these indicators would be classified as outcome measures. You could also develop a list of indicators for structures and processes related to the falls prevention process.

Table 3.1 provides examples of specific indicators and their related concepts.[4] For each concept, there are several different indicators that could be tracked. The decision as to which indicator is selected (from this list or a new list of indicators that a team might develop) depends on the questions that a quality improvement team is trying to answer. If you phrase the question in terms of the absolute volume of an activity, you might be interested in tracking a simple count of the number of events (e.g., the number of falls). If, on the other hand, you were interested in a relative measure, then you would be better off measuring falls as a percentage, or, better yet, as a rate. Life is full of choices. When it comes to indicator selection, there are more options than most people realize.

▼ **TABLE 3.1** Moving from a concept to a specific indicator

Concept	Potential indicators for this process
Patient falls prevention	• The number of patient falls • The percentage of patient falls • The patient falls rate
C-sections	• The number of C-sections • The percent of C-sections • The C-section rate
Care of surgical patients	• The percent of postop deaths (sorted by ASA class) • The number of days between the occurrence of a postop death • The percentage of unexpected returns to surgery • The number of days between unexpected returns to surgery
Care of coronary artery bypass graph (CABG) patients	• Intubation time—post CABG • The percentage of prolonged postop CABG intubations
Patient scheduling	• The average number of days between a call for an appointment and the actual appointment date • The percentage of appointments made within three days of the call for an appointment • The number of appointments scheduled each day • The number of days between a call for an appointment and the first appointment
Employee retention	• Total number of full-time equivalents (FTEs) • Percentage of employee turnover • Employee turnover rate • Average number of years employed by the organization • The percentage of new hires that leave during the first year
Employee evaluations	• The number of evaluations completed • The percentage of evaluations completed on time • Variance from due date of a completed evaluation

▼ TABLE 3.1 Moving from a concept to a specific indicator *(continued)*

Concept	Potential indicators for this process
Care of emergency patients	• The number of unplanned returns to the emergency department (ED) • The percentage of ED patients admitted as inpatients • The ED transfer rate • The patient wait time in the ED
Implementation of a restraint protocol	• The number of patients who had restraints applied • The percentage of patients placed in restraints • The restraint utilization rate
Documentation of histories and physicals (H&Ps)	• Transcription turnaround time • The time from patient admission to the physician-dictated H&P • The percentage of incomplete H&Ps
Medication usage	• The total number of medication orders placed each day • The number of medication orders that had an error • The percentage of orders with an error • The medication error rate • The number of wasted IVs
Customer satisfaction	• The number of patient complaints • The percentage of patients providing positive responses to a survey • The percentage of patients who indicated that they would recommend your facility to a family member or friend • The percentile ranking for employee satisfaction in a national database • The percentage of physicians indicating that your hospital is an "excellent" facility
Home care visits	• The number of home care visits • The average time spent during a home care visit • The percentage of time spent traveling during each home care visit • The number of visits per home care nurse • The number of bottles of home oxygen delivered
Pastoral care	• The number of patient encounters by the pastoral care staff • The number of minutes spent during a patient encounter • The percentage of inpatient admissions that have properly documented the patient's religious preference • The number of requests from nursing units for assistance

▼ **TABLE 3.1** Moving from a concept to a specific indicator *(continued)*

Concept	Potential indicators for this process
Delivery of oncology services	• The percentage of outpatient oncology patients that have to be admitted • An individual patient's platelet counts • The total cost to treat a cancer patient • Mood scale index scores for cancer patients
CQI training	• The number of participants attending a class • The percentage of cancellations • The percentage of no-shows • The information recall scores at 30 and 60 days
Ventilator management	• The number of patients on a ventilator • The percentage of patients placed on a ventilator • The number of days on a ventilator • The ventilator-associated pneumonia rate
Electronic access to information	• The number of PC stations in the organization • The minutes of system downtime • The percentage of physicians who regularly use online protocols • The number of visits (hits) to the organization's Web site
Outpatient testing and therapy	• The total number of outpatient visits • The wait time to have a blood draw (or any other procedure) • The percentage of outpatient procedures with a complication • The complication rate for outpatient procedures • The time it takes to complete a colonoscopy procedure
Lab production	• Lab turnaround time • The total number of lab orders • The percentage of inaccurate lab orders • The percentage of stat lab orders

Developing Operational Definitions

The real work of indicator development begins after you have selected a specific indicator. Now it is time to develop an operational definition. Personally, I find the specification of operational definitions to be one of the more interesting and intriguing aspects of indicator development. Every day we are challenged to think about operational definitions. They are not only essential to good measurement but also critical to successful communication between individuals. For example, if you tell your teenage son or daughter to be "home early" from a party, you will quickly understand the necessity of establishing a clear operational definition.

An operational definition is a description, in quantifiable terms, of what to measure and the specific steps needed to measure it consistently. A good operational definition:

- Gives communicable meaning to a concept or idea
- Is clear and unambiguous
- Specifies the measurement method, procedures, and equipment (when appropriate)
- Provides decision-making criteria when necessary
- Enables consistency in data collection

Some groups are better at developing operational definitions than others. For example, politicians typically do not want to have clear and unambiguous terms. Consider the following list of terms that are used frequently during political campaigns:

- A "fair tax"
- A "tax loophole"
- We need to "jump-start" the economy
- The "rich" need to give more to the "poor"
- The "middle class" needs tax relief
- We need to get this country "moving" again
- The "small farmer" needs economic support

All of these terms require clear operational definitions if there is to be a consistent understanding of what they mean and how we would measure them. In the political arena, however, the desire is to have a certain amount of ambiguity surrounding concepts and terms so that the person presenting the idea cannot be held to a single position or definition.[5]

On a more personal note, I was just reminded of how operational definitions play a major role in the way we communicate with each other on a daily basis. My 9-year-old daughter Devon and her friend Janine called up to me and asked, "When are you going to come down and race slot cars with us?" My answer would have made any politician proud. I responded confidently,

"Soon." That appeased them for about 15 minutes. Then they called up again, and this time when I answered, "Soon," they demanded to know how many minutes made up "soon." Even 9-year-old children understand the need for an operational definition.

One of the most interesting problems with an operational definition involved the Mars space probe. European scientists, using metric measurements and calibrations, built the probe. Scientists in the United States, using decimal units, navigated it. When the probe went around the far side of Mars and was ordered to go down to the surface for a closer look, it followed the programming commands but unfortunately augured itself right into the planet's far side. The difference between metric and decimal units of measurement created an inconsistent operational definition of the term "unit of distance." As a result, a multibillion-dollar project went up in Martian dust.

The most recent example of an ambiguous operational definition can be found with the term "terrorism alert level." The categories of level of risk developed by the Department of Homeland Security are as follows:

- Severe (red)
- High Risk (orange)
- Elevated (yellow)
- Guarded (blue)
- Low (green)

There is no doubt that people need to know if our nation is at risk for a terrorist attack. The problem is that the alert classification schema does not seem to have clear definitions of the various levels and the criteria for moving from one level to another. This ambiguity has led to confusion on the part of local officials and the public. One of the major challenges for the general public is trying to figure out what it means for them personally when the level is raised from "elevated" to "high risk." I saw a local news report one evening that demonstrated this confusion very clearly. The reporter asked a man (apparently picked at random on the street) what he plans on doing now that we are at the high risk alert level. The fellow commented that he was not going to do anything different because he did not know what the new level meant. Another example comes from the *Chicago Tribune* (February 8, 2003). A front-page headline on this date read, "U.S. Raises Terrorism Alert Level." The article then went on to say that the move to high risk was due to "specific intelligence received and analyzed by the full intelligence community." It stated that this new level of alert requires citizens to be "more alert." The problem from an operational definition point of view is that they have never defined what it means to be "more alert." Unfortunately, the ambiguity of the term "terrorist alert" probably means that people will become complacent and less vigilant whenever a warning is posted.

Healthcare has many terms that beg for more precise operational definitions. How does your organization define the following terms?

- A patient fall
- A restraint
- A good outcome for the patient
- A medication administration error
- A complete and thorough physical exam
- A good employee performance review
- Surgical start time
- An accurate patient bill
- A successful surgical outcome
- An organization that supports its workers
- A late food tray
- A clean patient room
- A quick admission
- A blameless culture for reporting errors

Consider one of these terms that has intrigued me for years—a patient fall. One of the first definitions I heard for a patient fall was "a sudden and rapid movement from one plane to another." This sounds like something you try to do at a busy airport rather than a negative patient outcome. It is not very precise and leaves a lot to the imagination.

I have frequently heard nurses talk about two basic types of falls: (1) partial falls and (2) assisted falls. *Partial falls* usually occur when the patient attempts to get out of bed and discovers that he or she does not have an adequate amount of strength to permit ambulation. In this case, the patient might stagger a little, slump back onto the bed, try to stand again, attempt to make it to the chair by the window, but end up collapsing to the floor. As I have explored this scenario with nurses and asked them if this constituted a partial fall, I get mixed responses. One meeting I especially remember produced two very different views of a partial fall. After describing the conditions of a partial fall, half of the nurses indicated that they would classify the situation as a partial fall because the patient did bounce around a little before ending up on the floor. Their reasoning was that the patient bounced around a little, came in contact with some furniture, and eventually ended up on the floor. The other nurses in the group reserved their opinion until they found out the answer to one question: "Did the patient's knee hit the floor?" If the answer was "Yes," then they agreed it would be a partial fall. If the answer to this question was "No," however, this group of nurses was not convinced that this was a partial fall. The knee touching the floor was the primary determinant of a "partial fall."

Assisted falls are even more interesting than partial falls. When I first heard this term I envisioned nurses getting so fed up with a patient that they gave him a gentle nudge and "assisted" him in falling. As I learned more about this topic, however, I came to realize that an assisted fall has nothing to do with the nurses causing the fall. It does, however, have a very distinctive operational definition. Here is the scenario. A patient decides to go for a walk tethered to his IV pole. The patient takes a few steps then announces to the nurse that he does not feel very well and that things are starting to move in circles. As the patient begins to sway the nurse moves into position, grabs the patient, and assists him to the floor. But is this really a fall? It seems to me it is more like a recline or possibly a lay-down. Most nurses I have worked with agree that being present when a patient is starting to go down and intervening to break the patient's fall constitutes an "assisted fall."

You can see the problem that all this poses for measurement. If you are part of a multihospital system or plan on comparing hospital outcomes, then you should make sure that each hospital is defining a patient fall in the same way. Without such consistency you will end up with apples and oranges at best and more likely apples and carburetors. The pieces will not be comparable, which means that ultimately the conclusions that are derived from the data are not accurate. All good measurement begins and ends with operational definitions.

Developing Data Collection Plans

I have separated this step from the actual collection of data because I do not believe that as an industry we have devoted enough time to thinking about the numerous factors that influence the success or failure of our data collection efforts. Most people want to move directly from "I have an indicator" to "Let's go get some data" without spending much time thinking about how to actually collect the data. From my perspective, planning for data collection should occupy upwards of 80% of your data collection time, and the actual act of collecting the numbers should consume about 20% of your time.

Data collection is not unlike other aspects of life that require planning. Whether the activity is painting a house, planting a garden, or going on a major vacation, preparation is key. If you do not spend enough time preparing a house, the paint will not last as long as you would like. Similarly, if you do not take time to properly prepare the soil in your garden, the seeds and young plants will not get off to a very good start. Finally, a major vacation (e.g., a cruise or a bed-and-breakfast tour of Ireland) usually requires more time to plan than the time you actually spend on the holiday itself. The act of data collection is very similar. Inadequately prepared data collection plans will usually produce unacceptable results. The data will be challenged, questioned, and/or seen as being rather useless.

There are several important data collection issues that require some elaboration, most notably stratification and sampling.

Stratification is one of the best things a team can discuss when building indicators, yet it is frequently overlooked. Stratification is the separation and classification of data according to selected identifiers. The objective of stratification is to create strata or categories within the data that are mutually exclusive and allow you to discover patterns that would not otherwise be observed if the data were all aggregated together. Frequently used stratification levels include:

- Day of the week
- Time of day
- Time of year
- Shift
- Type of order (stat versus routine)
- Experience of the worker
- Type of procedure
- Machine (such as ventilators or lab equipment)
- Severity of the patients
- Tenure of the staff

If you do not think about the factors that might influence the outcome of your data before you collect the data, you run the risk of having to try to tease out the stratification effect manually after the data have been collected. At this point not only is it too late to effectively address the stratification question, but you will also have to engage in rework and wasted time to even attempt to untangle the stratification questions. Figures 3.3 and 3.4 provide examples of stratification problems.

In Figure 3.3 there is a period of several data points in a row that are at relatively the same levels. Then there is a sharp drop in the data for two data points. This pattern demonstrates a clear problem with stratification. In this case, the revenue generated Monday through Friday at this hospital is markedly different from that generated on Saturday and Sunday. This hospital is clearly not a seven-day-a-week hospital. If you were to calculate the average revenue generated per day for this hospital you would get a misleading number. Although the overall mean would be skewed toward the weekday revenue side of the chart (because of the higher volume generated during this time as well as more days), it would not reflect the average generated during the weekdays. For this example, someone should have said before the data were collected, "Since we do not generate the same amount of revenue on the weekend as we do on weekdays, we should stratify the data into two categories—weekday revenue and weekend revenue—and analyze the data separately."

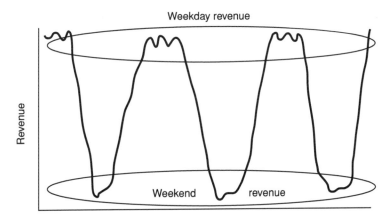

▲ **FIGURE 3.3** A stratification problem with tracking revenue

In the second example (Figure 3.4) we are looking at turnaround time (TAT) in the lab (the particular test does not matter at this point). The data reveal that the process displays extremes because the team did not separate the TATs for the day and P.M. shifts. They merely collected data and combined the two shifts, which are obviously different. In this case, the average TAT will fall exactly in the middle of the two extremes of data. The average TAT is a number that is absolutely meaningless. It is a mathematical artifact that is the result of two distributions of data—one high and one low. There should be one chart for the day shift TAT and another for the P.M. shift.

Stratification is an essential aspect of data collection. If you do not spend some time discussing the implications of stratification, you will end up thinking that your data are worse (or better) than they should be.

Sampling is the second key component of a data collection plan. Not every data effort will require sampling. If a process does not generate a lot of data, then you will probably analyze all the occurrences. This happens most often when the indicator is a percentage. For example, when we compute the percentage of C-sections for the month we typically do not use a sampling plan. We usually take all the C-sections for the month and divide this numerator by the total number of deliveries (the denominator) for the month. When a process generates considerable data, however (e.g., lab TAT for blood tests or all admissions during the month), a sampling plan is usually appropriate. From my perspective, sampling is probably the single most important thing that you can do to reduce the amount of time and resources spent on data collection.

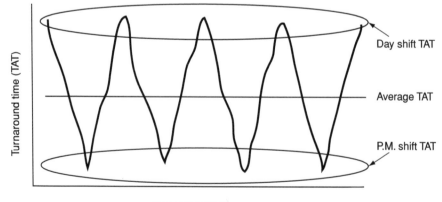

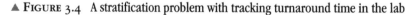

▲ **Figure 3.4** A stratification problem with tracking turnaround time in the lab

Sampling deals more with logic than statistics. Individuals trained in the social sciences are typically exposed to extensive training in sampling principles and concepts. Unfortunately, most healthcare professionals are given only a cursory foundation in this subject. The irony with this situation is that sampling is actually quite easy. Healthcare professionals would grasp sampling principles quickly if they were exposed to them throughout their formal training.

Try this simple test to demonstrate this point. The next time you are with a group of healthcare professionals, ask them, "Have any of you ever drawn a random sample?"[6] Rather quickly you will receive a bunch of positive nods. When you ask one of the people who was nodding rather energetically how they actually drew the random sample, they will usually announce rather proudly that they "picked every 10th chart." Selecting every 10th chart is a form of random sampling known as *systematic sampling* (described below), but it is a rather poor approach to random sampling that introduces bias into the sampling plan. The overall result can easily produce an inaccurate picture of your population.

The purpose of sampling is to be able to draw a limited number of observations and to be reasonably comfortable that they represent the larger population from which they were drawn. If you had all the time and money in the world you would never draw a sample. You would always do a complete enumeration of all cases. But time and resources are limited, so we draw samples.[7] Whenever you draw a sample, however, the key question is, "How much data do I need?" One of my professors in graduate school, Dr. Bob Bealer, had a great answer to this question. When asked by one of my fellow doctoral students how much data we should collect for our dissertation research, he merely answered, "As much as you must and as little as you dare." At the time I thought this was a clever and rather professorial response. But after spending many years trying to help healthcare professionals develop reasonable sampling strategies, I have come to realize that this was very practical advice. For example, if I wanted to check your weight by weighing you on only one day out of the year, would you say this is a representative sample of your true weight? As an aside, I should tell you that the day I have selected to weigh you is Thanksgiving Day after you eat. Most people would say, "No way do I want you to use my Thanksgiving Day weight." Their initial reaction would probably be correct. On the average, for example, adults eat more than 5000 calories on Thanksgiving Day. So most people would probably say, "If you are going to weigh me once, check me in the spring when I am trying to get back into my shorts or bathing suit." To be even more reasonable (reliable), I might weigh you every couple of weeks as they do in many weight control programs. In this way I would obtain a more representative sample of your weight as it fluctuates over time. Remember, as much as you must and as little as you dare.[8]

What happens if you draw a sample and it is not representative of the population from which it was drawn? Figure 3.5 shows the relationship between three samples and a population. The larger curve represents the total population of interest (e.g., all asthma patients returning to the emergency department within 24 hours). Curve A identifies a properly pulled sample of patients. The shape and location of this sample are very similar to the population. Curve C, on the other hand, represents a sample that was drawn with a negative bias. In this case, you could get the false impression that your results were much worse than they really were just because you pulled a sample that came from the negative end of the population curve. Similarly, Curve B depicts a positive sampling bias, which leads you to an overly optimistic conclusion. A well-designed sampling plan will not only produce data that are representative of the population but also save time and money for those collecting the data.

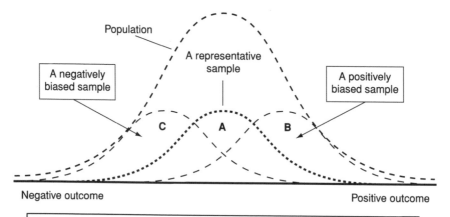

Ideally the sample will have the same shape and location as the total population but have fewer observations (curve A). A sample improperly pulled could result in a positive sampling bias (curve B) or a negative sampling bias (curve C).

▲ FIGURE 3.5 The relationship between a sample and the population

There are many ways to draw a sample. The key question you have to ask yourself whenever you want to draw a sample is, "How representative and precise do I need to be with this sample?" For example, if you have received numerous calls and complaint letters about the wait time in outpatient testing and therapy, you basically have two sampling options: (1) develop a statistically based sample that allows you to generalize to your total outpatient population, or (2) go out on any given day, grab a convenient handful of willing patients and ask them how they like your outpatient testing and therapy services. If the level of precision you need to answer this question is low, then option #2 is appropriate. If, on the other hand, you need to be very sure (statistically sure) that there is a problem in outpatient testing and therapy, then you need to formulate a more scientific approach to sampling.

Ishikawa, in his classic work *Guide to Quality Control* (1982), identifies four conditions for developing a sampling plan:

- Accuracy
- Reliability
- Speed
- Economy

These four criteria should serve as a fundamental checklist for building sampling designs. Not every sample will maximize all four criteria. There are times when accuracy will be the primary objective of sampling (e.g., when designing a randomized clinical trial). At other times reliability will become more important (e.g., when you are establishing a sampling plan for patient satisfaction and you want to be able to draw reliable samples each month or quarter). Speed may be essential when you have to sample a number of blood specimens to determine if there is a contamination problem. Finally, the economics of sampling will usually pose a challenge for everyone. Each time you draw a sample, whether it is a sample of medical records or a sample of patients, there are economic factors involved with the pull of data. Complicated sampling plans require more time, effort, and money. In the end, however, it all comes down to a fairly simple question—how can you pull an accurate, reliable, fast, and inexpensive sample? Obviously it is nearly impossible to obtain a sample that meets all four criteria simultaneously. Sampling, therefore, really consists of a series of compromises. It basically gets us back to Professor Bealer's words of wisdom, "As much as you must and as little as you dare."

Sampling methods are basically divided into two major categories—probability and nonprobability. Any standard research methods or statistics book will provide a review of sampling methods. I would encourage you to obtain several books on this topic to see how different writers classify and describe the various methods. Do not worry about the age of the book. Most of my books on sampling, for example, are 20 to 30 years old. Even when I pick up a new book on sampling, the terms remain virtually the same as those I find in my older books. The terms and approaches to sampling have remained rather constant since the late 1930s.[9] I do not intend to replicate in this book what can be found in may good references (Selltiz *et al.* 1959; Miller 1964; Weiss 1968; Campbell 1974; Hess, Riedel, and Fitzpatrick 1975; Babbie 1979; Ishikawa 1982; Western Electric 1985; Duncan 1986; Daniel and Terrell 1989; Gonick and Smith 1993). I will provide a brief review of the major sampling methods and let the reader explore the details.

Probability Sampling

Probability sampling is designed to provide the highest possible level of predictability and confidence in the sampled data at the most economical cost to the researcher. Although most people have some notion of what a probability or random sampling entails, many are unclear on the specific aspects of actually designing and selecting the sample. At the very foundation of probability sampling is trust: trust in statistical probability and the fact that when you draw a random sample you do not throw it away merely because it does not conform to your personal belief about what the data are supposed to tell you. I have drawn many random samples for people over the years. On numerous occasions I have been questioned about the "accuracy" of the samples because the individuals who requested the samples did not like the results. In their minds they thought they should be allowed to pick and choose what should be included (and excluded) in the sample. If they were to do this it would not make the sample a probability sample. Whenever judgment, purposeful intent, or convenience enter into the sampling plan, you have moved from probability sampling to nonprobability sampling, which will be addressed in the next section.

Campbell (1974:143) identifies three characteristics of probability sampling:

1. A specific statistical design is followed.

2. The selection of items from the population is determined solely according to known probabilities by means of a random mechanism, usually using a table of random digits.

3. The sampling error—that is, the difference between results obtained from a sample survey and that which would have been obtained from a census of the entire population conducted using the same procedures as in the sample—can be estimated and, as a result, the precision of the sample result can be evaluated.

There are numerous ways to draw a probability sample. They are all essentially variations on the simple random sample.

Simple Random Sampling

A random sample is one that is drawn in such a way that it gives every element in the population an equal and independent chance of being included in the sample. This is usually accomplished by using a random number table (usually found in the back of any good statistics book) or a computer-based random number generator (found in all statistical software programs and in many spreadsheet packages). Step-by-step procedures for drawing a random sample can be found in *Probability Sampling of Hospitals and Patients* (Hess, Riedel, and Fitzpatrick 1975) and in *Flaws and Fallacies in Statistical Thinking* (Campbell 1974). Even though this method is referred to as a "simple" random sample, the term "simple" can be a little misleading. The mechanics of drawing a random sample may not feel simple to those who have to number all the elements in the population and learn how to apply a random number table or a computerized random number generator.

As an alternative, you can simply write the names or numbers of the population elements on separate pieces of paper, place them in a bowl, and draw out the sample. I did this to develop a sampling plan for one of our medical groups. They wanted to sample the wait times of patients in one of their clinics, but they did not have the resources to sample every day of the week. They initially said they would pull a sample of patients every Monday. I advised them that this could produce biased results, because Mondays are typically more busy than other days of the week. So I wrote the days of the week (excluding the weekend) on five pieces of paper (all the same dimensions), placed them in a bowl, and then drew out a day of the week. The first day I pulled was a Wednesday. This meant that during the first week, a sample of patients would be pulled on Wednesday and their wait times to see the physician would be recorded. I placed the slip of paper with Wednesday written on it back into the bowl and drew another piece of paper. The second piece of paper had Friday written on it, which would be the sampling day during week 2. I replaced the piece of paper and repeated this process 23 more times to obtain a total of 25 sample days. To pull the sample of patients on a given day, I first asked the staff to run a report showing the actual volume of patient visits by day for the last six months. From this report we determined the minimum and maximum number of visits as well as the mean, median, and standard deviation (to see if the data approximate a normal distribution). We determined that the average number of visits each day was 74 with a minimum of 63 and a maximum of 86. I advised them to place the numbers 1 through 86 on pieces of paper and place them all in the bowl. We then proceeded to draw a subgroup (explained in Chapter 6) of 8 patients from the bowl for each sampling day. The first day to be sampled, for example, was a Wednesday. On this day the following 8 patients would have their wait times tracked: 43rd, 15th, 63rd, 2nd, 47th, 23rd, 18th, and 4th. Since the clinic basically knew how many patients they had scheduled for that day, they could identify those patients from the charts that had been pulled ahead of time. This allowed the staff to be prepared to track the various steps in the process for these patients (i.e., the time from check-in to being called by the nurse, time with the nurse, wait time to see the doctor, time with the doctor, and finally checkout time). In this example, two random samples were selected, one for the day of the week and another for the patients to be tracked within a selected day. By using the pieces of paper and a bowl, we were able to apply the principles and precision of probability sampling and avoid some of the complexity associated with using random number tables or computer-generated random samples.

Stratified Random Sampling

This method of sampling is not an alternative to simple random sampling but rather a variation on a theme. Simple random sampling assumes that the composition of the total population is unknown. A random selection process is seen, therefore, as the best way to obtain a "representative" sample. The problem is that the very nature of a random selection process could produce a sample that is not truly representative of the characteristics of the total population. This is where stratification comes into the picture. By stratifying the population into relatively homogeneous strata or categories before the sample is selected, you increase the representativeness of the sample and decrease the sampling error. Once the stratification levels have been identified, a random selection process is applied within each stratum. For example, you might stratify a hospital's patients into medical and surgical strata and then sample randomly within each group. This would help to ensure that one group was not over- or underrepresented in the sample.

Stratified Proportional Random Sampling

In this case, we are going to use the approach outlined for stratified random sampling, but we are going to add another twist. We are going to determine the proportion that each stratum represents in the population and then replicate this proportion in the sample. For example, if we knew that medical services represented 50% of the hospital's business, surgical services represented 30%, and emergency services represented 20%, then we would draw 50% of the sample from medical units, 30% from surgery, and 20% from the emergency department. This would produce a sample that not only was representative but also proportionally representative. This would further increase the precision of the sample and reduce the sampling error. The stratified proportional random sample is one of the more sophisticated sampling designs, but it does require knowledge of the population being sampled, and it can be more costly in terms of both money and time.

Systematic Sampling

Systematic sampling offers one of the easiest ways to draw a sample. It consists of numbering or ordering each element in the population and then selecting every kth observation after you have selected a random place to start, which should be equal to or less than k but greater than zero. For example, if you had a list of 500 medical records and you wanted to pull a sample of 50, you would pull every 10th record. To determine the starting place for the sample, you would pick a random number between 1 and 10. For argument's sake, imagine that when we do this we select the number 6. So to start our systematic sample we would go to the 6th medical record on our list, pick it, and then proceed to select every 10th record after this starting point.

Technically, this is known as a systematic sample with a random start (Babbie 1979:178). The most frequent ways to organize the elements are either alphabetically or chronologically. There are two major advantages of systematic sampling: (1) it is simple and (2) you only have to generate the first random number. This sampling method is what most healthcare professionals think of as a random sample. Although it is a form of random sampling, it does have certain limitations. The major problem with systematic sampling is that you are eliminating chunks of data that could provide knowledge about the process. If, for example, you are selecting every 10th record, you have automatically eliminated from further consideration records 1 through 9. You pick the 10th record, then skip 11 through 19 and pick number 20. The records in between the ones you select will never have a chance of being included in your analysis. If there is something that occurs regularly in the data or something that causes your data to be organized into bunches of, say, 7 or 8, then these records would be automatically eliminated from consideration. The other problem I have observed with this form of sampling in healthcare settings is that the people drawing the sample do not base the start on a random process. They merely pick a convenient place to start and then start applying the sampling interval they have selected. This introduces bias and greatly increases the sampling error.

Cluster Sampling

In cluster sampling the population is divided into mutually exclusive and exhaustive clusters, then a simple random sample is drawn within each cluster. On the surface this approach does not seem very different from stratification. Cluster sampling differs from stratified random sampling in that cluster sampling seeks to create "bunches" within the population. Sampling in this way is almost always less expensive than simple random sampling (which is not as focused). The other key distinctions between stratification and cluster sampling include: (1) with stratified sampling, a sample of elements is selected from within each stratum or category; (2) with cluster sampling, a sample of stratum is selected. Since the cluster sample is selecting a sample of stratum or categories, it is desirable to have each cluster be a small collection of the population. Cluster samples, therefore, should establish groupings that are as heterogeneous as possible. Stratified samples, on the other hand, attempt to create homogeneous categories (e.g., all medical and all surgical patients).

Another distinction with cluster sampling is that it is typically done with fairly large populations. This method could be applied, for example, to a large system that has 15 to 20 hospitals. Each hospital could be considered a cluster, or they could be grouped into regional clusters. A cluster sample also could be drawn in a large metropolitan area. Instead of looking at individual hospitals or hospital systems, you could divide the metropolitan area into regions (the clusters) and then sample patients within these regions. In Chicago where I live, for example, it would be possible to divide the metropolitan area into north, south, west, and urban core clusters (east would not work since Lake Michigan is located to the east of Chicago). If we did this we would not be so concerned with the individual hospitals and their organizational affiliations but rather with bundling people together into common geographic areas. With large populations, therefore, cluster sampling can be a very economical approach to sampling. Cluster sampling would not apply to the unit or department level because the population of interest (e.g., all hip- or knee-replacement patients) is not large enough to permit clusters to be created.

Nonprobability Sampling

Nonprobability sampling is typically used when the researcher is not worried about estimating the reliability and precision of the sample. This is not to say, however, that nonprobability samples do not serve a useful purpose. More specifically, nonprobability approaches to sampling can be used when:

- Probability samples are either too expensive to collect or too complicated for the question being asked
- There is no need to draw inferences or generalize to larger populations
- There is no need to estimate the probability that each element has of being included in the sample
- There is no need to have assurance that every element (e.g., patient) had an equal opportunity to be included in the sample
- The objective is to conduct an exploratory or descriptive study on an issue or process that has not been studied in detail
- You are testing a potential improvement strategy and want to run a quick pilot study (i.e., sending up a trial balloon to see if it has any hope of succeeding)

- Mechanical selection of the sample is not required; personal judgment and subjective choice are sufficient

The major forms of nonprobability sampling are convenience sampling, quota sampling, and judgment sampling. The basic objective with all of these methods is to select a sample that the researchers believe is "typical" of the larger population. The problem is that there is no way to actually measure how typical or representative a nonprobability sample is with respect to the population it supposedly is representing. In short, nonprobability samples can be considered "good enough samples" (i.e., they are good enough for the people pulling the sample).

Convenience Sampling

As the name implies, convenience sampling is designed to obtain a handful of observations that are readily available and convenient to gather. Convenience sampling is also referred to as "chunk" sampling (Hess, Riedel, and Fitzpatrick 1975:8) or accidental sampling (Selltiz *et al.* 1959:516; Maddox 1981:3). A classic example of convenience sampling is found in the "man on the street" interview conducted by TV stations. The local TV channel parks its action-cam van along a busy downtown street at lunchtime. The investigative reporter positions herself strategically and begins to scan the people that walk by. She knows that she needs to get at least four good comments from local citizens (her quota sample), so she eliminates anyone from consideration who looks like they would be (1) noncooperative, (2) argumentative, or (3) chatty without any substantive sound bites. Then she sees a likely candidate and strikes: "Hi, I'm from Channel 5 News and I'd like to know how you feel about (fill in the blank)." Okay, one down and three more to go (to meet the quota). So the search continues. There is no science behind this type of sampling. It produces a biased sample that is essentially a collection of anecdotes that cannot be generalized to larger populations. In technical terms, this is what is referred to as a convenient quota sample (i.e., I need a quota of four people and I'm willing to take anyone who is convenient and agrees to talk). In the healthcare setting, convenience sampling is used frequently, possibly too often. I have seen it used to pull a convenient sample of medical records, obtain patient satisfaction input (go grab a few people waiting in the emergency department and ask them how they feel about their wait time), or select a "typical" day to study call button response time. The primary question that someone should ask when a convenience sample is drawn is, "How important is it to know if the sample of elements we just selected are representative of the larger population?" If the consequences of being wrong do not matter, then the convenience sample might be good enough.

Quota Sampling

Quota sampling was developed in the late 1930s and used extensively by the Gallup organization to gain great recognition as well as ridicule (see note 9 for additional details on how Gallup benefited from quota sampling in 1936 and then was criticized in 1948 for its failure to predict accurately). If you ask healthcare professionals to describe quota sampling, they will probably tell you that it is merely a simple way to determine the total minimum number of elements needed in a sample (e.g., we need a quota of 5% of the medical records) or the total minimum amount of data that the team can afford to gather. These two factors, while part of quota sampling, are only part of the picture. Babbie (1979:196) nicely describes the steps involved in developing a quota sample:

1. Develop a matrix describing the characteristics of the target population. This may entail knowing the proportion of male and female, various age, racial, and ethnic proportions as well as the educational and income levels of the population.

2. Once the matrix has been created and a relative proportion assigned to each cell in the matrix, you collect data from persons having all the characteristics of a given cell.

3. All persons in a given cell are then assigned a weight appropriate to their proportion of the total.

4. When all the sample elements are so weighted, the overall data should provide a reasonable representation of the total population.

Theoretically, an accurate quota sampling design should produce results that are reasonably representative of the larger population. Quota sampling has several inherent problems, however, that are related primarily to how the cells in the quota matrix are actually populated. If, for example, the individuals collecting the quota samples are not particularly vigilant and honest about filling their quotas, the results will be biased. Remember, the actual selection of the elements to fill the quota are left up to the individual gathering the data, not to random chance. If the data collectors are not diligent and/or honest about their work, they will end up obtaining their quotas in a manner that is more like a convenience sample than a true quota sample. This happens frequently when quota samples are being collected in neighborhoods. The 2000 census in Chicago provided a good example of this type of bias. The census workers were given quotas to fill on the North Shore of the city. This is a rather wealthy area where it is not uncommon to find homes that are gated and monitored by security. Many of the census workers were not given access to these homes, even though they were technically in the cell they were supposed to obtain. Apparently pressured by the requirement to meet their quotas, the census workers creatively began to substitute other residents for the ones defined by the quota sample. As a result, the cells in question (i.e., neighborhoods) were underreported and not properly representative of the area (*Chicago Tribune*, July 5, 2000, "Census Shortcuts Alleged"). Another threat to the validity of the quota sample is that the patient population characteristics might be outdated and not reflect the current patient population. The final threat involves the process by which the data collectors actually gather the data. For example, if a quota sample was established to gather data in the emergency department but only during the day shift, you would run the risk of missing key data points during the afternoon and evening shifts.

Judgment Sampling

I saved the discussion of judgment sampling till the end because it can be viewed in two very different lights. If you approach sampling from an academic research perspective, then judgment sampling is regarded as having a low level of precision and statistical rigor. If, on the other hand, your objective is not academic research but rather quality improvement research (see Chapter 5 for additional details on this issue), then judgment sampling provides a useful approach to sampling. The academic view that judgment sampling (also referred to as purposive sampling) has a low level of precision is based on the fact that the sample is drawn on the basis of the knowledge of the person drawing the sample. No objective mechanical means are used to select the sample. The assumption is that experience, good judgment, and appropriate strategy can select a sample that is acceptable for the objectives of the researcher. An example of judgment sampling is seen every four years when a handful of states and communities are selected to be "pulse checks" on the presidential election. In this case, the assumption is that the people in Iowa and New Hampshire are "typical" of the rest of the nation and that the responses of these citizens provide a snapshot of how the American views the presidential candidates. Obviously the major challenge to judgment sampling is related to the knowledge and wisdom of the person making the judgment call. If everyone believes that this person exhibits good wisdom, then they will have confidence in the sample that the person selects. If, on the other hand, people doubt the person's wisdom and knowledge, then the sample will be discredited.

Now, consider the nonacademic use of judgment sampling. Deming considered judgment sampling to be the method of choice for quality improvement research. Langley *et al.* (1996:111) maintain that "A random selection of units is rarely preferred to a selection made by a subject matter expert." In quality improvement circles this type of sampling is also known as expert sampling or rational sampling. It essentially consists of having those who have expert knowledge of the process decide on how to arrange the data into subgroups and pull the sample. The subgroups can be elected either by random or nonrandom procedures, which is a major distinction between the quality improvement perspective and the academic view of judgment sampling. The other important distinction about Deming's view of judgment sampling is that the samples should be selected at regular intervals over time, not at a single point in time. Most sampling designs, whether they are probability or nonprobability, are static in nature. The researcher decides on a time frame then picks as much data as possible. In contrast, Deming's view of sampling was that it should be done in small doses (rather than large quantities) and pulled as a continuous stream of data (Deming 1950, 1960, 1975). The primary criticism of judgment sampling is that the "expert" may not fully understand all facets of the population under investigation and may therefore select a biased sample. The second criticism is that the sampling error cannot be measured. The final challenge is that the results of a judgment sample cannot be generalized to the larger population because the sample was not selected by random methods.

A review of the probability and nonprobability sampling methods is provided in Table 3.2. Developing a working knowledge of these sampling techniques will be one of the best ways to reduce the time spent on collecting data. Done correctly, sampling will also be a way to ensure that the data you do collect are directly related to your quality improvement efforts.

▼ TABLE 3.2 Advantages and disadvantages of various sampling methods

Sampling method	Description	Advantages	Disadvantages
Probability sampling			
Simple random sample	A sample that is drawn in such a way that every member of a population has an equal chance of being included. A random number table or a random number generator is typically used to actually pull the sample.	• Requires minimum knowledge of the population in advance • Free of possible classification errors • Easy to analyze the data and compute errors • Fairly inexpensive	• Does not take advantage of the knowledge the researcher might have about the population • There could be over- or underrepresentation of subgroups within the population • Typically produces larger sampling errors for the same sample than a stratified sample
Stratified random sample	The population is divided into relevant strata before random sampling is applied to each stratum.	• Helps to reduce the chances of over-/under-representing subgroups within the population • Allows you to segment the data into "buckets" during the analysis phase • Create more efficient samples • Reduces sampling error	• Requires knowledge of the presence of various characteristics within the population • Sampling costs can increase if knowledge of the population is shallow • If the strata are not highly homogeneous then sampling error goes up and efficiency goes down

▼ TABLE 3.2 Advantages and disadvantages of various sampling methods *(continued)*

Sampling method	Description	Advantages	Disadvantages
Probability sampling			
Proportional stratified random sample	The proportion (or percentage) of a particular stratum is determined in the population and then applied to the random sample.	• Adds even more precision than the stratified random sample • Increases sample representativeness • Creates very efficient samples • Reduces sampling error	• Requires more human and financial resources than other methods • Requires even more information about the population than stratified random methods
Systematic sample	Select every *k*th observation from the population after a random starting point has been selected.	• Very easy to conduct • Has "intuitive" appeal • Inexpensive to conduct	• Can produce bias due to periodic ordering of observation, which produces exclusion of segments of the population • Increased probability of sampling bias
Cluster sample	Clusters or "bunches" of the population are identified, and then random sampling is applied to each cluster.	• Can be low cost, especially if geographic clusters are used • If properly done, each cluster is a small model of the population • High level of practicality	• Clusters need to be as heterogeneous as possible • Typically has lower statistical efficiency • Large samples are often needed to ensure precision

▼ TABLE 3.2 Advantages and disadvantages of various sampling methods

Sampling method	Description	Advantages	Disadvantages
Nonprobability sampling			
Convenience sample	Observations are selected based on availability and convenience. Also known as "accidental" samples.	• Ease of obtaining a sample • Relatively low cost	• Extremely low generalizability • No way to determine sampling bias or sampling error
Quota sample	A population is divided into relevant strata. The desired proportion of samples to be obtained from each stratum is determined, and then a fixed quota within each stratum is set.	• Stratification effect is achieved if the strata are appropriately structured • In theory, the quota sample should be reasonably representative of the population • Human and financial costs can be kept to a minimum if the strata from which the quotas are to be drawn are grouped close together (reduces the amount of travel the data collectors have to perform in order to gather the data)	• The people assigned to collect the quotas need to be scrupulous, free from selection bias, and follow the prescribed sampling design (otherwise this method becomes a convenience sample) • It is difficult to guarantee that the quotas were filled accurately • In-depth knowledge of the population is required • Nonrandom selection of the quotas can also introduce bias
Judgment sample	Subgroups are drawn from a process over time based on expert knowledge. The subgroup samples can be drawn either by random or nonrandom procedures.	• Samples in a subgroup can be small (3–5) since many subgroups will be selected • Data collection costs can be reduced • Provides a dynamic picture of the data and serves as the basis for process improvement • Minimum stratification effect is achieved	• Sampling bias and sampling error cannot be calculated • Expert knowledge of the process or population is required • Generalization of the judgment sample to larger populations cannot be done • Personal bias enters into the selection of the sample

The Indicator Development Form

Now that we have addressed the major technical aspects of indicator development, it is time to think about a more formalized way to organize our indicator work activities. Figure 3.6 provides a list of questions that you should ask yourself and your colleagues as you embark on your quality measurement journey. These are the questions that I typically ask as we specify indicators. Although this list should stimulate a reasonably good dialogue about indicator development, it does not provide a very user-friendly template. Who wants to sit and slog through such a list? In 1996 Advocate Health Care wrestled with this very question.[10] We needed a template to provide our sites with a step-by-step guide to building indicators. So a colleague, Judi Miller, and I designed what we refer to as the Indicator Development Form©. This form has been modified many times as our sites have used the form and offered suggestions for its improvement. Some have rearranged the layout, and others have shortened it to fit on one page. It has also been distributed widely in this country and abroad.[11] Faulkner and Grey recognized the contribution that this template has made to the measurement field by using it as a model for indicator development in its *1999 Medical Quality Management Sourcebook* (Boyle 1998).

The Indicator Development Form© is presented in Figure 3.7. The form is divided into three major parts:

- Part I: Identification of an Indicator
- Part II: Indicator Development and Data Collection
- Part III: Indicator Analysis and Interpretation

Each part is summarized below.

Part I: Identification of an Indicator

This section is designed to get people talking about why they want to measure this particular indicator. Stated differently, out of all the things that you could measure, why do you want to measure this particular indicator?

1. What Process or Outcome Does This Indicator Measure?

In this section the name of the process being tracked or a related outcome should be identified (e.g., patient falls, medical record transcription, patient wait time, or timely discharge).

- What types of data will you be collecting?
- What processes will be monitored?
- What are the specific indicators?
- Have you developed objective names for these indicators?
- What are the operational definitions of the indicators?
- Why are you collecting these data?
- What value-added contribution will this indicator make to your work?
- Have you discussed the impact of stratification on the indicators?
- How often (frequency) and for how long (duration) will you collect the data?
- Will you employ sampling? If so, what sampling design do you propose?
- How will you collect the data? (Will you use data sheets, a survey, focus group discussions, phone interviews, or some combination of methods?)
- Will you conduct a pilot study?
- Who will actually collect the data?
- What costs (dollars plus time costs) will be incurred by collecting these data?
- Will collecting these data have any negative impacts on patients or employees?
- What is the current baseline for this indicator?
- Do you have targets and goals?
- How will the data be coded, edited, and verified?
- Who will perform these tasks?
- Will you tabulate and analyze these data by hand or by computer?
- How will these data be used?
- Who will have access to the raw data? To the final reports?
- Are there potential issues with HIPAA (patient confidentiality) or the Institutional Review Board (human subjects' reviews)?

▲ FIGURE 3.6 Questions to ask as you develop your data collection plan

Advocate Health Care
INDICATOR DEVELOPMENT FORM©

PART I: IDENTIFICATION OF AN INDICATOR

1. WHAT PROCESS OR OUTCOME DOES THIS INDICATOR MEASURE?

2. WHAT IS THE RATIONALE FOR THIS INDICATOR?
   (Why has this indicator been selected? What is the purpose of the indicator?
   Are there external/internal stakeholders who have influenced the selection?)

3. WHAT IS THE SPECIFIC NAME OF THIS INDICATOR?

4. LIST THE ORGANIZATIONAL UNIT(S), DEPARTMENT(S)/FUNC-
   TION(S) OR TEAMS TO WHICH THE INDICATOR APPLIES:
   (Examples: CQI Team, Department Name, System-Wide, Advocate Health
   Providers, etc.)

5. THIS INDICATOR WILL SATISFY THE FOLLOWING OBJECTIVE(S):
   CORE STRATEGIES:
   - Service Breakthrough
   - Work Life Quality
   - Clinical Excellence
   - Technology Leadership
   - Innovative Growth

6. THE INDICATOR IS DESIGNED TO MEASURE THE FOLLOWING
   DIMENSION(S) OF EXCELLENCE:

Appropriateness ___	Financial Viability ___
Availability/Access ___	Growth/Market Share ___
Continuity ___	Respect/Caring ___
Effectiveness ___	Timeliness ___
Efficiency ___	Other (Specify) ___

7. ARE THERE LITERATURE REFERENCES FOR THIS INDICATOR?
   YES ___ NO ___
   IF YES, SPECIFY SOURCE, DATE, ETC.:

▲ FIGURE 3.7   The Indicator Development Form

ADVOCATE HEALTH CARE
INDICATOR DEVELOPMENT FORM©
PAGE 2

PART II: INDICATOR DEVELOPMENT AND DATA COLLECTION

8. OPERATIONAL DEFINITION

Define the specific data collection method to be used, including:

1. Any special equipment to be used (computers, logs, etc.)

2. Specific criteria for all data to be collected

Remember: Include full definition with all inclusions and exclusions and specify all required data elements (e.g., patient types, financial class, data dictionary elements, DRGs, codes, clinical specialty).

9. DESCRIBE THE DATA COLLECTION PLAN:

- PERSON(S) RESPONSIBLE FOR COLLECTING THE DATA

- COLLECTION FREQUENCY

- DATA SOURCES (BE SPECIFIC)

- METHOD

10. DOES THE DATA COLLECTION REQUIRE SAMPLING?
    YES ___ NO ___
    IF YES, DESCRIBE THE SAMPLING PLAN:

▲ FIGURE 3.7   The Indicator Development Form *(continued)*

ADVOCATE HEALTH CARE
INDICATOR DEVELOPMENT FORM©
PAGE 3

11. IS THERE A CURRENT BASELINE DATA FOR THIS INDICATOR?
    YES ___ NO ___
    (Baseline data is the current actual measure of the indicator.)
    IF YES, WHAT IS THE TIME PERIOD FROM WHICH THE BASELINE
    IS OBTAINED?

    WHAT IS THE ACTUAL BASELINE MEASUREMENT?

12. IS THERE A TARGET OR GOAL FOR THIS INDICATOR?
    YES ___ NO ___
    IF YES, WHAT TYPE OF TARGET OR GOAL IS IT?
    • EXTERNAL TARGET OR GOAL?
    (Specify the number, rate, or volume, etc., as well as the source of the target/goal.)

    • INTERNAL TARGET OR GOAL DEVELOPED BY THE TEAM OR
      RECOMMENDED BY OTHER ADVOCATE SITES? (Specify the number,
      rate, or volume, etc., and rationale for the target/goal.)

PART III: INDICATOR ANALYSIS AND INTERPRETATION

13. DESCRIBE THE ANALYSIS PLAN:
    WHAT DESCRIPTIVE STATISTICS WILL BE USED?
    1. MEAN ___   2. MEDIAN ___   3. MODE ___   4. PERCENTAGES ___
    5. MINIMUM ___   6. MAXIMUM ___   7. RANGE ___   8. STANDARD DEVIATION ___
    9. TABULAR ANALYSIS ___   10. OTHER ___

    WHAT GRAPHS WILL BE USED?
    1. BAR CHART ___   2. HISTOGRAM ___   3. PIE CHART ___
    4. LINE CHART ___   5. RUN CHART ___   6. CONTROL CHART ___
    7. PARETO DIAGRAM ___   8. OTHER ___

14. DESCRIBE THE DATA REPORTING PLAN:
    • WHO WILL RECEIVE THE RESULTS?

    • HOW OFTEN WILL THEY RECEIVE THE RESULTS?

▲ FIGURE 3.7 The Indicator Development Form *(continued)*

2. *What is the Rationale for This Indicator?*

(Why has this indicator been selected? What is the purpose of the indicator? Are there external/internal stakeholders who have influenced the selection?)

This section is designed to answer a very simple question—Why do you want to measure this indicator? Try this the next time you are involved with a measurement effort. Just ask the team, "Given all the other things you could measure, why do you want to measure this particular indicator?" I guarantee that you will get some very interesting responses. One of the better ones I ever received was, "Because we have a form." Another good one was, "Because management wants it." Ideally you would like to hear someone say, "Because it represents a key aspect of what our customers expect from this process."

3. *What is the Specific name of This Indiactor?*

Naming indicators is an important component of indicator development that is frequently taken for granted. Some might ask, "What's the big deal? Just give it a name." Indicator names should be objective, and they should basically be nouns. What I find, however, is that many indicator names include adjectives and adverbs as well as targets and goals (e.g., H&P transcription turnaround time will be 12 hours or less). This produces what I call "thou shalts" (i.e., thou shalt perform this task in 12 hours or less or there will be consequences). Indicators named in this fashion identify the desired outcome. When you include the desired level of performance in the indicator name, you have basically built in a barrier or, worse yet, a threat. It sends a message to the workers that you had better do this or else. If the desired outcome is an unrealistic goal, the workers quickly figure this out. The indicator then becomes an unrealistic metric or a joke. Consider this example: I was working with a medical group on their indicators and asked a team what they intended to measure. A member of the team said that the indicator was, "No one should have to wait more than 30 minutes to see the doctor." My comment to the team was that this was not the name of an indicator but rather a threat. The indicator name should have been "wait time to see the doctor." Although it seems like a minor aspect of performance measurement, I believe that the naming of indicators sets the tone for the rest of the measurement journey.

4. *List the Organizational Unit(s), Department(s)/Function(s), or Teams to Which the Indicator Applies:*

Some indicators stay within a department or area. Others cut across departments. This section is intended to generate a discussion about the complexity of an indicator. For example, an indicator such as "the number of phone calls coming into the department" generally is contained within the department. On the other hand, an indicator such as "the number of hours it takes to get an emergency department patient into a bed on an inpatient unit" requires a number of departments to be involved. At a minimum it will involve the ED, the admissions office, the unit receiving the patient, and transportation. This indicator is fairly complex and will require considerably more effort than an indicator that is basically owned by a single department.

5. *This Indicator Will Satisfy the Following Objective(s):*

Core Strategies:
- **Service Breakthrough**
- **Work Life Quality**
- **Clinical Excellence**
- **Technology Leadership**
- **Innovative Growth**

Each indicator needs to be placed within the context of the organization's strategic plan. These five objectives represent Advocate's core strategies. If your organization wishes to adapt this form for its own purposes, then these five items need to be changed to reflect your own core strategies. Within Advocate, if an indicator cannot be mapped directly to one of these five core strategies, we do not spend resources to track it.

6. *The Indicator is Designed to Measure the Following Dimension(s) of Excellence:*

Appropriateness ____	Financial Viability ____
Availability/Access ____	Growth/Market Share ____
Continuity ____	Respect/Caring ____
Effectiveness ____	Timeliness ____
Efficiency ____	Other (Specify) ____

At Advocate, Excellence is one of our five core values (along with Compassion, Equality, Partnership, and Stewardship). Excellence is also one of the primary objectives of all quality improvement initiatives. This section of the form is designed to make explicit the reasons why this indicator is being measured. If the indicator can satisfy several aspects of Excellence, then the time and effort spent collecting it will be worthwhile.

7. Are There Literature References for This Indicator?

Yes ____ No ____
If Yes, specify source, data, etc.:

All too often, quality improvement teams forget to conduct a literature review to see if others have already worked on this indicator or the process it represents. There are many good journals on quality that can save you time and effort. The ASQ, for example, publishes *Quality Progress* on a monthly basis. There are also several other journals published by ASQ's professional divisions as well as a very rich offering of books and training materials offered through ASQ's Quality Press. JCAHO's quality journal is another good source of healthcare quality initiatives. Organizations such as the IHI, the National Patient Safety Foundation, and the Agency for Healthcare Research and Quality (AHRQ) all provide very comprehensive Web sites for quality applications and outcomes.

PART II: Indicator Development and Data Collection

8. Operational Definition

Define the specific data collection method to be used, including:

1. **Any special equipment to be used (computers, logs, etc.)**
2. **Specific criteria for all data to be collected**

Remember: Include the full definition with all inclusions and exclusions and specify all required data elements (e.g., patient types, financial class, data dictionary elements, DRGs, codes, clinical specialty).

This is essentially the heart and soul of the Indicator Development Form©. In this section you should indicate the components of the operational definition in very specific terms. If it involves a percentage, then the numerator and denominator should be described. Similarly, if the measure is a rate, then the rate-based statistic should be defined. The easiest way to do this is to take the indicator name (e.g., inpatient fall rate) and then say, "Inpatient fall rate is defined as (fill in the blank)." Remember to describe what is to be included (e.g., all inpatients, including pediatrics, and geriatrics and falls in the emergency department) and what is to be excluded (e.g., visitor falls in and out of the hospital, staff falls, and falls in the rehabilitation unit). The litmus test for a good operational definition is really quite simple. Just ask yourself, "How could someone get confused with this definition and collect wrong data?" If you have written a clear and unambiguous operational definition, then you will be able to avoid confusion during the data collection stage.

9. Describe the Data Collection Plan:

- **Person(s) responsible for collecting the data**

  It is not uncommon to arrive at this step in the process and realize that you have not made any provisions for actually collecting the data. Everyone seems to assume that someone else will do the dirty work of recording wait times or extracting documentation history from the medical records. Someone has to do the data collection. Frequently, however, there is a wonderful chain reaction when it comes to this task. Physicians assume that the nurses will collect the data. The nurses assume that the unit secretaries will complete this task. The unit secretaries hope (and pray) that several administrative interns will be assigned to the department for the summer and this job can be pawned off on them. If all else fails, the volunteers can be asked to do the data collection. Now think about this. If you have spent considerable time building the indicator's operational definition and data collection plan, why would you assume that some undetermined entity will magically appear and solve all your data collection problems? In Greek dramas this solution was referred to as the *deus ex machina* (the god from the machine) or the unexpected solution to a difficult problem.[12] If this aspect of the measurement journey is not determined prior to the collection of data, I can guarantee you that (1) it will not go smoothly and (2) the data gathered will be questionable.

- **Collection frequency**

  Frequency deals with how often you plan on collecting the data. Will you collect the wait time of every patient or develop a sampling strategy? Will you collect the wait time of all patients but only on Mondays? All these questions relate to the frequency of data collection. The other aspect of frequency relates to the duration of your data collection. How long do you plan on collecting the data? Will you do it for a week, a month, or several months? If you do not spend time discussing this issue, you will inevitably come to a point when someone says, "How long do I have to collect this stuff?"

- **Data sources (be as specific as possible)**

  Where do you plan on getting the data? Will it be manually collected, or will it come from an automated system? If it is to be a manual process, will it come from existing log sheets or the medical record, or do you have to create a new data collection tool? If it comes from an automated system, what segment of the automated system will be used (e.g., is it the registration system, the billing system, or the patient satisfaction system)?

- **Method**

  By what method do you propose to actually gather the data? For example, if you are tracking lab turnaround time, will the recorded time come from the watch of the individual who is recording the log-in time, the clock on the wall by the door, or the automated time stamp produced by the computer system? If the data are to be collected manually, do you have a procedure outlining how the person recording the data is supposed to identify the particular piece of data (e.g., the log-in time to the lab of a specimen) and then enter it into the logbook? For some of you this probably seems like a very left-brained, compulsive set of questions. If someone does not attend to the details, however, they will be ignored. This is why you need both left- and right-brained people on quality improvement (QI) teams. A team with all left- or all right-brained people usually does not achieve as much as teams that have a mix of perspectives. Sometimes you need vision and creativity, and sometimes you need structure and attention to details.

10. *Does the Data Collection Require Sampling?*

Yes _____   No _____
If Yes, describe the sampling plan:

Sampling was covered in considerable detail earlier in this section and in Table 3.3. Suffice it to say that increasing your knowledge of sampling will be an asset to your QI initiatives.

11. *Is There a Current Baseline Data for This Indicator?*

Yes _____   No _____
(Baseline data is the current actual measure of the indicator.)
If Yes, what is the time period from which the baseline is obtained?

What is the actual measurement?

Remember that the baseline is what the current process is producing. It is not what you want it to be or expect it to be. Baseline is a fundamental concept in medicine. We get a baseline on a patient before we start to prescribe medications or treatments. We basically want to know how the indicator is performing and what it is capable of producing under current conditions.

12. *Is There a Target or Goal for This Indicator?*

Yes _____   No _____
If Yes, what type of target or goal is it?

External target or goal?
(Specify the number, rate or volume, etc., as well as the source of the target/goal.)

Internal target or goal? Is it developed by the team or other sources?
(Specify the number, rate or volume, etc., and rationale for the target/goal.)

This is where you identify what you want or expect the indicator's performance to be. Targets are usually seen as short-term objectives (several months or 1–2 years). Goals, on the other hand, are usually designed for a little longer period of time, say 3–5 years. I have seen numerous examples, however, of how organizations have confused staff by not being clear on whether the new number was a target or a goal. Frequently people use the terms as if they were synonymous. It really does not matter if you use the term "target" or "goal." What is important is that you (1) use consistent terms that are understood by all members of the organization, (2) develop targets/goals that are reasonable, and (3) have a plan for how the targets/goals are to be achieved. As Deming pointed out frequently in his seminars and in his writings, "Goals are necessary for you and me, but numerical goals for other people, without a road map to reach the goal, have effects opposite to the effects sought" (1992:69).

PART III: Indicator Analysis and Interpretation

13. *Describe the Analysis Plan:*

What descriptive statistics will be used?

Mean _____	Maximum _____
Median _____	Range _____
Mode _____	Standard deviation _____
Percentages _____	Tabular analysis _____
Minimum _____	Other _____

What graphs will be used?

Bar chart _____	Run chart _____
Histogram _____	Control chart _____
Pie chart _____	Pareto diagram _____
Line chart _____	Other _____

The analysis plan can be divided into two parts. The first part may consist of preparing descriptive statistics on your data. This would be of value if you (1) have not collected the data before and need merely to describe what you have collected or (2) pulled a sample of data and need to determine if your sample is representative of the total population. The descriptive analysis can be accomplished with statistics (e.g., mean, median, mode, and standard deviation) or with descriptive graphics (e.g., a bar chart, pie chart, histogram, or simple line chart). The second aspect of the analysis plan is more analytic in nature. This consists of preparing run or control charts and evaluating the data for the presence of common or special causes of variation. The run and control charts are reviewed in Chapter 6.

14. Describe the Data Reporting Plan:

- **Who will receive the results?**
- **How often will they receive the results?**

After analyzing the data, the remaining question is, "What are you going to do with the results?" Data without a plan for action are useless. This section is intended, therefore, to identify the individuals who will receive the results, the frequency of distribution, and any issues related to the distribution of the data. If there are issues related to patient confidentiality or compliance with the Health Insurance Portability and Accountability Act (HIPAA), for example, these should be noted in this section. Finally, if the data collection effort had to be reviewed by the Institutional Review Board (IRB), this, too, should be discussed.

When a group or a QI team uses this template they usually end up with an indicator that not only fits with their objectives but also has the technical aspects of the indicator clearly outlined and any major data collection challenges identified. Once a single indicator has been finalized, it is time to think about how to organize multiple indicators and build a dashboard, which is the main subject of the next chapter.

Case Study: Transcription Turnaround Time

The following case study is designed to demonstrate how the principles addressed in this chapter can be applied to a very practical problem—transcription turnaround time for histories and physicals.

Situation

Imagine that you are the director of quality improvement at a medium-sized hospital. One morning you receive a call from your friend Becky, the manager of medical transcription, who asks if she can meet with you ASAP.

You sense that she is bothered by something and tell her that you will come to her office in an hour. You have known Becky for more than 8 years and are a little surprised when she dispenses with the usual pleasantries and jumps right into her concern. She tells you that several of the physicians have been complaining recently about transcription TAT. She even confides in you that she actually had a rather "energetic" exchange with the head of surgery about this issue earlier in the morning. Now Becky is asking for your help, she explains it as to, "get the doctors to realize that TAT is actually very good." To prove her point she shows you Figure 3.8. She points out quickly that the goal is to get the transcriptions completed in 12 hours or less. The graph demonstrates that over the last 10 months the transcription team has been able to meet this goal 92 – 99% of the time. So what is the big deal with the physicians? Why are they on Becky's case?

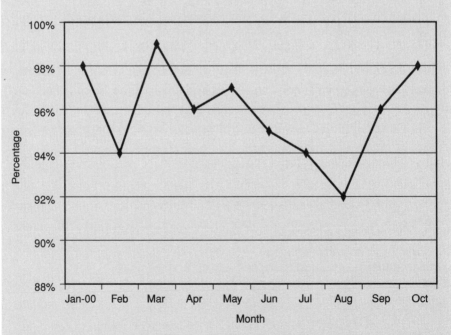

▲ FIGURE 3.8 Percentage of history and physical (H&P) transcription turnaround times completed within 12 hours

Diagnosis of the Problem

As you look at the title of Figure 3.8, the first thing that strikes you as confusing is that the indicator of interest is transcription TAT, yet Becky has presented the data as the percenage of H&P transcriptions completed within 12 hours. You also point out that she has actually violated one of the basic principles of naming an indicator—she created a "thou shalt" (H&P transcription TAT will be 12 hours or less). Her response is, "We have to have a goal; otherwise, the doctors will not take us seriously." You respond by saying that goals are critical to improvement initiatives but that they should not be built into the name of the indicator. Indicator names should be objective statements about what is to be measured, not what you want it to be. You also point out that by measuring TAT as a percentage, you are losing information about the true variation in the process. For example, consider the month of August in Figure 3.8. During this month 92% of the transcriptions were completed in 12 hours or less. What was the longest TAT in this month? You cannot answer this question because the measure is whether the transcriptions were completed in more than 12 hours or less than 12 hours. The longest TAT might have been 13 hours or 40 hours. But because of the way in which the indicator was developed, you will never know the answer to this question. You suggest that it would be useful, therefore, to look at the actual time (in hours) to transcribe H&Ps. Becky is so desperate for help that she agrees to do this even though she is not sure why.

The next day Becky comes to your office with Figures 3.9 and 3.10. Figure 3.9 shows the number of H&P reports completed each month, the total hours required to complete the transcriptions, and the average hours. Figure 3.10 presents these data as a line graph with the 12-hour goal as a reference line. Becky is quick to point out that this chart does not really tell a different story from her first graph. Figure 3.10 reveals that the transcription process has constantly performed below the goal of 12 hours. So what is the big deal with the physicians?

As you look at Figure 3.10 you notice what you believe is the big deal with the physicians. You see from the title of this chart that the process starts with dictation and ends when transcription is completed. You ask Becky a simple question: "What do the physicians care most about?" She looks at you in a quizzical manner and says, "I don't understand your

Summary Data Turnaround Time
January–October 2000
Average: Hospital and patients (from dictation to transcription)

	Number of H&P Reports	Total Hours TAT*	Average TAT Hours
January	500	5140	10.3
February	487	5734	11.8
March	498	4948	9.9
April	521	6024	11.6
May	517	5882	11.4
June	508	5913	11.6
July	489	5756	11.8
August	501	6031	12.0
September	517	5960	11.5
October	520	5850	11.3

Goal = 12 hours   *Hours are rounded up to the nearest hour

▲ FIGURE 3.9 Summary data by month for H&P turnaround times

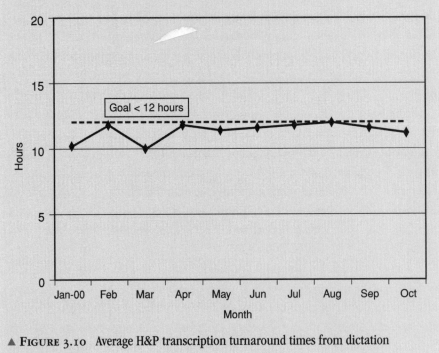

▲ FIGURE 3.10 Average H&P transcription turnaround times from dictation to transcription

question." You proceed to explain that the physicians probably do not care very much about the time from dictation to transcription but rather the time from dictation to posting the results on the computer or finding the results in the chart. Becky is very quick to point out that "now you're being unreasonable." She continues by explaining that they have never looked at the end piece of the process (i.e., transcription to posting of the results) because that chunk of time has never been very good, and it is something they do not feel that they have much control over. She concludes her comments by stating, "We look at what we do and expect someone else to take care of the rest of the process. It is not my problem that the people who are supposed to post the results don't do it according to the doctor's demands." You politely point out that the customers apparently do believe that the transcription department is responsible for making the posting of results happen in a timely manner. With reluctance Becky agrees to look at the process from dictation to charting, but she points out that there is no way that they can look at all the cases for these new starting and ending points. So you offer to help her pull a random sample of 60 cases per month.

The next Monday Becky sits in a quiet stupor in your office. She shows you Figure 3.11 and seems to be somewhere between shock and embarrassment. When you look at Figure 3.11 you start to understand why she is in this state of mind. It shows that the average TAT for all patients is somewhere around 18 hours—much higher than the goal of 12 hours. When you ask Becky about these results, she says that they are very surprising. Because you know her well, however, you quickly figure out that she is not being totally honest with you. She admits readily that she knew this all along, and that is why she decided to focus only on the dictation-to-transcription part of the process (this is where the embarrassment starts to settle in). So to cut the dead silence in the room, you offer another one of your brilliant quality measurement insights. Specifically, you ask if this process needs to be stratified. Becky is not quite sure where you are going with this question. You explain that it might be possible that the transcription process varies by day of the week or possibly by type of procedure. As you explore this idea with her, she indicates that it is possible that the TAT could vary by type of patient, namely, nonsurgical versus surgical H&Ps. When she says this you notice a slight hesitancy in her voice, but you are not sure why.

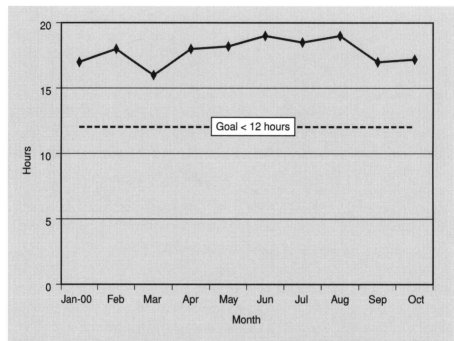

▲ FIGURE 3.11 Average H&P transcription turnaround times from dictation to chart

Much to your surprise, Becky returns to your office later that same day. She now has two new charts. Figure 3.12 shows the average TAT for non-surgical patients, and Figure 3.13 shows the results for surgical patients. As soon as you look at the charts you realize why Becky was a little embarrassed and hesitant. The answer to her problem is obvious. There is not one process occurring here but two: one for nonsurgical patients and another for surgical patients. The nonsurgical patients' H&Ps are turned around in roughly 21 hours, but those for the surgical patients have TATs of about 5 hours. No wonder the average for all patients is about 18 hours; it reflects the average of two very different processes.

So why the big discrepancy? It turns out that two of the surgeons were very upset with Becky and her department about eight months ago. They complained not only to the president of the medical staff but also to the CEO. Becky said she still remembers vividly the discussion she had with the CEO that day. In order to avoid that situation again, she made sure her staff gave preferential treatment to any H&P related to surgical procedures. As a result, the nonsurgical H&Ps received less attention, as demonstrated by the charts.

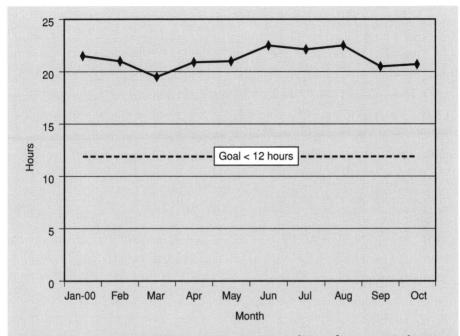

▲ FIGURE 3.12   Average H&P transcription turnaround times for nonsurgical patients from dictation to chart

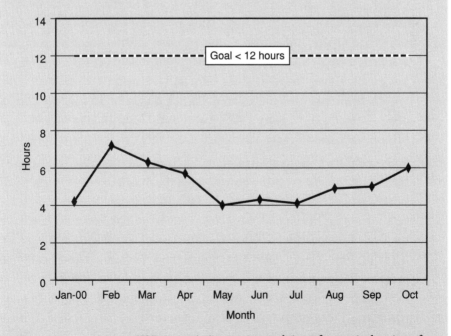

▲ FIGURE 3.13   Average H&P transcription turnaround times for surgical patients from dictation to chart

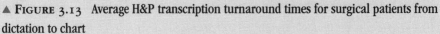

The Improvement Plan

Once Becky was over her cathartic release of pent-up angst, she was able to acknowledge readily that they set themselves up for this outcome. Obviously, one objective will be to maintain the performance of the surgical H&P TAT process. The challenge will be to work on the nonsurgical process and take steps to reduce this time to meet the goal of 12 hours or less. You agree to assist Becky by helping to create an improvement team, serve as the facilitator for the team, and guide them through the next round of data collection and analysis. Becky leaves your office not only feeling better about revealing the entire story behind this issue but also knowing that the team can do some things to improve the nonsurgical process.

Notes

1. When selecting indicators it is very important to keep the Pareto principle in mind (i.e., focus on the vital few and forget the trivial or common many). All too often, healthcare professionals tend to select entirely too many indicators. This usually means that the minutiae associated with collecting and analyzing the data wear the group down before they ever know if their efforts have made a difference. The Pareto principle and the related Pareto diagram (Plsek and Onnias 1989; Graham and Cleary 2000; Carey and Lloyd 2001) provide a useful approach to indicator selection.

2. The healthcare industry has huge databases to track the financial aspect of our business and relatively small databases to address questions related to quality. In contrast, a manufacturing company typically has relatively small financial databases and large databases to track the quality of its products. Why does this seem backwards? There are many historical and legitimate reasons why the financing of healthcare services has emerged as a very different system than the financing of manufacturing production. Manufacturing companies pay for inputs (resources), design and production, and marketing and distribution. They then set a selling price for the product, which is derived by

determining how much it costs to make the product and how much markup (profit) they think they can get. This model, unfortunately, does not work in healthcare. In healthcare we have costs that are then converted into charges sent on to the patient. Technically, the difference between costs and charges should be equivalent to profit in the manufacturing world (except because most healthcare organizations are not-for-profit, they do not use the term "profit" but rather "operating margin"). Very few patients actually pay for their healthcare services. Usually an insurance company, managed care organization, or some other fiscal intermediary (e.g., the Medicare and Medicaid programs) decides what they think is a "fair" reimbursement for a particular healthcare service. This approach essentially means that healthcare services are not market-driven commodities like manufactured products. So it is not surprising that we have large financial databases in the healthcare industry. The problem is that we are oftentimes trying to answer questions about quality with existing financial databases. This practice needs to change. Lengths of stay by diagnosis and average cost per discharge are not acceptable proxies for quality. We need to redesign the way in which we think about quality data and then take steps to start building quality-related databases.

3. Michael Millenson's book *Demanding Medical Excellence* (1999) provides an excellent overview of Dr. Codman's thinking and his efforts to develop performance measurement systems (see particularly pages 142–147). The JCAHO's book *The Measurement Mandate* (1993) also provides additional detail on Dr. Codman's life.

4. I want to thank my friend and colleague Judi Miller for her assistance in developing this list of processes and indicators. For several years Judi and I taught a class within Advocate Health Care on indicator selection and development. We also were asked to conduct workshops on this topic at the IHI's National Healthcare Forum. Her insights into medical records and hospital information management are greatly appreciated.

5. Increasingly politicians are being asked to clarify what they say and what they mean. It is not uncommon, for example, for a political candidate or an incumbent to have a reporter repeat what the politician said yesterday or last week about an issue and then ask them why they are now saying something different. The evening news is notorious for

playing a clip of what the president said last month and then showing that he said just the opposite today. Think how easy our Founding Fathers had it in this regard. It was probably very easy for them to take a position one day and another position the next. No one recorded their comments verbatim, and there were no cameras, videotapes, or recording devices. Operational definitions in George Washington's day could be very loose. Today, however, there is increasing scrutiny on the part of the public and a desire to have the politicians be more precise in their definitions of terms.

6. You will need to be clever in how you actually fit this into a conversation or a meeting, because most people will look at you in a strange manner if you just let the words "random sample" fly out of your mouth. One possible opening is to couch it in light of some vague reference to the public release of healthcare data and indicate that you read in the paper that there would be a "random sample of patients pulled from all admissions." Now you can innocently ask, "Have any of you ever drawn a random sample?" and it will seem to be consistent with your setup.

7. While it seems counterintuitive, it is possible to have too much data. There is frequently a belief (although it is generally a false belief) that if a little data is good, then a lot of data must be better. This is not always the case. For example, when a national news service conducts one of its "man on the street" surveys to test the political climate, or a national public polling agency conducts a survey of American opinions, how many people do you think they include in their sample? Typically they shoot for 1000 to no more than 2000 people. We have more than 280 million people in this country and they get only 1500 respondents. Why don't they get more? After a certain point the additional data does not add anything to the statistical precision of a study. It merely wastes resources and time. A general rule of thumb is that 30–50 observations (data points, survey respondents, or numbers) will start to produce a distribution. If you stratify your respondents by age, gender, race, region of the country, urban/rural status, education, income, and religious preference, which is what the national news polls do, then you need more than 30–50 observations in order to ensure that each level of stratification has sufficient data to enable the appropriate statistical

analysis. Telemarketers are experts at sampling. They can pinpoint down to the neighborhood area or census track level how many people represent the categories they need for their marketing study. A stratified proportional random sampling plan is put into place, the computer automatically dials the numbers, and your dinner is interrupted because you fit the sampling profile they need. But remember they do not need much data to complete their sampling plan.

8. I want to thank Dr. Bob Bealer for this phrase. While I was a doctoral student at Penn State University in the Department of Agricultural Economics and Rural Sociology, he used this phrase frequently. He used it when a student would ask, "How many pages do you want for this paper?" or when one of us would want to know how much data we needed to produce a "significant" result. Professor Bealer challenged us to think by using few words. He knew that the answers were rattling around somewhere within our developing brains. His skill was in providing a light for us to find the path. As much as you must and as little as you dare—it is a wonderfully simple phrase that relates to many aspects of life.

9. There are two classic stories about sampling that both the critics of sampling and its proponents have referenced for years. The first is the 1936 *Literary Digest* poll that predicted the landslide victory of Alf Landon over incumbent Franklin D. Roosevelt. Using a mailed sample of more than 2 million voters, the *Literary Digest* predicted that Landon would win by almost 15%. The mistake they made was in selecting the list of individuals for the sample (this is referred to as the sampling frame). The sample was drawn from telephone directories and automobile registration lists. These methods had worked in the past elections quite nicely. What the *Literary Digest* pollsters forgot was that in 1936 the nation was still feeling the negative effects of the depression and the more positive impacts of Roosevelt's New Deal program. The 1936 election witnessed an unprecedented turnout of poor voters. These people were not proportionately represented in the telephone and car registration lists because they could not afford such luxuries. The other key issue that the *Literary Digest* missed was that the poor voters were primarily Democrats while the more wealthy voters, who could afford cars and telephones, were primarily Republicans. In this same year, however, George Gallup correctly

predicted that Roosevelt would be the winner. Gallup's approach was based on using quota sampling, which ensured that samples were drawn from various segments of society (e.g., urban, rural, rich, poor, Republicans, and Democrats). As a result of this event, Gallup's credibility increased dramatically while that of the *Literary Digest* plummeted. The next major sampling fiasco occurred in 1948 when Gallup, and most other public opinion polling organizations, predicted that Thomas Dewey would be victorious over Harry Truman. What they all missed in this case was (1) that nearly all the pollsters finished their polling too soon and missed the late surge for Truman and (2) the people who in earlier polls said they were not sure who they would vote for decided to vote predominantly for Truman. The success that Gallup had in 1936 with quota sampling proved to be disastrous twelve years later. It was after the 1948 election that academic statisticians began a serious push for using probability theory as a basis for drawing samples. Today the use of probability sampling methods remains the accepted standard for drawing the least amount of data with the highest level of predictability and confidence.

10. Advocate Health Care is the largest integrated delivery system in the Chicago metropolitan area. Advocate is a faith-based system sponsored by the Evangelical Lutheran Church in America (ELCA) and the United Church of Christ (UCC). We have eight general acute care hospitals, two children's hospitals, the state's largest home health care organization, and three medical groups. Three of our largest hospitals are teaching facilities. There are more than 24,000 employees and more than 5000 physicians affiliated with Advocate. The corporate offices are located in Oak Brook, Illinois.

11. Ms. Miller and I have had the pleasure of being invited by the IHI to present workshops on this form at the IHI's National Quality Forum in 1997 and 1998. Attendance at the four workshops we presented totaled more than 600 people. In addition, I have had the opportunity to share this form with many healthcare organizations in this country and abroad. I have encouraged all of them to modify the form for their own use and adapt it to suit the culture they have created for measurement.

The goal is to get staff talking about indicators, about how they are selected and developed. If this form serves as a catalyst for discussing what an organization wants to measure, then as an industry we will all benefit. Remember, one of the hallmarks of quality improvement is that you should "steal shamelessly" from others. Always cite your sources and give credit to people for what they have developed, but use the knowledge of others as a springboard for your own initiatives.

12. The other alternative to the *deus ex machina* is found in the following story:

> **The Facts of Life**
> The story that follows is about four people named Everybody, Somebody, Anybody, and Nobody. There was an important job to be done and Everybody was asked to do it. Anybody could have done it, but Nobody did it. Somebody got angry about that because it was Everybody's job. Everybody thought Anybody could do it, but Nobody realized that Everybody blamed Somebody when Nobody accused Anybody.

I am not sure of the origin of this story. My mother gave me a copy of it when I first started college. At the time I accepted it graciously and tucked it away, thinking that it was one of those things mothers give their children as they go off to college and hope that it makes them think about how their actions affect others. That was back in 1966. Today, I still have the original piece of paper she gave me with this story typed on it. Over the years it is funny how many times I have pulled out this little piece of paper or run across it in a cluttered desk drawer and realized how relevant the lines are to so many aspects of life. Many of the challenges we face with data and measurement stem from the fact that the people who own the process do not take ownership of their data and the results produced by their processes. Inevitably, when I am involved with assisting people in developing their indicators, there will be a moment when their discussion about data collection makes me think of this story.

References

Babbie, E. R. *The Practice of Social Research.* Belmont, Calif.: Wadsworth, 1979.

Boyle, J. "Quality by the Numbers." In K. Coughlin (ed.), *1999 Medical Quality Management Sourcebook.* New York: Faulkner & Gray, 1998: 33–49.

Brooke, R., C. Kamberg, and E McGlynn. "Health System Reform and Quality." *Journal of the American Medical Association* 276, no. 6 (1996): 476–480.

Caldwell, C. *Mentoring Strategic Change in Health Care.* Milwaukee: Quality Press, 1995.

Campbell, S. *Flaws and Fallacies in Statistical Thinking.* Englewood Cliffs, N.J.: Prentice-Hall, 1974.

Carey, R., and R. Lloyd. *Measuring Quality Improvement in Healthcare: A Guide to Statistical Process Control Applications.* Milwaukee: Quality Press, 2001.

Codman, E. A. *A Study in Hospital Efficiency* (1917). Reprint, Oak Brook, Ill., Joint Commission on the Accreditation of Healthcare Organizations: 1996.

Daniel, W., and J. Terrell. *Business Statistics.* Dallas: Houghton Mifflin, 1989.

Deming, W. E. *Some Theory of Sampling.* New York: John Wiley & Sons, 1950.

Deming, W. E. *Sample Design in Business Research.* New York: John Wiley & Sons, 1960.

Deming, W. E. "On Probability as a Basis for Action." *The American Statistician* 29, no. 4 (1975): 146–152.

Deming, W. E. *Out of the Crisis.* Cambridge, Mass.: Massachusetts Institute of Technology Center for Advanced Engineering Study, 1992.

Donabedian, A. *Explorations in Quality Assessment and Monitoring. Volume I: The Definition of Quality and Approaches to Its Assessment.* Ann Arbor, Mich.: Health Administration Press, 1980.

Donabedian, A. *Explorations in Quality Assessment and Monitoring. Volume II: The Criteria and Standards of Quality.* Ann Arbor, Mich.: Health Administration Press, 1982.

Duncan, A. *Quality Control and Industrial Statistics.* Homewood, Ill.: Irwin Press, 5th ed., 1986

Gonick, L., and W. Smith. *The Cartoon Guide to Statistics.* New York: Harper Perennial, 1993.

Graham, J., and M. Cleary (eds.). *Practical Tools for Continuous Improvement. Volume 1: Statistical Tools.* Miamisburg, Ohio: PQ Systems, 2000.

Hess, I., D. Riedel, and T. Fitzpatrick. *Probability Sampling of Hospitals and Patients.* Ann Arbor, Mich.: Health Administration Press, 1975.

Institute of Medicine. *Crossing the Quality Chasm.* Washington, D.C.: National Academy Press, 2001.

Ishikawa, K. *Guide to Quality Control.* White Plains, N.Y.: Quality Resources, 1982.

Joint Commission on Accreditation of Healthcare Organizations. *The Measurement Mandate: On the Road to Performance Measurement in Health Care.* Oak Brook, Ill.: JCAHO, 1993.

Kaplan, R., and P. Norton. "The Balanced Scorecard—Measures That Drive Performance." *Harvard Business Review* (January–February 1992): 71–79.

———."Putting the Balanced Scorecard to Work." *Harvard Business Review* (September–October 1993): 134–147.

———."Using the Balanced Scorecard as a Strategic Management System." *Harvard Business Review* (January–February 1996): 75–85.

Langley, G., K. Nolan, T. Nolan, C. Norman, and L. Provost. *The Improvement Guide.* San Francisco: Jossey-Bass, 1996.

Maddox, B. "Sampling Concepts, Strategy and Techniques" Pennsylvania Department of Health, State Health Data Center, Technical report 81-1, July 1, 1981.

Mann, N. R. *The Keys to Excellence: The Story of the Deming Philosophy.* London: Mercury Books, 1989.

Miller, D. *Handbook of Research Design and Social Measurement.* New York: David McKay Company, 1964.

Plsek, P., and A. Onnias. *Quality Improvement Tools.* Wilton, Conn.: The Juran Institute, 1989.

Selltiz, C., M. Jahoda, M. Deutsch, and S. Cook. *Research Methods in Social Relations.* New York: Holt, Rinehart and Winston, 1959.

Shewhart, W. *Economic Control of Quality of Manufactured Product.* New York: D. Van Nostrand, 1931. Reprint, Milwaukee: Quality Press, 1980.

Weiss, R. *Statistics in Social Research.* New York: John Wiley & Sons, 1968.

Wheeler, D. *Understanding Variation: The Key to Managing Chaos.* Knoxville, Tenn.: SPC Press, 1993.

Western Electric Co. *Statistical Quality Control Handbook.* Indianapolis, Ind.: AT&T Technologies, 11th printing, 1985.

Chapter 4

Organizing Indicators into Strategic Dashboards

Most QI teams will create more than one indicator. If your organization has 10 to 15 teams, this means that you could be looking at managing 50 to 75 indicators (assuming that each team creates 5 indicators, which is usually at the low end of what teams want to track). So how do you go about organizing multiple indicators? First of all, you need a simple way to summarize the various indicators you have produced. Table 4.1 provides such a template. This matrix can be viewed as the summary version of your measurement efforts. You do not need (or want) to give the details documented in the Indicator Development Form© to the quality council or to senior management. They need a 40,000-foot view. As owners of the process you and your team members need to have the detail on each indicator. Groups listening to you explain your measurement plan, however, want to know the big picture, not the details.

Each row in Table 4.1 represents a single indicator. The columns identify the major pieces of information that need to be summarized about each indicator. Table 4.2 provides an example of a completed measurement plan matrix.[1] The objective of the team was to improve the assessment and treatment process for individuals entering the emergency department with chest pain. The basic question is, "Is this person having a real heart attack or is it a serious case of indigestion and heartburn?" Obviously you do not want to miss a diagnosis. But, on the other hand, you do not want to place a patient in an observation unit or admit them when all they have is a serious gas attack or indigestion. This team developed three measures: two related to accuracy and one related to cost. When it came time to present to the quality council or to the management team, all they had to do was place this grid on the overhead projector and describe what they were measuring. They would then provide their statistical analysis by showing control charts for each indicator. Once you have started to organize your indicators into a format that can be shared with others, you are well on your way to building what is known as a dashboard or instrument panel of strategic indicators.

▼ TABLE 4.1 Measurement plan matrix

Key concept	Specific measure	Operational definition	Data source(s)	Data collection • Schedule • Method • Responsible person(s)	Collaborating department(s)	Comments
Indicator #1						
Indicator #2						
Indicator #3						
Indicator #4						

▼ TABLE 4.2   An example of a completed measurement plan matrix for non-specific chest pain (NSCP) patients

Key concept	Specific measures	Operational definitions	Data source(s)	Data collection • Schedule • Method • Responsibility	Collaborating department/ division/ program	Priority/ comments
Accuracy of diagnosis	Percentage of patients who have a myocardial infarction (MI) or unstable angina as a diagnosis	Denominator = All patients entered into the NSCP path Numerator = Patients entered into the NSCP path who have acute MI or unstable angina as the discharge diagnosis	• Medical records • MIDAS • Variance tracking form	• Discharge diagnosis will be identified for all patients entered into the NSCP pathway • Quality Assurance and Utilization Review (QA-UR) will retrospectively review charts of all patients entered into the NSCP pathway; data will be entered into MIDAS system	• Medical records • QA-UR • Medicine	Must relate to total of patients entered in the pathway to obtain percentage

▼ TABLE 4.2 An example of a completed measurement plan matrix for non-specific chest pain (NSCP) patients *(continued)*

Key concept	Specific measures	Operational definitions	Data source(s)	Data collection • Schedule • Method • Responsiblity	Collaborating department/ division/ program	Priority/ comments
Accuracy of diagnosis	Number of patients who are admitted to hospital or seen in an Emergency Department (ED) because of chest pain within one week of discharge	Operational definition: One who reports during the call-back interview that they have been admitted or seen in an ED for chest pain during the past week	All patients who have been managed within the NSCP protocol throughout their hospital stay	• Patients will be contacted by phone one week after discharge • Call-back interview will be the method	• Research institute • Department of Medicine	
Cost	Total hospital costs per one cardiac diagnosis	Numerator = Total costs per quarter for hospital care of NSCP pathway patients Denominator = Number of patients per quarter entered into the NSCP pathway with a discharge diagnosis of MI or unstable angina	• Finance • Chart review	Can be calculated every three months from financial and clinical data already being collected	• Finance • QA-UR • Medical records • Performance Improvement Department	

Evolution of the Strategic Dashboard

The growing demand for healthcare data can be traced back to the early 1980s (see Chapter 1) when a variety of external groups began pushing for the development of healthcare report cards. Just like the report cards we received when we were in school, these summaries are intended to evaluate providers on a number of key indicators. Report card sponsors feel that these assessments are needed in order to make prudent decisions about which providers offer the highest quality at the lowest cost. As Nelson *et al.* (1995) point out, there are three primary groups that have led the development of healthcare report cards: (1) purchasers of care, (2) health service researchers, and (3) providers of care who are anxious to show that they are concerned about cost, service, and quality. To these three I would add a fourth: politicians. Without political support and sponsorship, the state data commissions, for example, would never have become a major provider of healthcare report cards.

Over the past 20 years, the demand for healthcare report cards has waxed and waned. Currently the push for the public reporting of healthcare data is once again on the rise. The problem with report cards, however, is that they are basically designed to produce data for judgment, not improvement. Report cards are usually derived from historical data that is aggregated and static in nature. They also have the uncanny ability to produce a wide variety of emotional reactions (i.e., unbridled joy if you receive a good grade, disappointment if you receive a bad grade, and fear that you might be given a poor grade). Nelson *et al.* provide the following portrait of the report card orientation (1995:157):

The Report Card image . . .

Who gets report cards?	Students
Who gives them?	Teachers
What is the focus?	Past performance
Who wins?	The A's
Who loses?	Everybody else
What's learned?	I'm above average, average, or below average

Placed within the healthcare context, report cards are typically produced by external groups and organizations. Those producing the report card may involve the providers in the development and design of the final product, or they may totally exclude the providers from the process. The primary objective is to rate and rank providers on selected indicators. Providers rated or ranked at or near the top are judged to be better performers than those further down in the list. It is not uncommon for percentiles to be used as the primary statistical determinant of performance. The major problem with the report card approach, however, is that they provide judgment about selected outcomes but do not "help providers know how to make improvements" (Nelson *et al.* 1995:157). Improvement requires not only a different approach to the collection and analysis of data but also a different way of thinking about what to do with data once you have it.

The alternative to the static report card is the development of a more dynamic performance measurement system that enhances decision making and encourages improvement strategies. Two terms have emerged to describe this alternative approach: the dashboard and the instrument panel. Some writers have favored the image of a car dashboard for this approach, and others have used the analogy of the instrument panel of an airplane. Regardless of the term, the concept that they are trying to promote is the same.

According to Bader (1993), Henry Berman, CEO of Group Health Northwest (Spokane, Washington), was the first to popularize the dashboard analogy. To understand this analogy, just think about how you use the dashboard of your car. The dashboard gives you real-time feedback on how you are doing right now. You really do not care about the past performance of your car. For example, when you drive down a street that you travel frequently, how often do you ask yourself, "Gee, I wonder what my average speed was when I traveled down this stretch of road last month?" Your concern is not with your speed last month, last quarter, or last year but with how fast you are going right now.

Nelson and his colleagues favor the instrument panel analogy. They write, "Just like the cockpit crew of a jet airplane need instrument panels to fly safely, health care delivery system leaders need instrument panels to manage wisely" (1995:157). The characteristics of an instrument panel are as follows:

Instrument Panel Image . . .

Who uses them?	The cockpit crew (pilot, copilot, navigator)
Who interprets the results?	The cockpit crew
What is the focus?	Present and future performance
What is the utility?	Real-time monitoring, predicting the future, and taking action

According to Nelson *et al.* (1995:158), "The instrument panel or dashboard metaphor has an entirely different aura from that of the report card. It has vitality, timeliness, and a clear-cut utility that is absent from report card thinking. A key feature is providing critical, real-time information to the user to prompt wise decisions and—if need be—make rapid midcourse corrections." The decision to create an instrument panel or dashboard rather than a report card is based on much more than semantics. Although there are obvious differences in the intent of each approach (judgment versus improvement), there are also major differences in the ways in which data are collected, tabulated, and displayed.

Robert Kaplan and David Norton have developed a third concept to describe the organization of key strategic indicators. They have coined the term the "balanced scorecard" as their organizing rubric. In 1992 they published the first of a series of articles defining the balanced scorecard, its components, and how they envision its use. Subsequent articles provided examples of companies applying their ideas (1993) and how their framework can be used to create a strategic management system (1996). Although the terminology is different from that used by Nelson and his colleagues, Kaplan and Norton also see the balanced scorecard as "the dials and indicators in an airplane cockpit." They continue their analogy by stating, "Reliance on one instrument can be fatal. Similarly the complexity of managing an organization today requires that managers be able to view performance in several areas simultaneously" (Kaplan and Norton 1992:72).[2]

In their first article (1992) Kaplan and Norton identified the following benefits of developing a balanced scorecard:

- It brings together, in a single management report, many of the seemingly disparate elements of an organization's strategic agenda.
- It helps to reduce information overload by focusing on the "vital few" indicators.
- It helps to guard against suboptimization by forcing senior managers to consider all the important measures together and lets them see whether improvement in one area may be achieved at the expense of another.
- It puts strategy and vision, rather than control, at the center of an organization's effort.
- It is based on an understanding of interrelationships between functions, not on the performance of individual functions or units.

- It provides an opportunity for organizational learning at the executive level.

Nugent *et al.* (1994) demonstrate how this process works by describing the creation of an instrument panel to monitor and improve CABG surgery. In this classic article, they walk the reader through the selection and definition of key indicators for CABG surgery and then show how control charts can be used to understand the variation that lives in the process. Although the authors focus on the details of how to create a dashboard, one of the side benefits of the article is to show how the instrument panel concept can be applied to a very specific clinical procedure and its related outcomes.

More recently, the Health Care Advisory Board published a comprehensive report entitled *CEO Dashboards: Performance Metrics for the New Health Care Economy* (2000). This document has emerged as a general guide for the development of healthcare dashboards. It addresses the following issues:

- The problem of inadequate performance measurement
- Elements of an effective dashboard
- Recommendations for rapid dashboard development
- Dashboards of leading hospitals and health systems

Based on their research, the Health Care Advisory Board identified four key elements of an effective dashboard:

- Building a dashboard around a balanced set of performance measures
- Selecting a fairly austere set of measures (i.e., keeping it simple by selecting the vital few measures, usually 15–30)
- Presenting data in graphic displays (rather than tabular formats)
- Developing action triggers (i.e., setting targets and goals that trigger the need for action)

They then proceed to summarize the leading categories for organizing healthcare dashboards:

- Financial performance
- Operational effectiveness/efficiency
- Quality (clinical and service quality)
- Satisfaction (patient and family as well as employee and physician satisfaction)

Examples of specific indicators that characterize each of these four categories are also provided. The report concludes with actual examples from health systems, stand-alone hospitals, and academic medical centers.

Designed correctly, the dashboard (or instrument panel) can be used to meet not only internal management needs but also those demands made on providers by external groups interested in building report cards. If an organization builds what Caldwell (1995) refers to as a "strategic measurement deployment matrix," it will be able to measure key indicators at various levels within the organization and then have the capability to roll these measures up into overall summary measures that also satisfy external requirements. Dashboards and instrument panels can be used to navigate correctly at 30,000 feet or at the departmental or even frontline levels. The choice in how you structure your dashboard(s) is up to you.

Focusing on the Vital Few

One of the major challenges with creating a dashboard is parsimony (what the Health Care Advisory Board calls austerity). I have seen many organizations create a dashboard that contains 50 to 80 indicators. A dashboard with this many indicators is counter to what the concept of the dashboard is trying to achieve. Again, consider the dashboard of your car. There are a few vital indicators that you rely on regularly, most notably the speedometer and fuel gauge. After these two indicators, the rest of the dashboard gauges may (or may not) be of importance to you. Hopefully you pay some attention to the temperature gauge, but you probably do not give much consideration to your electrical system status indicators or the accumulating mileage indicator (a.k.a. the odometer). Then there is the tachometer. This is probably the most useless indicator on your dashboard, especially if you are driving an automatic transmission vehicle.[3]

The Pareto principle provides a good conceptual and organizational framework for selecting dashboard indicators. The Pareto principle (named after the Italian economist Vilfredo Pareto, circa 1840) basically states that for any event (or problem) a small number of factors will account for a majority of the reasons why the event (or problem) occurred. Out of the Pareto principle emerged the 80/20 rule (i.e., 80% of the problem is due to 20% of the causes). The Pareto diagram (for construction see Graham and Cleary 2000; Plsek and Onnias 1989) is used most often to prioritize opportunities for

CQI teams (Carey and Lloyd 2000). Its primary goal is to identify the *vital few* and separate these causal factors from the *common* or *trivial many* (the things that do not matter). The Pareto principle applies very well, however, to the dashboard concept. Dashboards should be populated with the vital few, not the trivial many. Yet all too often organizations decide that nearly everything they measure needs to be placed on the dashboard. In this case, their dashboard looks more like the instrument panel of a space shuttle or a 747 jumbo jet. Although you may not be able to achieve the simplicity of a moped's dashboard, which has about three indicators, you certainly do not need the complexity of the space shuttle. From my perspective, I believe that a parsimonious dashboard should consist of 10–15 indicators.

If you are interested in obtaining examples of dashboards, I would suggest that you obtain a copy of the Health Care Advisory Board's *CEO Dashboard* report and contact several of the organizations listed in the report. Because my system was one of the systems included in the *CEO Dashboard,* I have included several examples of dashboards we have developed. Again, I offer these only as illustrations. They can be used as a basis for discussion of both the contents of the dashboard and the display formats. But they should not be accepted automatically as the preferred template for a dashboard. Each organization needs to develop and design dashboards that not only meet their short- and long-term objectives but also, most importantly, fit with the organization's culture. The dashboards for Advocate Health Care include our strategic and clinical excellence dashboards (Figures 4.1 and 4.2). These examples merely list the indicators that are collected and the format for displaying the basic dashboard. The strategic dashboard is populated with the actual value for each time period. Figure 4.2, the clinical excellence dashboard, does not report actual numbers but performance-to-goal identifiers. If a site is at or better than the identified goal, then a star is placed in that site's cell. Short-term performance is depicted by arrows that indicate the current direction of the indicator compared with the last reporting period. Both of these dashboards are static in nature. They are designed to provide a snapshot of where the organization is currently positioned on key indicators. The primary customers of these two documents are the board, senior management, and site operations managers. All employees, however, do have access to the results on the Advocate intranet. Behind each dashboard is a series of graphs that show how each indicator has been performing over time and the relationship of the indicator to its goal.

Indicator sets	Frequency	Baseline	Current	Short-term goal	Long-term goal
System health					
Spiritual care (from patient satisfaction survey results) Clinical integration (out-of-network) Operating margin Debt/asset ratio					
Service breakthrough					
Overall patient satisfaction percentile Willing to recommend percentile					
Work life quality					
Associate satisfaction percentile					
Clinical excellence					
Clinical quality index Research and CME performance Graduate medical education performance Cost per adjusted discharge					
Technology leadership					
Percentage of aligned physicians electronically linked to advocate					
Innovative growth					
Net ambulatory revenue as percentage of total net revenue Inpatient market share Covered lives market share					

▲ FIGURE 4.1 Advocate Health Care's strategic dashboard

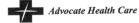 **Advocate Health Care**

Clinical Excellence Indicators - Goal Achievement Executive Summary
(Date Issued 00/00/00)*

Indicator/(System Goal)													
Clinical Effectiveness	SYSTEM	Bethany	Christ	Good Samaritan	Good Shepherd	IMMC	LGH	South Suburban	Trinity	AHC	AMG	Dreyer	HHC
Hospital Ratio (93.0%)													
Days per 1000 Medicare patients (AHC 1125/Dreyer 1225)													
Percent of acute hospitalization of home health patients (<23%)													
Asthma Management	SYSTEM	Bethany	Christ	Good Samaritan	Good Shepherd	IMMC	LGH	South Suburban	Trinity	AHC	AMG	Dreyer	HHC
Percent of asthma readmissions within 30 days of inpatient discharge (6%)													
Percent of asthma ED revisits within 3 days of discharge (2%)													
Baby Advocate: Childhood Immunizations	SYSTEM	Bethany	Christ	Good Samaritan	Good Shepherd	IMMC	LGH/AMG	South Suburban	Trinity	AHC	AMG	Dreyer	HHC
90% children immunized at 2 years of age (7/7 indicators)													
Congestive Heart Failure Management	SYSTEM	Bethany	Christ	Good Samaritan	Good Shepherd	IMMC	LGH	South Suburban	Trinity	AHC	AMG	Dreyer	HHC
Percent of CHF readmissions within 30 days of inpatient discharge (JCAHO definition of CHF) (7.3%)													
Percent of ACE inhibitor use (CHF coordinator defined CHF population) (80%)													
Deep Vein Thrombosis (DVT) Prophylaxis	SYSTEM	Bethany	Christ	Good Samaritan	Good Shepherd	IMMC	LGH	South Suburban	Trinity	AHC	AMG	Dreyer	HHC
Percent of patients at risk for DVT that receive pharmacological prophylaxis and/or IPC devices (80%)													
Percent of patients at risk for DVT receiving drug prophylaxis that receive recommended pharmacological dosage (90%)													
Diabetes Mellitus Outpatient Management	SYSTEM	Bethany	Christ	Good Samaritan	Good Shepherd	IMMC	LGH	South Suburban	Trinity	AHC	AMG	Dreyer	HHC
Percent of diabetic patients receiving annual HgA1c screening blood test (100%)													
Percent of diabetic patients receiving annual LDL-C screening blood test (100%)													
Influenza Prevention	SYSTEM	Bethany	Christ	Good Samaritan	Good Shepherd	IMMC	LGH	South Suburban	Trinity	AHC	AMG	Dreyer	HHC
Percent of Medicare managed care patients immunized (65%)													
Percent of associates immunized (50%)													
Labor and Delivery Patient Safety	SYSTEM	Bethany	Christ	Good Samaritan	Good Shepherd	IMMC	LGH	South Suburban	Trinity	AHC	AMG	Dreyer	HHC
Percent of new hires trained within 6 months in neonatal resuscitation (100%)													
Percent of new hires trained within 6 months in fetal heart rate monitoring (100%)													
Mammography Management	SYSTEM	Bethany	Christ	Good Samaritan	Good Shepherd	IMMC	LGH	South Suburban	Trinity	AHC	AMG	Dreyer	HHC
Cycle time from abnormal mammogram to diagnosis (H-17 days/MG 16 days)													
Percent of non-surgical biopsies (increase from baseline)													
Medication Error Prevention	SYSTEM	Bethany	Christ	Good Samaritan	Good Shepherd	IMMC	LGH	South Suburban	Trinity	AHC	AMG	Dreyer	HHC
Number medication errors reported per 100 adj admissions (increase reporting by 10%)													
Number adverse drug events reported per 100 adj admissions (decrease rate by 10%)													
Number medication errors related to active administration reported per 100 adj admissions (decrease rate by 10%)													
Nosocomial Infection Prevention	SYSTEM	Bethany	Christ	Good Samaritan	Good Shepherd	IMMC	LGH	South Suburban	Trinity	AHC	AMG	Dreyer	HHC
Percent of surgical site infections within 1 year of total hip and/or knee procedures (1.3%)													
ICU central line-associated bloodstream infection rate (5.6)													
ICU ventilator-associated pneumonia rate (8.0)													
AHRQ Focus Areas	SYSTEM	Bethany	Christ	Good Samaritan	Good Shepherd	IMMC	LGH	South Suburban	Trinity	AHC	AMG	Dreyer	HHC
Use of pre-anesthesia equipment checklist													
Percent of patients on inpatient anticoagulation protocol for the management of DVT or PE													
Dissemination of outpatient anticoagulation protocol to relevant medical staff													
Percent of eligible patients that received peri-operative beta blocker therapy													
Surgical antibiotic prophylaxis: a) Percent of surgeries with antibiotic prophylaxis given in appropriate time period													
Surgical antibiotic prophylaxis: b) Surgical site infections using Standardized Infection Ratio													

↑↓ = Indicates improvement or decline compared to 1 year ago
TBD = To be determined
ND = No data submitted for current period
= Not applicable or No cases
★ = Achieved goal
= Below goal

*Data reporting periods vary by indicator. Please refer to the **February 2003 Indicator by Site Report** for details. To access on intranet: Click on Clinical Excellence: Periodic Reports - Current near the bottom of home page, click on Indicator by Site Report

▲ **Figure 4.2** Advocate Health Care's clinical excellence dashboard

The Role of Benchmarking

Once you have defined a specific indicator, collected data, and analyzed the variation in the data (see Chapters 5 and 6 for discussions on variation), you are ready to find out just how good your performance really is. This can be accomplished by using comparative reference data (e.g., a national norm from a patient satisfaction vendor's database) or by benchmarking. Unfortunately there seems to be considerable misunderstanding within the healthcare industry on the nature and intent of benchmarking. The simple message about benchmarking is that it is not about numbers—it is about improving practices and processes that ultimately lead to better outcomes.

It is about the transformation of the organization's culture and the way it does business. Benchmarking is about understanding the relationships between structures, processes, and outcomes. Unfortunately, I have seen too many healthcare professionals think that benchmarking is strictly about meeting a numeric target or goal (i.e., a benchmark). Before the month is over, I bet that you will hear someone say, "Here is the benchmark we need to hit by the end of the next quarter." When you hear a statement like this, you are basically hearing confusion between the concepts of a benchmark (a noun) and benchmarking (a verb). In such cases, the confusion goes even deeper because it usually involves confusion over the relationship of targets and goals to benchmarks and the benchmarking process. This confusion was highlighted recently in a newsletter published by the Mihalik Group (2003). In a brief article entitled "When Is a Performance Goal a Benchmark?" they make the following conclusions: "Occasionally there is some confusion over the correct use of the term 'benchmark.' A benchmark is a measure of best performance against which an organization's performance is compared. A benchmark, however, is never derived from average or aggregate performance. Because it represents the best, a benchmark must refer to the performance of only one organization." All too often I have seen organizations use an average or aggregated number as *the* benchmark. It not only flies in the face of what good benchmarking is supposed to achieve but also leads to confusion within the organization.

I believe there is a real need within the healthcare industry to clarify these concepts. Let us start our discussion by addressing the terms "target" and "goal." In a general sense, targets are short-term markers of achievement that are met over the span of several months or possibly years. Goals are more long term in nature, usually in the range of three to five years. A target or a goal can be based on a benchmark (the noun) if it is derived from an organization that is considered the "best of the best."

Benchmarking, on the other hand, is a completely different concept. Benchmarking uses numbers and data, but if you stop at the numbers you will never achieve the potential that benchmarking offers. Benchmarking is a way to identify and understand best practices that enable organizations to realize new levels of performance. Confusion over these concepts leads an organization to accept a number, either from an internal source or an external consultant, as "*the* benchmark." This orientation typically leads to a fairly singular focus on the numbers (outcomes) without giving due consideration to the interplay of the structures and processes that produce the numbers. Although you will hear organizations claim, "We are benchmarking," this statement usually means that they are hoping that they hit the selected metric but have not developed a strategy for achieving this ethereal number. The end result is usually confusion within the ranks and unrealistic expectations on the part of management and the board (especially if the organization has paid a large fee to an external consulting group that produced the "benchmark numbers").

The most widely referenced work on benchmarking is Robert Camp's classic book *Benchmarking: The Search for Industry Best Practices That Lead to Superior Performance* (1989). Camp traces the history of benchmarking, clearly defines what it is (and is not), outlines the steps in the benchmarking process, and then offers a series of examples of how successful companies have engaged in benchmarking. In the preface of his book, Camp introduces the Japanese term *dantotsu,* which loosely translates as striving to be the "best of the best." Camp (1989:3) points out that "We in America have no such word, perhaps because we always assumed we were the best."

Essentially a benchmark reflects an absolute measure of superior performance against which all other performances can be judged. Although benchmarks have been identified in other industries (e.g., the Ritz-Carlton Hotels, Motorola, L.L. Bean, Ben & Jerry's, or Toyota might be considered benchmarks), there is little consensus on which organization is consistently *the* best in healthcare and the standard to follow. How an organization becomes a "benchmark" is what benchmarking is all about. Camp (1989:10) provides the following formal definition of benchmarking: "Benchmarking is the continuous process of measuring products, services, and practices against the toughest competitors or those companies recognized as industry leaders."

He continues with a more direct working definition of the concept: "Benchmarking is the search for industry best practices that lead to superior performance" (1989:12). According to Camp, benchmarking is more about understanding practices that lead to performance than selecting a number to achieve. He puts it this way: "Benchmarking metrics are seen as a result of understanding best practices, not something that can be quantified first and understood later" (1989:13).

Frequently in healthcare, however, we do exactly what Camp cautions against. We look at current performance and then quickly pick a new level of performance that is a desired end state. In many instances, the decision-making process goes something like this: "We are currently at 80% on completed histories and physicals for outpatient surgery, so next quarter we expect it to be at 85%. No, maybe we should pick 90%? Oh, what the heck, let's use 100% as the target."[4] The basic problem with this approach to setting targets or goals is that little thought is given to how the new level of performance will be achieved. In most instances this leads to what Deming referred to as the creation of arbitrary numeric targets and goals, which demoralize the workers and mislead the organization. On this point Deming wrote, "Goals are necessary for you and for me, but numerical goals set for other people, without a road map to reach the goal, have effects opposite to the effects sought" (Deming 1992:69). Benchmarking is one of the best ways to develop a road map for achieving new performance levels.

Camp outlines five phases of benchmarking and ten related specific steps. These are summarized in Figure 4.3. The key to understanding these phases and their related steps is that they have to be seen as an ongoing process, not as something that the organization does once before moving on to the next popular management solution. The other important aspect of applying Camp's benchmarking framework is the recognition that although benchmarking is a structured process, it is first and foremost a search for knowledge and learning. Organizations looking for a silver bullet will quickly abandon benchmarking as being too detailed and involved. They will find it much easier to merely issue a memo that says, "Next year's performance targets will be 5% higher than this year's!"

Planning phase

Step 1:   Identify what is to be benchmarked

Step 2:   Identify comparative companies

Step 3:   Determine data collection methods and proceed with collecting data

Analysis phase

Step 4:   Determine current performance "gap" between your organization and the comparative companies

Step 5:   Project future performance levels (where do you want to be?)

Integration phase

Step 6:   Communicate benchmarking findings and gain acceptance within your organization

Step 7:   Establish functional goals for your organization

Action phase

Step 8:   Develop action plans (the road map for achieving new levels of performance)

Step 9:   Implement specific actions and monitor progress (start to change organizational practices and the culture)

Step 10: Recalibrate benchmarks based on changes in the organization and in the external environment

Maturity phase

This final phase occurs when the practices of the comparative companies have become integrated into the day-to-day functioning of your own organization. When your organization has reached this phase it may be sought out as a benchmark.

Adapted from: Camp, R. *Benchmarking: The Search for Industry Best Practices That Lead to Superior Performance.* Milwaukee: Quality Press, 1989.

▲ FIGURE 4.3   Benchmarking phases and related steps

A Comment on the "New" Business Management Strategies

Baldrige Criteria for Performance Excellence, Six Sigma, and ISO registration are new terms that have entered into the lexicon of corporate America. Most of the organizations using these business strategies, however, have been in the manufacturing and industrial sectors. Few healthcare providers have actually explored the utility of these new business management strategies until 2002, when SSM Health Care (based in St. Louis, Missouri) became the first healthcare provider ever to win the Baldrige Award (see *Quality Progress,* April 2003, for details). All of a sudden, healthcare CEOs became curious about the Baldrige Award and what it takes to win it. The mistake most organizations make about the Baldrige Award, however, is that they assume Baldrige is about getting an award. In fact, it is not about the award at all. It is about changing the organization's culture and demonstrating that quality principles permeate all facets of the organization. It is about getting external, objective evaluations on the extent to which your organization demonstrates excellence. Gaining Baldrige status is not something that is achieved in a year or two. The SSM system, for example, spent more than ten years preparing for the Baldrige application and review process (Smith, July 2003). Their journey suggests that they are emerging as one of the first real "benchmarks" in healthcare.

There are seven criteria that drive the Baldrige process:

- Leadership
- Strategic planning
- Focus on patients, other customers, and markets
- Information and analysis
- Staff focus
- Process management
- Organizational performance results

These seven criteria are viewed as an integrated set of factors that create a system. The challenge for any healthcare organization is to demonstrate that all seven components are integrated in both form and function. If an organization's written application is accepted, they are then eligible for a possible site visit by a multidisciplinary team of examiners.

If the organization scores well during the site visit, then they become eligible for consideration as a finalist in their division. While for some the Baldrige process seems overly complicated, all the steps in the process are well thought out and seen as being vital in determining whether the organization clearly demonstrates systems thinking and quality integration.[5] From my perspective, if healthcare leaders are serious about making quality a central aspect of their organizational strategy, then they will embrace the Baldrige criteria, conduct a Baldrige self-assessment, and initiate steps to achieve Baldrige recognition. An excellent way to start preparing for Baldrige is to participate in your state's quality award process. The state quality awards are patterned after the Baldrige process and provide a wonderful way to find out if your organization is structured to produce quality outcomes.

Six Sigma is the second business management strategy that has captured the attention of many organizations. In fact, if the volume of written material is any indication of the importance of a topic, then Six Sigma will certainly have to receive the award for the most important topic in American business. New publications are announced almost daily, as are new consulting firms willing to help your organization become a Six Sigma company.

Six Sigma has engendered considerable debate within quality and managerial circles. Some claim that it is the answer to America's business problems, and others have argued that it is merely a fad. In an editorial in *Quality Progress*, Blanton Godfrey (2002:6) stated, "We should remember that the concept of Six Sigma quality has been around for 16 years. If it's a fad, it's a long lasting one." He concludes that, "For many, Six Sigma is the latest name for a comprehensive set of philosophies, tools, methods and fundamental concepts." Joseph Juran seems to take a similar view. In an interview published in *Quality Digest* (Patton 2002) Juran, when asked, "What do you think of Six Sigma?" made the following comment: "From what I've seen, it is a basic version of quality improvement. There is nothing new there. It includes what we used to call facilitators. They've adopted more flamboyant terms, like belts with different colors. I think that concept has merit to set apart, to create specialists who can be very helpful. Again, that's not a new idea." (21)

From my experience, it seems that most healthcare professionals have limited knowledge of Six Sigma. Juran made a similar observation by stating, "Most people don't even understand what Six Sigma means" (Patton, 2002). The limited familiarity healthcare professionals have gained with the Six

Sigma concept usually comes from reading articles and books on or by Jack Welch, former CEO of General Electric (GE). They have read how Six Sigma saved GE (supposedly) millions of dollars and created a world-class organization.[6] Upon reading these accounts, many healthcare CEOs started to wonder if Six Sigma could possibly solve some of their financial and customer service challenges. Before "doing Six Sigma," however, it is important to understand what it is.

There are basically two ways to view Six Sigma. The first is as a statistic, and the second is as an organization-wide program. As a statistic, Six Sigma refers to calculating what is known as process capability (AT&T Technologies 1985; Wheeler 1995). AT&T describes process capability as "the normal behavior of a process when operating in a state of statistical control; the predictable series of effects produced by a process when allowed to operate without interference from outside causes. Process capability may be expressed as a percent defective or as a distribution" (AT&T Technologies 1985:45). Basically, process capability is designed to answer the following question: "How capable is the process of meeting the specifications of the customer?" When output of the process does not meet the specifications of the customer (i.e., the VOC), then the process produces defects and its capability is hampered. Eliminating defects is a mark of performance excellence. Yet most organizations are quite happy if they are able to produce 3 sigma output (i.e., 66,807 defects per million opportunities). Movement to 6 sigma levels of performance, on the other hand, produces 3.4 defects per million opportunities (Harry and Schroeder 2000). By comparison, most recent estimates of healthcare performance suggest that we are performing somewhere between 2 and 3 sigma levels of performance (i.e., 308,537 to 66,807 defects per million opportunities).

There are two ratios used to measure process capability. They are referred to as C_p (the capability ratio) and C_{pk} (the centered capability ratio). Wheeler (1995:192–193) provides a detailed description of the formulae for computing these ratios and their uses. My purpose at this point is merely to introduce these statistical concepts as they relate to Six Sigma. Readers interested in the specific applications of these statistics can refer to AT&T Technologies (1995) and Wheeler (1995).

The second approach to Six Sigma, although using statistics as a tool, goes way beyond the statistical notion of defects per million opportunities. Six Sigma as a program is an all-encompassing approach to performance excellence. According to one of the leading experts in Six Sigma thinking, Dr. Mikel Harry, "the biggest reason for the incredible buzz about Six Sigma throughout the business community has been its astonishing success at dramatically improving a company's bottom-line profitability" (Harry and Schroeder 2000:viii). To achieve Six Sigma success, Harry and his associates have developed over the last 15 years what they refer to as the Six Sigma Breakthrough Strategy. This strategy consists of a series of steps that (1) reveal how well products perform and how well services are delivered, and (2) show companies how to improve their processes and maintain the gains they achieve (Harry and Schroeder 2000:7).[7] According to Harry and Schroeder (2000:22), the Breakthrough Strategy is grounded in eight steps or stages: Recognize, Define, Measure, Analyze, Improve, Control, Standardize, and Integrate. From the list of eight, they define what they call the "four core phases"—Measure, Analyze, Improve, and Control (M-A-I-C).

A commitment to Six Sigma, as it was first developed by Motorola, advanced by GE, and then made popular by Six Sigma consultants, is a very complex and resource-intense program. It has its own language (e.g., Champions, Master Black Belts, Black Belts, and Green Belts), leadership development pathways, tool sets (e.g., standard quality improvement tools like flowcharting and control charts, as well as benchmarking), and standards for advancement and expected levels of involvement of all employees. On this last point it is a fairly well-known story that in January 1998 Jack Welch sent a message to all GE managers stating that if they were interested in being promoted, they had to achieve Black Belt or Green Belt status within seven months. This probably explains why GE trained (during Welch's tenure) more than 10,000 employees each year in Six Sigma principles and skills.

There has clearly been a lot of buzz about the potential of Six Sigma to solve all of this country's healthcare problems. My major concern is that whatever good Six Sigma can offer the healthcare industry is being overshadowed by an aura that positions Six Sigma as a quick fix to the issues that plague our industry. Six Sigma is not a quick fix; it is not inexpensive to implement (e.g., I have heard estimates of anywhere from $20,000 to $30,000 to train one person as a Six Sigma Black Belt), and it is not something you decide to achieve by the end of the month. Finally, it appears that only large companies have the resources (people and dollars) to fully implement Six Sigma strategies in a manner similar to what GE and Motorola have done. In the 2003 Six Sigma Survey conducted by *Quality Digest* (Dusharme 2003) the author of the study concludes, "Ninety percent of the companies that do implement Six Sigma are units, divisions or sites of larger organizations. Of those, three-quarters belong to organizations with more than 2,000 employees." Yet according to the 1997 U.S. Census Bureau, 98% of all U.S. companies had fewer than 20 employees, and 82% grossed less than $1 million in sales in 1992 (Dusharme 2003:24). Although Six Sigma could benefit small companies, they do not usually have an extra half million dollars or more to pay for the basic training of Green and Black Belt experts, and they do not have sufficient depth in their employee ranks to send several of them off for four months of training.

So, in terms of the relevance of Six Sigma to healthcare, I think the jury is still out. *Quality Digest* recently published two articles that suggest that Six Sigma does have a place in the nonmanufacturing sectors. The first article (Smith, May 2003) concludes that Six Sigma is "proving to be a useful tool in environments that focus more on people and less on product (23)." In the second article on this topic, Spanyi and Wurtzel (2003) describe how Six Sigma is for "the rest of us" (i.e., not just for large manufacturing firms like Motorola and GE).

My friend and colleague Dr. Ray Carey has nicely summarized the challenges of applying Six Sigma to healthcare organizations (2003:155–157). He points out three major difficulties:

1. *Setting specification limits* in healthcare organizations is difficult. Remember Six Sigma as a statistic requires calculating process capability ratios (C_p and C_{pk}), which are based on having specification limits. Because there are very few processes in healthcare that have clearly established specification limits upon which all providers agree, this is a major challenge.

2. *Hospitals are organized very differently from industry.* Specifically, many of the people who work at a hospital, for example, are not employed by the hospital. This creates a situation, particularly in not-for-profit hospitals, where the CEOs do not have the same level of power as CEOs in industry. As Carey concludes, "Hospital CEOs cannot mandate that everyone become a 'quality lunatic' as Jack Welch did at GE" (2003:156).

3. A primary goal of Six Sigma is to *improve profitability*. Given the financial difficulties of most healthcare organizations, however, the annual objective is not to end up in the red. Improving profits (or operating margins, as most not-for-profit healthcare providers refer to them) seems like a remote possibility for most. Thus, as Carey concludes, "Because both hospitals and physician groups often see money spent on improving quality as coming out of the bottom line, rather than contributing to it, there is less willingness to commit time and money to improving care" (2003:157).

I believe that Six Sigma thinking has the potential to improve the quality of healthcare services and outcomes. I am doubtful, however, that our industry will have the patience and/or resources to apply this methodology in a fashion that parallels what has been done at GE and Motorola.

The final business strategy currently in vogue is ISO registration. Although virtually unknown to most healthcare organizations, ISO (the International Organization for Standardization) has become a major force in manufacturing and industry. According to the "Quality Glossary" *(Quality Progress,* July 2002:52), ISO is "[a] network of national standards institutes from 140 countries working in partnership with international organizations, governments, industry, business and consumer representatives to develop and publish international standards. ISO acts as a bridge between public and private sectors." Companies can apply to become ISO registered, which means that they have met the agreed-upon international standards for quality. It is not uncommon, for example, to see a banner across a manufacturing firm's entrance that proclaims "ISO 9000 Registered Company."

There are many versions of ISO, and companies that were certified under an earlier version (e.g., ISO 9001:1994) can transition to the more current version (e.g., ISO 9001:2000) by documenting that they have adapted the new standards (Ketola and Roberts 2001; Wright 2001; Dusharme 2002; Stahan 2002; Vavra 2002). There are some specialized areas within healthcare (e.g., bioengineering, laboratory services, nuclear medicine, or freestanding ambulatory surgery centers) that could avail themselves of ISO and the detailed documentation processes that accompany ISO registration. In my travels and reading of the literature on this topic, however, I have not come across a hospital or health system that has become ISO registered. Some have suggested that ISO registration could be used as a substitute for accreditation by JCAHO, especially because companies that purchase health-care services are more familiar with ISO than they are with JCAHO. To date, however, ISO registration has had very little impact on the healthcare industry.

If CQI is to be an integral part of an organization's way of doing business, then there need to be individuals within the organizations who are skilled in:

- Executing the details associated with indicator development (described in the previous chapter).
- Summarizing the details of indicator development into cogent dashboards that meet the needs of management and the board.
- Anticipating how new ways of thinking (e.g., benchmarking, Baldrige, Six Sigma, and ISO) can be applied to the delivery of healthcare services.

It is essential, therefore, that the executive leadership team decides how they will structure, support, and staff CQI deployment throughout all levels of the organization. It is very easy to give lip service to the concept of the CQI but a challenge to make it become a part of the very fabric of the organization. Even well developed indicators are of little value if they are not integrated into daily work life and seen as an essential part of each department's quality journey.

Notes

1. This example comes from Advocate Lutheran General Hospital in Park Ridge, Illinois. I particularly want to thank Dr. David Cook, who at the time this set of indicators was developed, was the leader of the Non-Specific Chest Pain Team. Dr. Cook and his team not only did a great job of defining the indicators but also provided leadership in how they organized their indicators. Their efforts served as a template for others within the system to follow.

2. Although Kaplan and Norton continue to make major contributions to strategic planning and performance measurement, the majority of their work has been directed toward for-profit companies with the objective of returning profits to stockholders. Their ideas are certainly relevant to healthcare organizations (especially their notion about creating a balanced set of measures), but the term "scorecard" is so similar to the

concept of the report card that it often leads to confusion about the meaning and intent of the scorecard concept. Is it designed for judgment or improvement? Nelson *et al.* (1995) classify the balanced scorecard as a "hybrid" of report card and instrument panel thinking. Personally, I believe the concept of the dashboard or instrument panel is much more appropriate for healthcare organizations. As stated earlier in this chapter, there are plenty of groups that want to develop scorecards or report cards on healthcare providers in order to pass judgment on our performance. It is my belief, therefore, that healthcare providers need a more robust set of terms and tools to guide our improvement efforts. Within my own organization, for example, we have made a conscious decision to use the term "dashboard" as the organizing rubric for our various indicator sets. It is much more dynamic in nature, supports our commitment to quality improvement, and helps management and staff feel less threatened by performance measurement.

3. Personally I think the car manufacturers place the tachometer on the dashboard merely to fill space. I grew up driving a standard transmission car. In these vehicles a tachometer has utility. After a while, however, you get to know the sound of the engine and the shifting patterns so well that you really do not need a tachometer to tell you the engine RPMs (revolutions per minute). You shift by feel and sound. But in a vehicle with an automatic transmission, the tachometer serves no functional purpose because the engine is structured to shift at predetermined RPMs. So what purpose does the tachometer serve? Your guess is as good as mine. For example, my wife has a floral design business. She drives a minivan to deliver her designs and arrangements. The largest indicator on the dashboard of this van is the tachometer. Every time I drive this vehicle, I wonder why this dashboard gauge is so prominent. Look at your own vehicle and see how many of the indicators and warning lights you actually use. There will be only a vital few that you use regularly.

4. I am constantly amazed at how we decide on new levels of performance. Most often we seem to think in increments of 5 or 10. If the performance last year was X then X plus 5% or 10% should do for next year. We do this with budget cuts, as well, but in this case it is usually reductions of 5% or 10%. The next time you are involved with setting

new levels of performance, instead of using the traditional 5% or 10% increments, propose that you use unconventional increments (e.g., 4.75% or 6.875%). This may at least get people thinking about why they pick the numbers they do. An even better approach, however, would be to understand current performance by making a control chart, evaluating the process capability, and establishing new targets through objective statistical means.

5. For additional details on the Baldrige process and the criteria for healthcare, contact the Baldrige National Quality Program in Gaithersburg, Maryland, at (301) 975-2036, or visit their Web site at *www.quality.nist.gov*. You should specifically ask for the *Health Care Criteria for Performance Excellence*.

6. For an alternative perspective on the GE Six Sigma program, see "The Emperor's New Woes Revisited: What Has Six Sigma Done for General Electric?" *(Quality Digest*, August 2001:80). The anonymous author of this article is not only critical of the Six Sigma approach but also claims it is "all just hype to fool the stock analysts who are too timid or too ignorant to say, Hey look, Jack [Welch] has no clothes..." This is only one person's opinion, but it offers a very different view from what most of the literature about GE's Six Sigma program has been saying.

7. As an aside, it is interesting to note that this summary is probably what prompted Juran to say that Six Sigma offers nothing new (i.e., the underlying principles and methods of Six Sigma are very similar to what Juran and Deming were teaching companies for decades).

References

American Society for Quality. "Rx for Excellence." *Quality Progress* (April 2003): 42–49.

AT&T Technologies. *Statistical Quality Control Handbook*. Indianapolis: Western Electric Co., 1985.

Bader, B. "CQI Progress Reports: The Dashboard Approach Provides a Better Way to Keep Board Informed About Quality." *Healthcare Executive* 9, no. 5 (September/October 1993):8–11.

Caldwell, C. *Mentoring Strategic Change in Health Care.* Milwaukee: Quality Press, 1995.

Camp, R. *Benchmarking: The Search for Industry Best Practices That Lead to Superior Performance.* Milwaukee : Quality Press, 1989.

Carey, R., and R. Lloyd. *Measuring Quality Improvement in Healthcare.* Milwaukee: Quality Press, 2000.

Carey, R. *Improving Healthcare with Control Charts.* Milwaukee: Quality Press, 2003.

Deming, E. *Out of the Crisis.* Cambridge, Mass.: Massachusetts Institute of Technology Center for Advanced Engineering Study, 1992.

Dusharme, D. "Time Is Running Out." *Quality Digest* (July 2002): 23–32.

———."Six Sigma Survey." *Quality Digest* (February 2003): 24–32.

Godfrey, B. "Why Six Sigma?" *Quality Progress* (January 2002): 6.

Graham, J., and M. Cleary (eds.) *Practical Tools for Continuous Improvement.* Miamisburg, Ohio: PQ Systems, 2000.

Harry, M., and R. Schroeder. *Six Sigma.* New York: Doubleday/Currency, 2000.

Health Care Advisory Board. *CEO Dashboards: Performance Metrics for the New Health Care Economy.* Washington, D.C.: The Advisory Board Company, 2000.

Kaplan, R., and D. Norton. "The Balanced Scorecard—Measures That Drive Performance." *Harvard Business Review* (January–February 1992): 71–79.

———."Putting "Putting the Balanced Scorecard to Work." *Harvard Business Review* (September–October 1993): 134–147.

———."Putting "Using the Balanced Scorecard as a Strategic Management System." *Harvard Business Review* (January–February 1996): 75–85.

Ketola, J., and K. Roberts. "Demystifying ISO 9001:2000." *Quality Progress,* Part 1 (September 2001): 65–70 and Part 2 (October 2001): 44–47.

The Mihalik Group, LLC. "When Is a Performance Goal a Benchmark?" *The Mihalik Globe* 7, no. 2 (Summer 2003): 1–2.

Nelson, E., P. Batalden, S. Plume, N. Mihevc, and W. Swartz. "Report Cards or Instrument Panels: Who Needs What?" *Journal on Quality Improvement* 21, no. 4 (1995): 155–166.

Nugent, W., W. Schults, S. Plume, P. Batalden, and E. Nelson. "Designing an Instrument Panel to Monitor and Improve Coronary Artery Bypass Grafting." *The Joint Commission Journal on Quality Improvement* 1, no. 2 (1994): 57–64.

Patton, S. "Juran: A Lifetime of Quality." *Quality Digest* (August 2002): 19–23.

Plsek, P., and A. Onnias. *Quality Improvement Tools.* The Juran Institute, Wilton, Conn.: 1989.

Smith, K. "Six Sigma for the Service Sector." *Quality Digest* (May 2003): 23–28.

———."Putting"Quality Conversation with Sister Mary Jean Ryan." *Quality Digest* (July 2003): 45–46.

Spanyi, A., and M. Wurtzel. "Six Sigma for the Rest of Us." *Quality Digest* (July 2003): 23–26.

Stahan, J. "Transition to ISO 9000:2000." *Quality Progress* (March 2002): 27–30.

Vavra, T. "ISO 9001:2000 and Customer Satisfaction." *Quality Progress* (May 2002): 69–75.

Wheeler, D. *Advanced Topics in Statistical Process Control.* Knoxville, Tenn.: SPC Press, 1995.

Wright, T. "ISO 9001 Without Tears." *Quality Progress* (August 2001): 57–61.

Chapter 5

Tapping the Knowledge that Hides in Data

In the previous chapter we focused on building indicators that allow you to listen to the VOP. Now we need to address the question "What do I do with the data once I have it?" The answer is really quite simple—understand the variation that lives in the data. This is best achieved by building a knowledge and skill base around the following topics:

- Data versus information
- Research for efficacy
- Research for effectiveness and efficiency
- Static versus dynamic approaches to data analysis
- Understanding variation
- Common and special causes of variation
- Statistical process control (SPC) methods
- Making the appropriate management decisions when presented with common and special causes of variation

This chapter addresses the first four bullets. The next chapter discusses the last four points.

Data Versus Information

Although we live in an information age, it is interesting to observe how many people do not clearly understand the difference between data and information. I have been in many meetings where someone says, "We need more data," and I am thinking, "No, you have enough data; what you really need is more information." Similarly, I have heard people say, "We need more detailed information." What they really should have said, however, is "We need more detailed data." This issue was central to a recent discussion I heard on National Public Radio (NPR). The topic was the creation of the new cabinet-level Department of Homeland Security. The NPR announcer was interviewing various congressmen and senators on the merits of such a department. Quickly the discussion turned to the ability of the United States to obtain useful "data and information" on terrorist groups. One congressman stated that he thought we needed more data on individuals thought to be threats to this country. He proposed keeping all of this data in a massive database that the new department would manage. According to one of the senators interviewed, however, the problem was not having enough information on various terrorist groups. Finally, an official from one of the bureaus that would fall under the new department said that the central problem was that they did not have enough people who knew how to turn the massive amounts of data they already have into useful information. The lack of consensus on this data versus information issue was readily apparent even in the summary by the NPR reporter. He kept using the two words as if they were synonyms, indicating to me that he really did not understand the difference between the two concepts, even though this was the primary theme of the report.

The distinction between data and information is more than mere semantics. The two concepts are quite different from each other. I have always found Austin's (1983:24) distinction between data and information to be extremely useful: "Data refers to the raw facts and figures which are collected as part of the normal functioning of the hospital. Information, on the other hand, is defined as data, which have been processed and analyzed in a formal, intelligent way, so that the results are directly useful to those involved in the operation and management of the hospital." Data are the bits and bytes that we collect in an effort to measure the performance of a process. Data are not information. Information, on the other hand, can only be produced by submitting data to an inquiry process that is grounded in deductive (from the general to the specific) and inductive (from the specific to the general) thinking. The classic approach to data-based inquiry is referred to as the scientific method (Lastrucci 1967).

Figure 5.1 depicts the key steps needed to gather data and turn it into useful information for decision making.

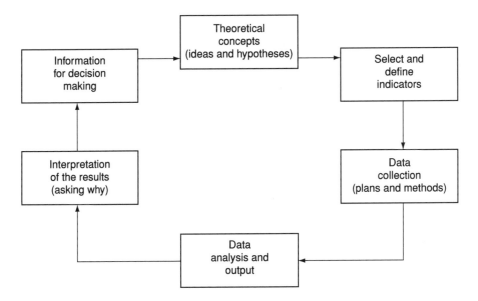

▲ FIGURE 5.1   The process of gathering data and turning it into information

Step 1: Theoretical Concepts

All scientific inquiry begins with theoretical concepts (ideas and hypotheses). These concepts are either derived from abstract thinking about the world and the way it works (e.g., theoretical physics) or generated from data that enable the researchers to propose theories based on the observed patterns in the accumulated data. Sometimes the theories people pose are merely variations on existing theories. For example, the basic theories about germs and their impacts on human populations have been around for thousands of years, yet each year there are new and subtle modifications to fundamental theories about germs and their impacts on the human body (Block 2001:3–17).[1] Existing theories become modified or refined as additional research is performed and data are placed into context of the theoretical principles. At other times, however, the theoretical concepts present new thinking, which then creates the foundation for debate. The human genome project, for example, will undoubtedly spawn new theories about human genetics that were not considered 5 or 10 years ago. Whether a theory has been around for a while or is relatively new, the real test of any theory or hypothesis lies with the empirical evidence that can be assembled to test the validity and reliability of the idea.

Step 2: Select and Define Indicators

The next step in turning data into information is to select a key set of indicators (key quality characteristics) that purport to measure the theoretical concepts under investigation and then reach consensus on an operational definition of each indicator.[2] This step was discussed in detail in Chapter 3, but several key points are worth repeating. First, I believe that this is one of the major challenges healthcare professionals face when attempting to measure what they do. Second, not devoting sufficient time to clarifying operational definitions usually leads to: (1) confusion over what the numbers really mean, (2) challenges to the results, and/or (3) a desire to "kill the messenger" because the data do not fit certain individuals' views of reality (e.g., this is seen frequently when a politician fires his or her public opinion pollster because the results of the poll do not match the politician's self-perception). Finally, improving operational definitions is not that difficult. It is not a statistical issue but rather one of logic and consensus. The healthcare industry has some of the best-educated professionals in this country. Reaching consensus on operational definitions, therefore, should be relatively easy. I believe the reasons we perform poorly at this step include:

- The lack of formal training in the specification of indicators
- Time constraints (i.e., we have to get the data now, so why waste time talking about the indicators?)
- A fatal assumption that "Everyone knows what a (fill in your favorite indicator name) is, so why do we need to discuss it further and waste time?"

If we do nothing more than improve our endeavors in this area, we will be making a significant enhancement to our measurement efforts.

Step 3: Measurement and Data Collection

The basic principles of measurement and data collection were reviewed in Chapter 3. Issues such as stratification, sampling, the role of pilot tests, the duration and frequency of data collection, respondent and data collector bias, and data collection methods are all critical to the success of this step. These issues are all too often overlooked when conducting both quantitative and qualitative studies.[3] I have seen teams develop well-defined indicators and then come to a screeching halt because they did not think through all the details related to data collection. Data do not magically collect themselves and then conveniently populate a database on their own. Someone has to do it.

Step 4: Data Analysis and Output

Failure to develop a well-thought-out data analysis plan will lead a team to sit on their data and hope that it will eventually hatch something they can use. What happens all too often, however, is that when the data are not subjected to analysis, they become antiquated and eventually obsolete. A well-designed and executed analysis plan allows a team to move to the next important step—interpretation.

Step 5: Interpretation of the Results

This is what the previous three steps were designed to achieve. To use the analogy of a fine dinner, the first three steps constitute the appetizer, soup, and salad. Interpretation is the main course. The first three steps relied on a combination of machine power and brainpower. Interpretation relies entirely on the machine that sits on top of your shoulders. Interpretation basically seeks the answer to one simple question: why? This is the point at which the data and the theory are compared to each other. Do the analytic results support the theories (hypotheses) I developed initially? If not, are my data correct and my theory wrong or vice versa? This is also the point at which previous research and data play key roles. Are my results consistent with what others have found? Are they consistent with what I have found when I did similar studies? Interpretation discussions should involve issues of reliability and validity (Selltiz *et al.* 1959; Campbell and Stanley 1966; Forcese and Richer 1970; Blalock 1971). This is the point at which all your hard work should pay off, because it sets the stage for the final piece of the puzzle.

Step 6: Information for Decision Making

If interpretation is the main course, then this step represents dessert. This is what you have been working toward (which, interestingly enough, is also how many people regard dessert). Being able to develop action plans for improvement, based on a well-executed measurement journey, is the foundation for CQI. The PDSA cycle (Deming 1992; Gaucher and Coffey 1993; Langley *et al.* 1996) as well as Deming's notion of profound knowledge (Schultz 1994:18–27) all identify taking action (decision making) as the primary goal of CQI. The previous four steps are designed to bring you to this point. Unfortunately, many QI initiatives never complete this step of the journey. CQI has been labeled by some as taking too long to demonstrate improvement. My experience has convinced me that when this occurs, it is usually a result of the team's lack of knowledge of how to turn data into information or a management structure that merely wanted to have the data confirm their view of reality. Just as we would not proceed with knee replacement surgery without a properly skilled and trained surgical team, we should not proceed with QI initiatives without a properly skilled and trained measurement team. Making appropriate decisions in the 21st century requires data and information. The steps are clear, but sometimes the path is obstructed with roadblocks.

Research for Efficacy

Although the scientific method forms the foundation for all credible research, there are many roads that can lead the researcher from raw data to useful information for decision making. In 1996 Robert Brooke and his colleagues wrote an extremely useful article that succinctly differentiated two basic roads that can be traveled for scientific inquiry. The first road takes the researcher down the traditional path of inquiry, which relies on experimental and quasi-experimental designs (Campbell and Stanley 1966; Weiss 1972; Posavac and Carey 1980). This is essentially what Brooke and his colleagues call research for *efficacy*.

In healthcare, efficacy studies are frequently used to test the ability of a particular drug, treatment, procedure, or protocol to improve medical conditions. For example, a researcher might pose the following questions about a new drug:

- Is this drug capable of producing the desired effect?
- Will this drug act differently with different types of patients (age, gender, race, etc.)?
- Does a 5-mg dose of the drug produce different results than a 10-mg dose?

Every time healthcare researchers conduct a randomized clinical trial to compare the impact of a new drug or a protocol, they are conducting research for efficacy purposes. A typical study might involve testing the effect of a new blood pressure drug on two groups of patients. One group would receive the drug and be labeled as the experimental group. The other group would receive a placebo and would be referred to as the control group. Baseline blood pressure readings would be obtained on each group, as well as demographic information about their current physiological condition, family history, and activities of daily living. After a period of time, the two groups would have their blood pressure levels measured again, and statistical tests would be performed to see if there is a "significant" difference between the two groups. The demographic and other patient characteristics would be used as control variables (i.e., they are used in an effort to "hold constant" all the other factors that might play a role in blood pressure variation).

If we really wanted to increase the precision of this type of study, we would establish matched samples of patients (i.e., we would make every possible effort to have the members of the experimental and control groups be similar in gender, age, race, socioeconomic status, and so on). The participants would be randomly assigned to the experimental and control groups, and then steps would be taken to make the study a double-blinded trial. The double-blinded component means that neither the participants nor the researchers know which group gets the drug and which one gets the placebo. This is done in order to minimize bias, increase the validity of the results, and thereby enhance the researcher's ability to answer the efficacy question.

The study design I have just described is a classic approach to research. In a design of this type, the goal is to test the null hypothesis (H_o) that there is no difference between the experimental and control groups with respect to the blood pressure drug. Statistical analysis of the before and after blood pressure readings for the two groups allows the researchers to either accept or reject the null hypothesis and test for statistical significance (Selltiz *et al.* 1959:415–418; Morrison and Henkel 1970; Babbie 1979:486–487).

Although some traditional research studies are based on time-series analysis (Ostrom 1978; McDowall *et al.* 1980), the majority of studies intended to test efficacy are not designed to monitor moment-to-moment fluctuations in an observed process or outcome. Instead, they typically obtain rather large sample sizes (i.e., 100 or more in the two comparison groups), let weeks or months transpire as the research trial is allowed to run its course, and then see if the two comparison groups show a significant statistical difference. The focus of most experimental and quasi-experimental designs, therefore, is on static comparisons (i.e., comparison of data sets that are fixed at discrete points in time).

In summary, the primary purpose of research for efficacy purposes is to build knowledge by testing theories against empirical evidence. The research results may not have immediate or even readily apparent practical outcomes. For example, research done in the vacuum of space by astronauts has produced amazingly pure crystals, but scientists are not sure what they can actually do with this new knowledge on earth. It will be added to the rest of the body of knowledge about crystal formation, and someday someone will figure out how to use this knowledge for practical purposes.

Research for Effectiveness and Efficiency

The second major research pathway discussed by Brooke *et al.* (1996) is one that seeks to determine the *effectiveness* and *efficiency* of a process that is producing outcomes in a dynamic or real-time fashion. Mosser *et al.* (1997) refer to this type of approach as measurement for improvement.[4] This is the path that leads to quality improvement or quality control research.

When healthcare professionals receive training in research designs and statistical methods, the approach described in the previous section is usually the standard frame of reference (i.e., research for efficacy). In my mind this is one of the primary reasons why many healthcare professionals seem to have a strong proclivity to focus on comparing two numbers and asking if one is different from the other. Research for efficacy purposes is designed to answer this question. As quality improvement thinking started to creep into the healthcare industry, however, a new way of turning data into information started to unfold for the healthcare professional.

Based upon the ideas of Shewhart (1931), Deming (1992), and Juran (1988, 1989), QI research takes a very practical approach that seeks to answer questions about efficiency and effectiveness of a process over time instead of whether one number is different from another (i.e., the efficacy question). The quality practitioner asks many of the same questions posed by those conducting efficacy research. In fact, they are both interested in answering a fairly simple question that was posed recently by Benneyan *et al.* (2003): What can be concluded from sets of measurements taken around the time of a change, given that these measurements would likely show variation even if no direct intervention to actually change the process had been introduced in the first place?

What separates the QI researcher from the traditional (efficacy-oriented) researcher are the following key characteristics:

- The QI researcher is more concerned with solving practical problems than building new theoretical models.
- The QI researcher views data from a dynamic perspective rather than from a static or aggregated perspective.
- The QI researcher uses small samples of data but selects them at more frequent points in time.
- The QI researcher relies more on graphical displays of data than on statistical equations and tests of significance.

Although there are clear differences between the two approaches, it must be noted that both research for efficacy and research for effectiveness are interested in being able to say something about the generalizability and/or sustainability of an improvement beyond the immediate time period under study. Because the researcher for efficacy relies primarily on large samples of data that are usually fixed in time (i.e., static comparisons), it is often difficult to move beyond two or three data points when conducting an analysis. Research for QI (i.e., effectiveness and efficiency), on the other hand, is not focused on how the numbers performed at fixed points in time (e.g., "How do April's numbers for this year compare to those from last year?" or "Is the average for this year statistically different from that of last year?") but rather on "What can I learn from today's process to predict where the process will go tomorrow or next week?" QI practitioners are more concerned with the present and the future than the past. They will take a dynamic approach to the data rather than a static approach.

The Debate Is Silly

Contrary to some misconceptions, QI research is a legitimate field of statistical inquiry. I have had discussions with several rather staunch supporters of the more traditional academic approaches to research and statistics who have implied that quality improvement research and approaches to research and statistics who have implied that quality improvement research and SPC methods are less rigorous forms of statistical inquiry. I even had an individual state rather emphatically in class one day that SPC was "kiddy statistics" and not worthy of further consideration.

The scientific method lies at the heart of all good research, whether it is done in real time or on large static comparison groups. All research designs and methods have utility. It is up to the individual researcher to build a knowledge base that allows him or her to know which design, method, and/or statistical technique is most appropriate for the questions that need to be answered. Consider an analogy from the surgical field. The surgeon has many tools available for surgery. The challenge is not to use all of them just because they are there or to state unequivocally that one tool or method is superior to all the others. Instead, the real challenge is to have knowledge of all the tools and methods and know when to use the right tool at the right time to solve the problem at hand. It is the same way with research. The question or problem being addressed should be the primary driver for deciding which research design or methods are appropriate for turning data into information. Some research methods and tools are best suited to answer questions related to efficacy. Others are more appropriate for questions related to effectiveness and efficiency. The wise researcher should know enough about each approach to know when to use one approach and not the other. The questions, not the statistical tools or methods, should drive the research endeavor.

Static Versus Dynamic Approaches to Data Analysis

The basic data challenge that we face in healthcare is that we have historically relied on aggregated data and summary statistics to understand the quality of what we do on a day-to-day basis.[5] Such an approach basically leads the researcher to a static way of thinking about data analysis and interpretation. For decades we have been using methods and tools that are best suited for efficacy research, judgment, or accountability and trying to use these tools to answer quality improvement questions. It is not surprising, therefore, that many healthcare professionals have become frustrated with QI. From my perspective, they are simply using the wrong tools and thinking to understand the variation that lives in their data.

Static approaches to data analysis focus on using aggregated data and tend to compare the most recent data point with a previous data point (usually the last month or quarter). If the current data point is regarded as being better than the last data point, then all is right with the world. If, on the other hand, the current data point is determined to be worse than the previous result, then management concludes that all is not right with the world. If both data points are the same number, what do you conclude?

The essential point to remember is that *aggregated data, presented in tabular formats or with summary statistics, will not help you measure the impact of process improvement or redesign efforts.* It is just that simple. Deming was very clear on this point. He stated, "Students are not warned in classes nor in the books that for analytic purposes (such as to improve a process), distributions and calculations of mean, mode, standard deviation, chi-square, t-test, etc. serve no useful purpose for improvement of a process unless the data were produced in a state of statistical control" (1992:312). Aggregated data, therefore, can only lead to judgment, not to improvement. The healthcare industry has a long and rich history of using data for judgment. For example, it is not uncommon for a hospital or a health system to compare the current month's results on a particular indicator to those for the same month a year ago. There is also a tendency to compare the average for this year (e.g., length of stay for a particular diagnosis) with the average from last year. Although this may have some utility for making determinations on incentive or bonus payout programs, it has very little to do with quality. Quality happens on a moment-to-moment basis. It is determined by the workers who deliver care at the bedside, the registration desk, and the blood draw station. Administrators and managers who rely on aggregated data to make decisions, therefore, are not really focused on quality. They are focused more on making judgments about the difference between two numbers rather than on how the numbers perform over time. Because variation exists in all that we do, the chances are quite high that two data points will differ. To paraphrase Deming, if you have two data points, there is a very high probability that one will be different from the other.[6]

If aggregated data are your primary frames of reference, then two data points are all you will need to make a conclusion about performance. If, for example, the result at Time 2 is better than the result at Time 1, then management will probably conclude that things must be getting better. What people fail to recognize when they do this, however, is that two numbers do not determine quality, a trend, or a "significant difference." Again, if you have two numbers, it is very likely that one will be different from the other. So, when healthcare professionals look at the most recent data point and determine success (or failure) in light of the data point's relative position to the previous data point, they will celebrate to excess, punish themselves beyond necessity, or take comfort in the fact that the numbers have not changed. Such an approach to data leads organizations to reward and punish workers for things over which they may have no control. It leads an organization to suffer from what I call the "good dog/bad dog" syndrome. Caught up in this syndrome, an organization will establish incentives and rewards that are not unlike Pavlov's approach to training his dogs. If the numbers are good and where I want to see them, I will reward you with a bonus or an incentive (good dog, you salivated on command; here, have a biscuit). On the other hand, if the numbers are not good (by whatever criteria I use to judge goodness), then you do not receive the reward (bad dog). This syndrome can drive an organization crazy. It is a complex syndrome that encompasses an organization's views on intrinsic and extrinsic motivation (Kohn 1986, 1993; Deming 1992), incentive programs, performance reviews, compensation practices, and data analysis.[7]

Figure 5.2 demonstrates the major difference between static and dynamic displays of data. Imagine that your hospital is interested in gaining a better understanding of its CABG outcomes. Historically you have evaluated your performance in this area by comparing the annual percentage of mortality. The top portion of Figure 5.2 depicts how you have typically looked at these data. Note that for the last two years you have had essentially the same percentage of mortality. So what do you conclude from this comparison? The answer is easy—this year is the same as last year. The overall average leads you to the conclusion that nothing has changed.

Now look at the lower portion of Figure 5.2. In this chart we observe the CABG mortality percentages as they occurred over the 12 months of each year. What do we observe? We note that last year the CABG mortality was on a constantly increasing trend upward and that this year the percentage of mortality has been on a downward trend. How is it that you can have two averages that are essentially the same and two monthly patterns that are fundamentally different? The answer is simple. The top part of Figure 5.2 presents data in a static fashion, but the data shown in the lower part of the figure are depicted in a dynamic fashion. Because quality is about efficiency and effectiveness, we need to look at data in dynamic rather than static fashion. This means, therefore, that we need to plot data over time rather than aggregate the data into summary statistics.

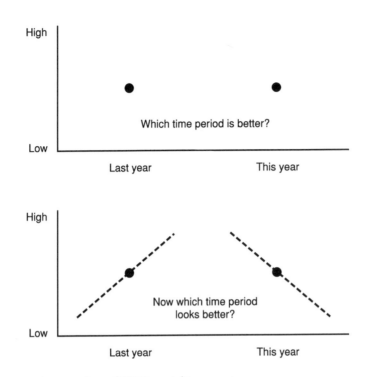

▲ FIGURE 5.2   A comparison of CABG mortality percentages

Figure 5.3 provides another example of why static approaches to variation should not be used for quality improvement. Imagine that Figure 5.3 represents two parts of the turnaround time (TAT) process for a particular lab test. Process A (the top chart) is the TAT from when the physician writes the lab order until the specimen is received in the lab and logged into the computer. Process B, on the other hand, is the in-lab processing time. If you only showed the aggregated distributions, represented by the bell-shaped curves on the far right side of the graphics, you would conclude that the two processes are exactly the same. Both curves have the same width and height and are centered at the same point. In fact, these two distributions could have the same mean, median, mode, and standard deviation. Applying aggregated or static thinking to these data would lead the researcher to conclude that the two processes are the same.

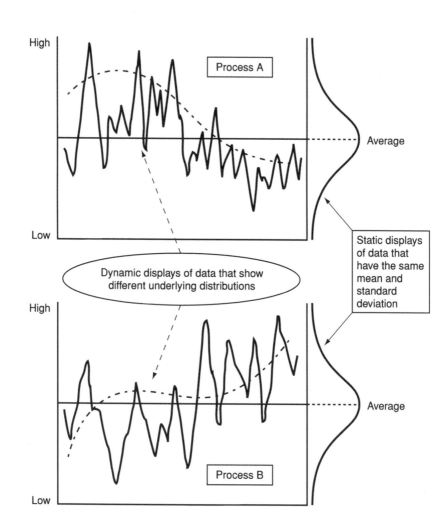

▲ FIGURE 5.3 Static versus dynamic data displays

If we look at these data from a dynamic point of view, however, we would arrange the lab test in chronological order and observe the TATs as they occurred over time. These data are shown in the main body of the charts as the solid line that fluctuates up and down around the centerline (average). When we look at the data in this manner, we see that Process A has shifted downward over time while Process B has been migrating gradually upward. The dashed lines imposed on each chart show these directional patterns.

How is it that the two summary curves on the far right side of the graphic are exactly the same, yet the data in the main body of the graphs show that

TATs for each individual lab test present two very different patterns? The answer is rather simple. The aggregated distributions (the bell-shaped curves on the far right of the charts) are static displays of data that merely summarize where the data are centered (the average) and the spread of the data (typically reported as the minimum and maximum values, the range, and/or the standard deviation). The main body of the charts, however, represents dynamic displays of data that essentially show how Processes A and B vary over time. The static displays, represented by the bell-shaped curves, have basically aggregated time out of each process.

A medical example will help to further clarify these distinctions. Using dynamic displays of data is equivalent to hooking patients up to telemetry monitors and tracking their vital signs moment by moment. Consider, however, what patient monitoring would look like from a static point of view. First, we add up all of the patient's heartbeats during his or her length of stay. Next, we would totally ignore the telemetry strips and calculate the average number of heartbeats and the standard deviation for the patient. Finally, we would want to know if the average number of heartbeats for the current patient was significantly different from the average of a patient who was in the same bed last month or last quarter. This aggregate or static approach to patient care might save the nurses some charting time and could be seen as a way to save money, but it would be irresponsible. Medical practice is more concerned with dynamic than static displays of data. Yet in healthcare we have a very long and rich history of using static displays of data to make conclusions about healthcare quality.

The objective in QI research, therefore, is to understand how the data present themselves over time. This is how effectiveness and efficiency are determined and how quality improvements are made. In short, the use of aggregated data will not allow the researcher to:

- Understand the variation that lives within the data
- Understand the underlying distribution that produced the observed average (i.e., you can obtain the exact same average from two entirely different distributions, as shown in Figure 5.3)
- Evaluate the impact of process improvement/redesign efforts

Although these issues might not be critical to researchers conducting efficacy studies, they are essential information to those interested in efficiency and effectiveness of a process. Another example will help to highlight the distinction. Suppose you were interested in calculating the average height of a group of people. You measure everyone as they come into the room and determine that the average height is 5 feet 11 inches tall. You then have everyone stand up and discover that half the people are professional basketball players and the other half are fourth grade students. We quickly conclude that there are no people in the room who are 5 feet 11 inches tall. What we have is a distribution that has two extremes with an average that does not match any of the individuals in the room. The average height is mathematically correct, but it does not provide a clear picture of the underlying nature of the distribution that produced the average. This is the basic problem of aggregated data.

The up and down fluctuation in data may be the result of random variation, which is an inherent part of any process, or it may result from periodic special causes or a true shift in process performance. The data may be up one month and down the next. Unfortunately, organizations spend a considerable amount of energy rewarding (and punishing) employees because first the numbers are up, then they are down. Quality is not about judging whether one data point is different from another. It is about sustained improvement over time and about shifts in process performance resulting from deliberate interventions. Dynamic, not static, approaches to data provide the road to knowledge about the quality of healthcare outcomes, processes, and services. Healthcare organizations can enhance their QI efforts dramatically if they do nothing more than make a deliberate effort to increase their knowledge and use of dynamic displays of data.

Case Study: The Monday Morning Dilemma

It is Friday afternoon and you have already started thinking about the relaxing weekend that lies ahead. Then the phone rings. Within seconds of picking it up, you realize that this is the call you had anticipated but wished would not come on a Friday afternoon. Your boss is calling to remind you about the management meeting on Monday. Typically this would not be a major event, but this time, for you, it will be. It seems that the numbers for your facility are "below expectations" for the past month, and you have to explain why your facility is not meeting its targets. You thank your boss for the reminder and, as you hang up, you remember what happened to your friend Scott when he had to go through this ordeal the previous month. At that time, your numbers looked fine. In retrospect, all you can really remember about that day was how pale Scott looked as he tried to explain why his numbers were below average. You also remember thinking how this whole affair reminded you of an inquisition.

Now as you sit in a numb stupor looking out your window, you realize that your time has come. Suddenly your secretary sticks her head in your office and brings you back to reality by saying, "I'm out of here; have a nice weekend." "Oh sure," you think, "I'll have a nice weekend. I'll spend all my time trying to develop a list of reasons why my numbers are not acceptable. I'll spend all weekend worrying about the inquisition on Monday!"

This is obviously a situation you do not want to be in. Yet stories like this are legendary in organizations that do not understand variation. So what would you do? You basically have two choices. First, you could develop a list of reasons why your numbers do not live up to expectations. This usually consists of one or more of the following tactics: (1) developing a series of complex sentences that try to divert attention from the numbers, (2) pointing fingers at other factors (some real and some imaginary), (3) blaming individuals (who are usually not attending the meeting) for poor work habits and low motivation, and (4) throwing yourself on the mercy of the inquisition court.

The second and more preferable choice is not to waste your time trying to explain why this month's numbers are different from last month's numbers. The reason they are down this month is that they *were* up last month. Variation occurs in all that we do. Therefore, you will drive yourself and all those around you absolutely crazy if you try to explain (rationalize) why two data points are different. If the performance of the process over time is unacceptable, then change the process. Focusing on aggregated numbers without understanding how they vary over time is a futile exercise. This type of thinking typically fosters competition between units and departments, builds barriers between individuals, and, most importantly, undermines the delivery of quality care. It is reflective of what Wheeler (1993:vi) refers to as "numerical illiteracy." According to Wheeler, "Numerical illiteracy is not a failure with arithmetic, but it is instead a failure to know how to use the basic tools of arithmetic to understand data. Numerical illiteracy is not addressed by traditional courses in primary or secondary schools, nor is it addressed by advanced courses in mathematics. This is why even highly educated individuals can be numerically illiterate" (vi).

Fortunately there is a cure for numerical illiteracy. It involves the following three remedies:

- Understanding variation
- Distinguishing common from special causes of variation
- Using SPC methods

If you inoculate yourself with these simple remedies (as opposed to spending your time trying to justify/rationalize why this month's number is lower than last month's number), you will be in a much better position to really explain what is occurring with the numbers on Monday morning. The details related to these three remedies are presented in the next chapter.

Notes

1. There are documented accounts in the Bible, for example, of directives to be clean in body as well as in the preparation and storage of food. Disinfectants are referenced by Aristotle and Homer and in Hindu medical teachings. The "modern" era in infection control can be traced back to the work of Swiss physician Paracelsus (1493–1541) and most notably to Girolamo Fracastoro (1478–1553), who wrote a three-volume set on the nature of infection and its transference from person to person. Block (2001) provides a wonderful review of the key steps in the development of this branch of medicine. Not only is this account extremely interesting but it also demonstrates the fundamental connection between theory and experience.

2. I say, "purport to measure" because all measurement is subject to bias and error. Deming claimed that there is no such thing as a "fact." He wrote (1992:292), "There can be no operational definition of the true value of anything. An observed numerical value of anything depends on the definitions and operations used. The definitions and operations will be constructed differently by different experts in the subject matter" (see Chapter 3 of this book for a more detailed discussion of operational definitions). It is reasonable to conclude, therefore, that all measurement is merely proxy for what it intends to measure.

3. Although this book deals primarily with topics related to conducting quantitative studies, the field of qualitative analysis should not be overlooked. Qualitative methods have been able to add great depth and richness to a variety of social, psychological, and anthropological research efforts.

4. Mosser and his colleagues (1997) identify "The Three Faces of Performance Measurement" as (1) measurement for research, (2) measurement for accountability, and (3) measurement for improvement. Category 1 basically coincides with what Brooke *et al.* refer to as efficacy studies (i.e., experimental and quasi-experimental research designs). Category 3 (measurement for improvement) equates directly to what Brooke *et al.* refer to as studies for effectiveness and efficiency, which will be addressed in this section. I would strongly encourage the reader to become familiar with both of these articles. They represent, in my opinion, two of the best short articles on clarifying the different approaches to research and the pros and cons associated with each approach. Mosser *et al.* sum it up best when they write, "We are increasingly realizing not only how critical measurement is to the quality improvement we seek but also how counterproductive it can be to mix measurement for accountability or research with measurement for improvement" (1997:135).

5. The traditional summary statistics are basically divided into two categories. The first consists of measures of central tendency, the mean, the median, and the mode. The second category consists of measures of dispersion, which usually include the minimum value, the maximum value, the range (the difference between the maximum and the minimum values), and the standard deviation. Any basic statistics book will provide the details on how to calculate these measures.

6. This statement was taken from the author's personal notes while attending a four-day Deming seminar ("Quality, Productivity, and Competitive Position") in Indianapolis, August 11–14, 1992.

7. In this chapter I do not intend to elaborate on the issues of intrinsic and extrinsic motivation. These topics were briefly addressed in Chapter 2. I do believe that if an organization does not have a healthy debate on how it intends to approach motivation and rewards, it will be haunted by this indecision and its culture will suffer. The dominant writer on this topic is Kohn (1986, 1993).

References

Austin, C. *Information Systems for Hospital Administration.* Chicago: Health Administration Press, 1983.

Babbie, E. R. *The Practice of Social Research.* Belmont, Calif.: Wadsworth, 1979.

Benneyan, J., R. Lloyd, and P. Plsek. "Statistical Process Control as a Tool for Research and Health Care Improvement." *Journal of Quality and Safety in Healthcare* 12, no. 6 (2003): 458–464.

Blalock, H. (ed.). *Causal Models in the Social Sciences.* Chicago: Aldine, 1971.

Block, S. *Disinfection, Sterilization, and Preservation.* Philadelphia: Lippincott Williams & Wilkins, 2001.

Brooke, R., C. Kamberg, and E. McGlynn. "Health System Reform and Quality." *Journal of the American Medical Association* 276, no. 6 (1996): 476–480.

Campbell, D., and J. Stanley. *Experimental and Quasi-Experimental Designs for Research.* Boston: Houghton Mifflin, 1966.

Carey, R. *Improving Healthcare with Control Charts.* Milwaukee: Quality Press, 2003.

Carey, R., and R. Lloyd. *Measuring Quality Improvement in Healthcare: A Guide to Statistical Process Control Applications.* Milwaukee: Quality Press, 2001.

Daniel, W., and J. Terrell. *Business Statistics for Management and Economics.* Boston: Houghton Mifflin, 1989.

Deming, W. E. *Out of the Crisis.* Cambridge, Mass: Massachusetts Institute of Technology Center for Advanced Engineering Study, 1992.

Forcese, D., and S. Richer. (eds.). *Stages of Social Research: Contemporary Perspectives.* Englewood Cliffs, N.J.: Prentice-Hall, 1970.

Gaucher, E., and R. Coffey. *Total Quality in Healthcare.* San Francisco: Jossey-Bass, 1993.

Hu, T. *Econometrics: An Introductory Analysis.* Baltimore: University Park Press, 1973.

Johnson, P., and R. Jackson. *Modern Statistical Methods: Descriptive and Inductive.* Chicago: Rand McNally & Company, 1959.

Juran, J. *Juran on Planning for Quality.* New York: Free Press, 1988.

———. *Juran on Leadership for Quality.* New York: Free Press, 1989.

Kerlinger, F., and E. Pedhazur. *Multiple Regression in Behavioral Research.* New York: Holt, Rinehart and Winston, 1973.

Kohn, A. *No Contest.* Boston: Houghton Mifflin, 1986.

———. *Punished by Rewards: The Trouble with Gold Stars, Incentive Plans, A's, Praise, and Other Bribes.* Boston: Houghton Mifflin, 1993.

Langley, G., K. Nolan, T. Nolan, C. Norman, and L. Provost. *The Improvement Guide.* San Francisco: Jossey-Bass Publishers, 1996.

Lastrucci, C. *The Scientific Approach: Basic Principles of the Scientific Method.* Cambridge, Mass.: Schenkman, 1967.

McDowall, D., R. McCleary, E. Meidinger, and R. Hay. *Interrupted Time Series Analysis.* Beverly Hills, Calif.: Sage, 1980.

Morrison, D., and R. Henkel. (eds.). *The Significance Test Controversy: A Reader.* Chicago: Aldine, 1970.

Mosser, G., L. Solberg, and S. McDonald. "The Three Faces of Performance Measurement." *Journal on Quality Improvement* 23, no. 3 (1997): 135–147.

Namboodiri, N., L. Carter, and H. Blalock. *Applied Multivariate Analysis and Experimental Designs.* New York: McGraw-Hill, 1975.

Ostrom, C. *Time Series Analysis: Regression Techniques.* Beverly Hills, Calif.: Sage, 1978.

Posavac, E., and R. Carey. *Program Evaluation: Methods and Case Studies,* 4th ed. Englewood Cliffs, N.J.: Prentice-Hall, 1980.

Schultz, L. *Profiles in Quality.* New York: Quality Resources, 1994.

Selltiz, C., M. Jahoda, M. Deutsch, and S. Cook. *Research Methods in Social Relations.* New York: Holt, Rinehart & Winston, 1959.

Shewhart, W. *Economic Control of Quality of Manufactured Product.* New York: D. Van Nostrand, 1931. Reprint, Milwaukee: Quality Press, 1980.

———.*Statistical Method from the Viewpoint of Quality Control.* Washington, D.C.: George Washington University, Graduate School, Department of Agriculture, 1939. Reprint, New York: Dover, 1986.

Van de Geer, J. *Introduction to Multivariate Analysis for the Social Sciences.* San Francisco: W. H. Freeman and Company, 1971.

Weiss, C. *Evaluation Research: Methods of Assessing Program Effectiveness.* Englewood Cliffs, N.J.: Prentice-Hall, 1972.

Wheeler, D. *Understanding Variation.* Knoxville, Tenn.: SPC Press, 1993.

———.*Advanced Topics in Statistical Process Control.* Knoxville, Tenn.: SPC Press, 1995.

Chapter 6

Overcoming Numerical Illiteracy

Variation (var'-i-a'shun), n 1. Act or instance of varying; change in the form, position, state, or qualities of a thing; modification, mutation, or deviation, or an instance or example of such. 2. Extent to which a thing varies; amount or rate of change.
Webster's Collegiate Dictionary, fifth edition, 1946

In the previous chapter the concept of numerical illiteracy was introduced. In this chapter four specific steps for overcoming numerical illiteracy are described:

- Understanding variation
- Distinguishing common from special causes of variation
- Using SPC methods
- Making the appropriate management decisions (when presented with common and special causes of variation)

Understanding Variation

Understanding variation requires two types of knowledge. First, you need to be comfortable with conceptual issues related to understanding variation, and then you need to have knowledge of how various statistical methods and tools can assist you in understanding variation. Let us begin by considering variation from a conceptual point of view.

Variation exists in all that we do, even in the simplest of activities. For example, consider writing your name. This is a simple activity that you probably do each day. Imagine that your annual performance review, however, was based on being able to write the first letter of your first name three times with no variation in the form, structure, or overall appearance of the letter. If you are able to perform this simple task, you will receive a 50% increase in your salary. Remember that there can be no variation in the letters. Give it a try. Now here is the second part of your performance evaluation. Place your pen or pencil in your opposite hand and write the same letter three times. How many of you passed the performance evaluation test? If you are like me, your results look something like this:

Bob's left hand   Bob's right hand

The three letters on the right were done with my dominant (right) hand. Although these letters look similar, they are not identical. There are subtle variations in the curves, where the loops intersect another part of the letter, and in the size of the letters (the middle letter B is a little smaller than the other two). Now compare these three letters with the three I wrote with my left hand. The differences are obvious. There is not only obvious variation between the two sets of letters but also the variation within the left-handed letters is greater than the variation within the right-handed set. You might even think that two different people wrote these two sets of letters.

So it is very likely that none of us would receive the 50% pay raise. Why? It is because variation exists in all that we do. Sometimes we are quick to recognize this fact, but at other times we act as though there should be no variation. Our society is full of great examples of how we understand (and frequently do not understand) variation. Consider the following list of processes and outcomes. How much variation do you expect to see in each of these items? A lot? A little? None?

- Snowflakes
- Twins
- Siblings (not twins)
- Your commute to work
- The stock market
- Your household expenses each month

- A patient's blood pressure readings
- Bowling or golf scores
- A patient's heartbeat
- Your weight throughout the year
- Patient satisfaction results
- A department's monthly expenses compared to budget

If you are like most people, you probably feel that all of these items will exhibit some form of variation. The snowflakes usually receive the following response: "No two snowflakes are alike." This clearly states that we perceive extreme variation among snowflakes (although I am not aware of any research that has been done to corroborate this popular conclusion). We have all heard and said this snowflake statement many times. But how does this clear position on variation play out across the other items? When I have asked these questions in class, most participants tend to say that even with identical twins there is some variation—subtle variation, not unlike the variation found when writing three letters with your dominant hand.

More variation usually comes into play as people describe siblings. One of the classic lines related to this point is, "I can't believe they came from the same gene pool!" To me this is a signal of more widespread variation. The responses to variation associated with the remaining items on the list typically depend, to a large extent, on personal experiences (e.g., How long is your commute? What stocks have you purchased recently? How skilled are you at golf?). The historical experiences you have had with these items will typically guide your estimates of the amount of anticipated variation. This is exactly what Deming meant when he said, "the past is helpful to us only if it helps in the future, if it predicts" (quoted in Schultz 1994:23).

The last two items in the list presented above (i.e., patient satisfaction results and monthly expenses compared to budget) deserve a few additional comments. Even though patient satisfaction scores are typically derived from sample data, which requires an understanding of sampling error, many people seem to think that patient satisfaction scores will (or should) keep going up. The very nature of variation, however, implies fluctuation in the numbers. Sometimes the numbers go up, sometimes they go down, and sometimes they may remain constant. Sometimes the differences between scores can be great, but at other times they can be small. The variation in patient satisfaction scores may reflect a normal or abnormal distribution. The point is that assuming, wishing, hoping, or even praying that the patient satisfaction scores constantly go up is a clear demonstration of the lack of understanding of variation. In this case, the desired state (i.e., improving scores) is being confused with the objective evaluation of the variation that lives within the data.

When people do not understand variation they will demonstrate a number of rather unique behaviors. Most of these behaviors can be grouped into one or more of the following categories.

1. **People will see trends where there are no trends.** There are many popular views on what constitutes a trend so that people end up confused about the true nature of a trend. For example, it is not uncommon for the media to describe a "trend" in fashion, dining, or cars. Most of these references have little to do with statistical trends. At best they reflect opinions about fads, marketing plans, or buying patterns of consumers. Every day the media reports about an upward or downward trend in something. More often than not, this simply refers to the fact that the most current number is higher (an upward trend) or lower (a downward trend) than the previous number. So what constitutes a trend? The simple answer is that a trend is an unusually long series of consecutive data points constantly going up or constantly going down. The key word here is constantly. A true statistical trend is defined by an ever increasing or decreasing set of numbers (Western Electric Company 1985; Pyzdek 1990; Carey and Lloyd 2001; Carey 2003). This is why many people see trends where there are no trends. They look at two or three numbers that appear to be going up and call it an upward trend. Yet the total number of data points in the analysis and the number that were constantly going up would actually determine if a trend was present. The specific rules for determining a trend will be discussed later in this chapter. An example of a correctly identified trend appeared in the *Chicago Tribune* on July 15, 2001. On the front page that day there was the following headline: "Crime falls in Illinois for 6th year in a row." The article then went on to describe the constantly declining crime rate from 1995 through 2000. I found this to be a major accomplishment because journalists typically use only two or three data points to determine a trend.

2. **People will try to explain natural variation as special events.** At an earlier point in time I thought that improperly defining a trend was the most prevalent problem that we needed to address. Over the years,

however, I have changed my mind. I now believe that trying to explain natural variation as special events is a much more pervasive problem. This behavior can be found everywhere: in staff meetings, board meetings, casual conversations, and the media. Our society prides itself on being "action oriented." So when a group is presented with data, it will look for anomalies or special events so that they feel justified in taking action.

I had a physician in a class one day who described this behavior very nicely. As I finished explaining the differences between common (natural) variation and special cause variation, he blurted out, "I explain natural variation as special events." When I asked what he meant, he explained that when his diabetic patients come to see him for checkups, he is prone to change their medications when he notices the slightest up or down movement in their blood glucose readings. He also noted that his patients seem to have rather wide swings in their readings—wider than the ranges his partners reported for their patients. As we processed these insights, he came to the conclusion that his patients were probably experiencing wider variation because he was, in fact, trying to explain natural variation as special events. He continued his own self-assessment by concluding that he was overreacting to both high and low blood glucose readings. In both cases he was attributing special cause status to readings that were essentially common cause. The result of treating natural variation as if it were special cause is that you increase variation. When I asked him why he thought he did overreact to natural variation, he made two comments. First, he said that he was basically taught to react to each data point. Second, he thought his patients would think he was not a "good" doctor unless he took action when they came to see him. Over the years, this physician and I have become good friends. He is now a staunch supporter of what Shewhart and Deming were trying to teach people—that variation exists.

Every day you will find people who try to explain natural variation as special events. The inevitable outcome of such behavior is overreacting to the numbers, which leads to tampering and ultimately to increased variation in the process. This principle has been best demonstrated by Deming's Monte Carlo experiments with the funnel (Deming 1992:327–332). The objective of the funnel demonstration is to drop a series of marbles through a funnel and see where they land on a target placed beneath the funnel. The setup for this demonstration is shown in Figure 6.1. Deming identified four rules to guide the dropping of the marbles, all of which produced very different patterns of variation. The rule of most interest to us right now is Rule 4 of the funnel. In this case, the funnel is adjusted to drop the next marble over the spot where the previous marble came to rest. Rule 4 basically states that the variation in the system will "explode" (Deming's term) if you keep changing the position of the funnel on every subsequent drop of a marble. This essentially amounts to tampering by overreacting to individual data points without understanding how they all fit together to form a system of variation. Deming described Rule 4 as follows: "Rule 4 will yield a random walk. The successive drops of the marble resemble a drunk man, trying to reach home, who falls after each step and has no

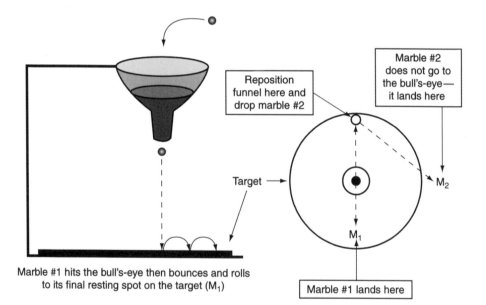

Marble #2 does not go to the bull's-eye — it lands here

Reposition funnel here and drop marble #2

Target

M_2

M_1

Marble #1 hits the bull's-eye then bounces and rolls to its final resting spot on the target (M_1)

Marble #1 lands here

Measure the distance from marble #1 (M_1) to the bull's-eye. Then swing the funnel an equal distance in the opposite direction and drop marble #2 at this point. The assumption is that the 2nd marble will follow the same course as the first one and end up in the bull's-eye. But marble #2 does not go where marble #1 went. So measure the distance that marble #2 is from the bull's-eye and swing the funnel an equal distance in the opposite direction. Continue this procedure until you have dropped at least 50 marbles.

▲ FIGURE 6.1   The funnel demonstration

idea which way is north. He steps in any direction, with no memory. His efforts eventually send him by faltering steps further and further from his target" (1992:329).

If you dropped all the marbles without ever adjusting the position of the funnel, you would end up with the minimum amount of variation and a stable process. This situation describes Rule 1 of the funnel. In this case the process variation is at a minimum because natural variation was not interpreted as special events. In a word, there was no tampering. The reader is encouraged to spend time reading the details of this demonstration and becoming familiar with all four rules of the funnel. They will provide critical knowledge about the subject of variation.

An example from healthcare will help to anchor Rule 4. Imagine that you are the manager of an outpatient clinic. You have been tracking the average wait time by day for several weeks. As you review the figures, you notice that the average wait time yesterday was higher than it was the day before. So you call the staff together and tell them that this higher wait time is unacceptable. Your response to this increased wait time is to adjust the staffing patterns to improve efficiency. The next time you look at the data you observe that the average wait time was lower than it had ever been during the past month. So you change the staffing patterns to "lighten up" on everyone's workload. What have you accomplished? By trying to force every day's average wait time to be like the previous day, you have been demonstrating Rule 4 of the funnel. You have overreacted to both the high and low average wait times and adjusted the process without knowledge of the system's performance. The prudent manager would first plot the data on a control chart and then determine if the process exhibited common or special causes of variation.

This tendency to try to explain natural variation as special events is demonstrated in nearly all walks of life. For example, consider the following illustrations from the newspaper industry. The first example comes from front pages of two newspapers on the same day. On September 1, 1998, the morning edition of the *San Francisco Chronicle* had the following headline: "Panic hammers market." It was accompanied by a picture of a stock market analyst holding his head in dismay at the plunging stock quotes. This was accompanied by multicolored graphs of rapidly dropping stock prices. The evening edition of the

San Francisco Examiner, however, told a very different story. Its head-line read, "Stocks bounce back." The article went on to explain how the stock market "soared" late in the closing hours of the day to over-come the panic that had occurred that morning. The morning drop and the afternoon rise were merely natural fluctuations in the data. Neither one was a special event.

The second example comes from the *Wall Street Journal* (September 19, 1997).[1] The headline read, "Trade deficit surges 25% to 10.3 billion." The article goes into great depth describing how the trade imbalance with Japan is the "largest in two years" and that the "Chinese gap widens to 9%." There is very colorful language in the ar-ticle about how the trade deficit has "ballooned" to $10.3 billion. The two-and-a-half-page article does not paint a very positive picture for our economy. They even showed a little line graph depicting the deficit over time. The article based its 25% "surge" conclusion on a compari-son of the most recent deficit with the previous time period's deficit. If one computed a percentage change between these two time periods, it was in fact about a 25% increase (from roughly $8.2 billion to $10.3 billion). If they had placed the data on a control chart, however (which they did not do), they would have realized that the deficit over the 25-month period (July 1995 through July 1997) was nothing more than common cause variation. Figure 6.2 shows that the average deficit over the study period was $8.9 billion with an upper control limit (UCL, to be described later in this chapter) of $13.4 billion and a lower control limit (LCL, also to be described later) of $4.4 billion. The average, along with the UCL and LCL, basically describes what is known as the capability of the process. Stated differently, the deficit process, on the average, will continue to be about $8.9 billion per year. It could go as high as $13.4 billion or as low as $4.4 billion, which represents the variation in the deficit process.

The question is not "What are you going to do about a 25% surge in the last two data points?" but rather, "Are you satisfied with an an-nual average deficit of $8.9 billion with a potential swing of anywhere between $4.4 and $13.4 billion?" If the government is willing to accept this process capability, then they should do nothing because the process will continue to perform in this manner into the future. If, on the other hand, they do not like the fact that this nation will continue to

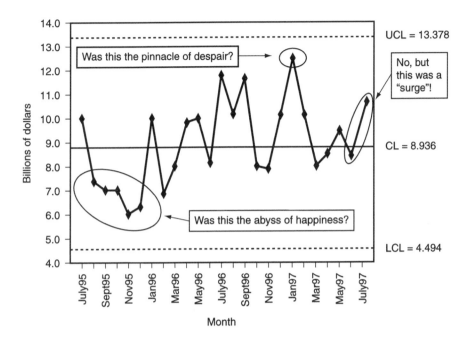

▲ **FIGURE 6.2** Deficit spending from July 1995 through July 1997

have an annual deficit of roughly $9 billion, then they should take steps to (1) shift the average deficit to a lower level of performance, or (2) reduce the variation in the entire process and thereby bring the UCL and LCL closer together.

Regardless of the action plan, the key learning point in this example is that the newspaper clearly saw natural variation as a special event. Actually, I am a little surprised that they did not pick up on earlier data patterns and give them top billing in this article. For example, the month of January 1997 had the highest deficit during this entire study period. Why did they not label this as the "pinnacle of despair"? They could have said that prior to this point there was a "sudden and rapid upward trend followed by a sudden and rapid precipitous fall in the deficit." If the month of January 1997 was the highest deficit, why did they not also highlight the period from August through December 1995, when the deficit was below the average for five straight months? If January 1997 was the pinnacle of despair, then this five-month period of relatively low deficit spending must surely have been the "abyss of happiness." In short, the deficit will never improve by seeing events as special when in fact they represent nothing more than random or common cause variation.[2]

3. **They will blame and give credit to people for things over which they have no control.** This is probably one of the most damaging aspects of not understanding variation, because it has a direct and immediate impact on the workers. Consider Bill, the manager of the outpatient testing and therapy department. You see him in the cafeteria and he looks rather depressed. You ask him why he seems down, and he tells you that his boss just chewed him out because the monthly patient satisfaction scores were lower this month than they were last month. The next month you also happen to run into Bill, who is in a very good mood. You say, "Bill, good to see that you are happier than the last time I saw you. What's going on to make you this happy?" Bill responds, "Well, the boss likes the patient satisfaction scores this month and he just told me I could buy pizza for everyone in the department to celebrate." With an inquisitive look on your face you ask, "Wow, what did you do to increase the scores?" Bill responds with a puzzled look, "Nothing. I guess we just lucked out this month." Unfortunately, I have been the recipient of this type of behavior and have observed many other individuals who have tried to cope with this form of numerical illiteracy.

   Behaviors surrounding budget variances provide another classic example of this behavior. Organizations will typically take a budget and divided it into 12 equal segments. The average monthly expected expense figure is then presented to the manager as the "target" for each month's actual expenses. Everyone knows that the actual expenses will not be exactly the same every month (i.e., no variation from target). Organizations that understand variation recognize this fact. But some organizations act as though there should be no variation from the expected average monthly budget figure. When a given month's expenses are above the average expected expenses for the month, the manager of that area is usually blamed and required to write a lengthy memo explaining why there is variance above the expected average. For the manager, this behavior creates confusion, because there will frequently be praise and potentially rewards when the department's budget is below the target. It gets even more confusing, however, when the manager is blamed when the budget is above the expected average but receives no credit when it is below the target for each month. Why is there no requirement for a memo when the budget is below the target?[3]

4. **They will find it very hard to understand past performance, make predictions, and/or make improvements.** CQI is based on these three activities. Yet if an organization approaches the analysis of data from a static rather than a dynamic point of view, then there is a very high probability that they will not be able to understand past performance, make predictions, and/or make improvements. Demonstrating skill in these behaviors requires an understanding of where measures have been, where they are now, and where they will go in the future. The answers to these questions cannot be found in summary statistics and tests of significance. They can only be found in knowledge of variation and SPC methods.

Distinguishing Common from Special Causes of Variation

These examples should help to highlight some of the inconsistencies we have when it comes to understanding variation. Once we begin to think about the nature of variation and how it plays a major role in our daily lives, however, we will be in a much better position to actually start distinguishing between two very distinctive types of variation, common and special cause variation.

The origins of SPC can be traced back to the early 1920s, a time when this country was struggling with a fairly basic question: How can you increase production and maintain quality? The man who helped answer this question was Dr. Walter Shewhart. Shewhart argued that all work could be viewed as a series of interrelated processes. Because customers are the recipients of process output, it stands to reason that organizations that focus on maintaining efficient and effective processes will meet and exceed customer expectations. Shewhart's recommendation for creating efficient and effective processes was very simple. He maintained that if you understand the variation that occurs within a process, you will be able to make appropriate management decisions that will produce quality products and services. Shewhart distinguished two types of variation: assignable and unassignable. These terms were later revised by Deming to the more popular terms common and special causes of variation (Shewhart 1931; Deming 1992; Schultz 1994). Deming (1992:314) classified common cause variation as "faults of the system" and special causes as "faults from fleeting events."

Common cause variation is random variation that results from regular, natural, or ordinary causes. Common cause variation affects all outcomes of the process and results from the regular random rhythm of the process. It produces processes that are stable or "in control." One can make predictions, within statistical limits, about a process that has only common cause variation (this is often referred to as the process capability). In a common cause state there are no indications of special cause, because the variation results only from chance fluctuations in the data. The key thing to remember with common cause variation is that it does not mean that the performance of the process is acceptable. It only means that the process is stable and predictable. A process can be predictably bad. For example, a patient may have blood pressure readings that are stable and very predictable but at an unacceptably high level (e.g., a systolic pressure that averages 165 with a minimum at 155 and a maximum at 175). The same could be true for cholesterol or blood glucose levels. In all these cases, we would need to shift the various process outputs to more acceptable levels of performance. This is what quality improvement is designed to do. Remember, though, common cause means stable and predictable, not necessarily acceptable.

Special cause variation, on the other hand, results from irregular or unnatural causes that are not inherent in the process. Special cause variation affects some but not necessarily all outcomes of a process. When special causes are present, a process will be classified as "out of control" and, therefore, unstable. Wheeler (1993) refers to special causes as "signals" that a process is in a state of chaos. The future performance of a process that exhibits special causes will be unpredictable. This is why improvement strategies should not be applied to processes exhibiting special cause variation. Because they are unstable and unpredictable, attempts to improve them will only lead to wasted time, effort, and money. The response to special causes of variation should be to investigate the origin of the special causes, determine why they occurred (conduct a root cause analysis), and then take steps to eliminate them from the system.

Several healthcare examples should help to clarify these two types of variation. When a patient is connected to telemetry, variation in his or her vital signs will be observed. In fact, there is great concern if variation is not observed and the patient is considered to be a "flat line." If the patient's heartbeat is observed at 59, then 61, then 60, and so on, there is no need for immediate concern. This is what would be called common cause variation. It represents normal fluctuation in the heartbeat process. If, on the other hand, the patient's heart rate starts to climb and goes from 65 to 70 to 75, continues past 100 beats per minute, and settles at around 140 beats per minute, this would usually be seen as a signal that the patient is exceeding normal variation. At some point the patient would move from a common cause state to one that reflects special cause variation, and action would be taken to correct the heart's rhythm and bring it back into a common cause level of performance. Action would not be taken, however, while the patient was demonstrating acceptable common cause variation.

Now consider a trauma patient who is brought into the emergency department (ED). The patient has a severe head injury, is hardly breathing, and has lost a considerable amount of blood. As you are examining him you also notice that he is wearing a medical bracelet indicating that he is diabetic. What is the first thing on the minds of the ED team? What would they do for this patient? They would focus their efforts on "stabilizing the patient." They would work to get the patient breathing under his own power, stop the bleeding, and deal with the head trauma. What they would not do is gather around a flipchart and brainstorm ideas about how this patient might improve his diet to have better control of his diabetes. The patient came in as a special cause, and the team would work to get the patient into a common cause state of affairs where he would be stable and predictable.

In summary, the basic points that Shewhart (1931) taught about these two types of variation were as follows:

- Variation exists in all that we do
- Processes that exhibit common or chance causes of variation are predictable within statistical limits
- Special causes of variation can be identified and eliminated
- Only processes that exhibit common cause variation can be improved
- Attempting to improve processes that contain special causes will increase variation and waste resources

Using SPC Methods

Understanding variation from a conceptual point of view provides only a start. If you are truly interested in overcoming numerical illiteracy, then you have to understand the variation that lives in the data and then take the appropriate action(s) based on whether you identify common or special causes of variation. Decisions about taking action can be greatly enhanced by using the simple tools that Shewhart created in the early 1920s, the run and control charts.

What Is a Run Chart?

The run chart is a very simple statistical tool that can be created without complicated formulae or even using computers. There is basically only one way to make a run chart. It is a plot of data over time with the unit of time (e.g., day, week, or month) always plotted on the horizontal or x-axis and the indicator (the key quality characteristic) always plotted on the vertical or y-axis. The data are arranged in chronological order, and the centerline of the chart is the median.[4] Figure 6.3 shows the basic elements of a run chart.

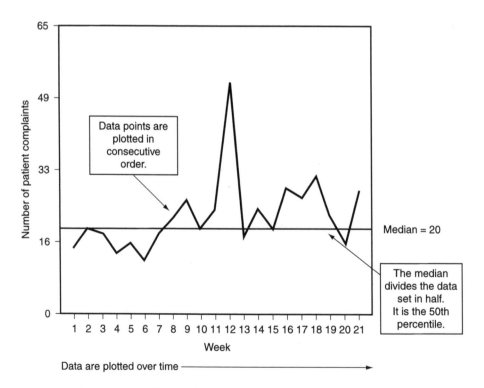

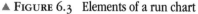

▲ FIGURE 6.3 Elements of a run chart

Once you have laid out a run chart, the first question to be asked is, "What is a run?" A run is defined as one or more consecutive data points on the same side of the median. Figure 6.4 shows how runs are determined. The first thing to do is to identify the data points that fall exactly on the median. These data points are noted but not included in the determination of a run. In Figure 6.4 there are three data points that fall exactly on the median value of 20. These three data points are highlighted as black diamonds and eliminated from further consideration.[5]

In the example shown in Figure 6.4 there were 21 total data points (i.e., we have the total number of patient complaints each week for 21 weeks). Note, however, that 3 of these data points are on the median (a value of 20). So we subtract these 3 data points from the total of 21 and end up with 18 "useful observations." Now we are ready to identify the actual "runs" in this data set.

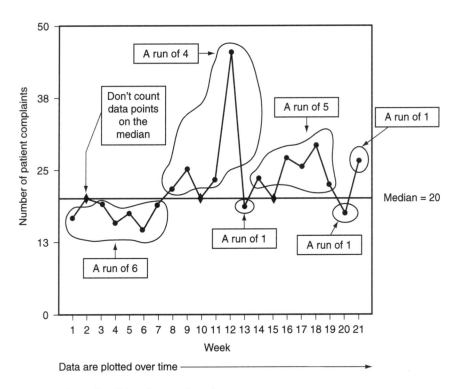

▲ Figure 6.4 Identifying the number of runs

In Figure 6.4 circles have been drawn around the runs. Six runs are present in the data. Three of the runs contain multiple data points, and the other three reflect a run of one. Remember that a run is defined as one or more consecutive points on the same side of the median. The other technical point to remember when counting runs is that because you have eliminated data points that fall on the median, these data points do not get included in the determination of a run. You can see this in Figure 6.4. Note that the circles do not include the data points on the median (the median data points are identified by gray squares).

When people are just starting out with run charts, they have a tendency to (1) include the data point on the median in the run, or (2) count the data before the point on the median as one run and then count the data after the point on the median as a second run. The first run in Figure 6.4 contains six data points. It does not contain seven data points, which would include the median data point, and it does not reflect two separate runs broken by the second data point, which falls on the median. Note that the other method for determining the number of runs is to count the number of times the line connecting the dots crosses the centerline and add one (to this number). In Figure 6.4 the line crosses the centerline five times. If you add one to this number you get six, which is the number of circles drawn around the runs. These two methods should always produce the same result. If they do not, then one of your methods for determining the number of runs is flawed.

Once we have identified the number of runs on the chart, the next question that most people ask is "so what? I've made this nice little line graph and circled some clusters of data, but why did I do it?" What can we learn from the number of runs? The answer should be obvious. The number of runs allows you to answer the primary question: "Does the chart exhibit common or special causes of variation?" This question is answered easily by applying four simple tests that allow you to determine if special causes are present in your data.

- **Test #1—too few or too many runs.** A special cause is defined as too little or too much variation in a data set. This first test is designed to help you make this determination. The first thing that you need to determine is the number of "useful observations." As stated above, this is determined by subtracting the number of data points on the median from the total number of data points. Once you have determined the number of useful observations in your data set, you refer to a table

(Table 6.1) to identify the minimum and maximum number of runs. If the number of runs on your chart falls between this minimum and maximum, you do not have a special cause.

▼ TABLE 6.1   Test #1—too few or too many runs

Use this table by first calculating the number of "useful observations" in your data set. This is done by subtracting the number of data points on the median from the total number of data points. Then find this number in the first column. The lower limit for the number of runs is found in the second column. The upper number of runs can be found in the third column. If the number of runs in your data falls below the lower limit or above the upper limit, then this is a signal of a special cause.

Number of useful observations	Lower number of runs	Upper number of runs
15	4	12
16	5	12
17	5	13
18	6	13
19	6	14
20	6	15
21	7	15
22	7	16
23	8	16
24	8	17
25	9	17
26	9	18
27	9	19
28	10	19
29	10	20
30	11	20
31	11	21
32	11	22
33	11	22
34	12	23
35	13	23
36	13	24
37	13	25
38	14	25
39	14	26
40	15	26

Returning to our example in Figure 6.4, we see that we have 18 useful observations (21 total data points minus 3 on the median). If we look up 18 useful observations in the first column of Table 6.1, we see that the lower number of runs should be 6 and the upper number of runs should be 13. That is, if we have between 6 and 13 runs, the data do not contain a special cause. In the case of Figure 6.4, we noted a total of 6 runs. This matches the minimum number of runs and we conclude, therefore, that our data successfully meet Test #1. Stated differently, there is a sufficient number of runs to reflect a random or common cause process.

- **Test #2—a shift in the process.** When do you know if a process has really moved to a more desirable level of performance? If you suffer from numerical illiteracy, you will probably think that one or two data points that are "better" (however defined) constitute a shift to an improved level. When looking at a run chart, however, the key to defining a shift in the process is when you have a run that has too many data points. I know what you are thinking: "So, how many data points is 'too many'?" If you have fewer than 20 data points on your chart, 7 or more data points are typically considered too many. More than 20 data points on the chart requires 8 data points in a run for that run to be too long. Figure 6.4 has a total of 21 data points, which means we would look for a run that has 8 or more data points to define a shift in the process. The longest run contains only 6 data points, so we conclude that there is not a shift in the process. Figure 6.4 also passes Test #2.

- **Test #3—a trend.** This is probably one of the more difficult tests to apply because of all the popular notions about what constitutes a "trend." People love to find a trend. This issue was discussed earlier in this chapter and will not be elaborated further in this section. The key point to remember, however, is that a trend is an unusually long series of consecutive data points constantly going up or constantly going down. Pyzdek (1990) and Western Electric (1985) offer two of the better references for identifying a trend. If you have 8 or fewer data points on your chart, 5 consecutively increasing or decreasing data points define a trend. If you have 9–20 data points on your chart, 6 or more data points constantly increasing or decreasing constitute a trend. Finally, if you have more than 20 data points, the standard requirement for a trend is 7 or more. The other two key points to remember when identifying a trend are (1) you count data points on the median and (2) you ignore points that repeat the previous value. In Figure 6.4 we are looking for 7 data points constantly increasing or decreasing because we have 21 total data points. There are only 4 data points constantly increasing in Figure 6.4 (data points 6–9), which does not reflect a trend.

- **Test #4—stratification.** Stratification can be a problem if you have not spent enough time up front thinking about how your data should be collected. This point was discussed in detail in Chapter 3. This test will let you know if you did not do a good job of specifying your data collection procedures. Stratification is defined as a cyclical pattern of up and down data points that forms a sawtooth or zigzag pattern. In healthcare stratification typically results from a data collection problem. For example, the data collectors forgot to separate the data by shift (day, afternoon, and night), by day of the week, or by type of patient (medical versus surgical). What happens in these cases is that multiple processes confound the data. For example, one piece of the process (day shift) performs at a high level while the other segment (night shift) performs at a lower level. In this case, stratification looks like this:

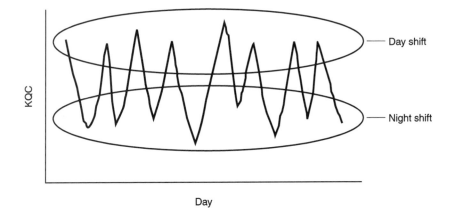

From a statistical point of view, 14 or more consecutive data points fluctuating up and down define stratification. This pattern requires point-to-point, up and down movement. If you have two data points going up in a row, this would break the point-to-point fluctuation and you would not have a stratification problem. This stratification pattern is not found in Figure 6.4.

In summary, Figure 6.4 passes all the run tests. This leads us to conclude that the data in Figure 6.4 reflect common cause variation and that the chart therefore depicts a process that is stable and predictable. But, as we will see in the next section on control charts, this conclusion may require a closer evaluation.

What Is a Control Chart?

Like run charts, control charts are graphic displays of process variation as it lays itself out over time. There are two key distinctions between run and control charts, however. First, the run chart is not as sensitive to special causes as the control chart. This is because the run chart is not sensitive to extreme values in the data. Because the centerline on the run chart is the median, the chart basically allows you to classify the data points as being only above or below the median. The actual distance a data point is from the centerline is not an issue on a run chart. Therefore, if one data point is two units above the median and another point is 22 units above the median, they will both be treated the same because they are both on the same side of the median. The logic for this decision is related to the definition of a run (i.e., one or more data points on the same side of the median). If these same two data points were placed on a control chart, you would notice a difference because the centerline on the control chart is the mean or average of all the data points. By using the mean, therefore, we are ensuring that the distance of each data point from the centerline will be considered in determining if special cause variation exists.

The presence of control limits on the chart is the second major difference between run and control charts. The UCL and LCL basically define the boundaries of the variation around the mean. These lines are drawn parallel to the centerline. The control limits provide the basis for (1) additional tests to identify special causes and (2) determining the capability of the process.[6] Figure 6.5 shows the basic elements of a control chart and one of the tests to identify a special cause (i.e., a data point exceeded the UCL, signaling too much variation in the data).

There are many useful books on the statistical theory behind control charts, how to construct them, and how to interpret the results. Readers interested in these detailed topics should consult Western Electric (1985); Duncan (1986); Ishikawa (1989); Pyzdek (1990); Montgomery (1991); Wheeler and Chambers (1992); Wheeler (1993 and 1995); Blank (1998); Benneyan (2001); Carey and Lloyd (2001); Carey (2003); and Benneyan, Lloyd, and Plsek (forthcoming). For my purposes, however, there are two issues that do require a brief review: (1) deciding which control chart to use and (2) identifying special causes. If the reader does not have at least a working knowledge of these two topics and some familiarity with the key terms associated with them, it will be very hard to fully appreciate what the charts are trying to tell you and how they can help you avoid numerical illiteracy.

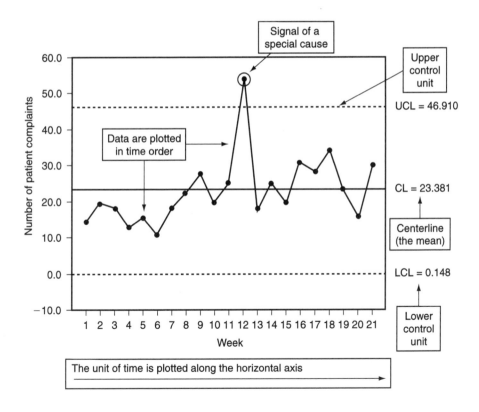

▲ FIGURE 6.5 Elements of a control chart

Deciding Which Control Chart to Use

Although there is only one way to make a run chart, there are numerous ways to make a control chart. This variety is summarized in the following passage:

> There are at least a dozen different types of control charts in common use in manufacturing and other industry, with three or four new types being developed each year. The various types differ by the statistic plotted (e.g., averages, percentages, counts, moving averages, cumulative sums, etc.) and the distribution assumed (e.g., normal, binomial, Poisson, geometric, etc.). Other control charts have been developed for special-purpose applications (e.g., naturally cyclic processes, short run processes, start-up processes, risk-adjustment applications, rare events, etc.). All have different formulae for calculating centerlines and control limits. Regardless of the complexity or underlying statistical theory, however, most control charts have the same visual appearance (a chronological graph of frequent process data with a centerline, UCL, and LCL) and are interpreted in a similar way. (Benneyan, Lloyd, and Plsek 2003:464)

If there are all these different types of control charts, how do you decide which one is best for your data? Although it may seem confusing on the surface, there are some rather simple rules to help make this decision.

The first thing you need to do is determine the type of data you are collecting. There are basically two types of data: (1) continuous (variables or measurement) data and (2) attribute (discrete or count) data. Continuous data, as the term implies, can be measured along a continuous scale. The most recognized version of a continuous scale is a ruler. It is marked with equal intervals that can be divided into as many subdivisions as your calibration instruments will permit. With continuous data you can perform all the mathematical functions. Data measured this way can be either whole numbers or decimals. Examples of continuous data include:

- Wait times in the ED
- Turnaround time in the lab
- Blood pressure readings
- Coumadin levels (international normalized ratios)

- Blood glucose readings
- The number of procedures or tests performed
- The number of surgeries done each day
- Financial measures such as operating margin or expenses
- Duration of a surgical procedure

Note that although I have chosen to use the term *continuous* to define this first type of data, it is also referred to as *measurement data* or *variables data*. The term is a matter of preference. What is important is the concept and how you start to visualize data.

Attributes data (also know as discrete or count data) are essentially "bucket data." Unlike measuring a patient's weight on a continuous scale, attributes data are looking at characteristics that can be classified into categories or "buckets." For example, any time you are measuring mortality you are using attribute data (the patient is either alive or dead). Similarly, pregnancy is an attribute measure. There are only two outcomes: the woman either is pregnant or not pregnant. Attribute data can be classified further into two subdivisions: *defectives* and *defects*.

Defectives (also known as nonconforming units) require that you have a count of the number of items that were acceptable and the number that were not acceptable. The unacceptable items become the numerator and the denominator is the total number of items observed. When you know how many items out of the total are unacceptable, you can either plot the number of defective items on your control chart or you can compute the percentage of defectives. When we compute a percentage, therefore, we are basically determining what proportion the numerator is of the denominator. The standard terminology used in most control chart books to define defectives is that you know both the *occurrences* of the defective product or service (the numerators) and the *nonoccurrences* (the denominators). Knowing these two pieces allows us to calculate a percentage or proportion of defectives. Keep in mind that when you use percentages you are comparing the same types of items, products, or services. If you are looking at the percentage of late food trays, for example, you will have the number of late food trays as the numerator and the total number of food trays produced as the denominator. In this case you have trays divided by trays—like divided by like. This is important to keep in mind because as we move next to define defects, this condition will not hold.

Defects pose an intriguing challenge. Defects occur and can be counted. But how do you count all the nondefects? Stated differently, you know when a defect occurs (the occurrence), but you do not know when the nondefects or nonoccurrences happen. I know you are thinking, "This makes no sense." When I first heard this statement it did not make a lot of sense to me, either. Examples should help to clarify this concept. Look down at the rug in your office or in your family room. How many spots or stains do you see? For argument's sake I will imagine that you found some spots or stains on the carpet. Now count the number of nonstains on the carpet? How did you do? If you are like most of us, you could not count the nonstains. This is an unknown.

When the highway department records traffic accidents, they do the same thing. They can count the occurrences (accidents) today, but they have no idea how many nonaccidents there were today. There are times, therefore, when we know the occurrence of an event but the nonoccurrences are unknown and unknowable. In healthcare we experience this situation with patient falls, needle sticks, nosocomial infections, medication errors, and liability cases. We only know when the event happens. Think of needle sticks. A staff member comes into your office to report that he just stuck himself. After you try to calm him down and explain the next steps you will take, you do not say, "Oh, by the way, how many times didn't you stick yourself today?" Similarly, if a nurse asked a patient, "How many times didn't you fall today?" he or she would probably get a rather confused look from the patient.

When you are dealing with defects you need to remember that a count of the number of falls, needle sticks, or medication errors gives you a numerator, but you do not have a denominator. So you cannot compute a percentage. The statistic of preference in this case is the rate. A rate is a ratio (a numerator and a denominator), but the two numbers you are using are not alike. For example, when we compute an inpatient falls rate by month, we have the number of inpatient falls (including multiple falls) for the month as the numerator, and the denominator is usually the total number of patient days for the month. Now we have falls divided by days, two unlike things. The resulting number is reported as so many falls per 1000 patient days. Any time you report that there are so many of this per 1000, 10,000, or 100,000 of that, you have just created a rate. Most of the patient safety measures fall into this category (e.g., patient fall rate, restraint rate, needle stick rate, or medication error rate). The other characteristic of a rate is that the numerator of a rate can be larger than the denominator. For example, it is possible that you could have 130 falls for 100 patients. This is because an individual patient could fall more than once.

After determining whether your data are variables or attributes, the next step is to decide which control chart is most appropriate for your data. There are seven basic control charts that are regularly described in the literature and taught in most classes and seminars on SPC. After working with the charts for more than 10 years, however, I have found that 5 of the 7 charts are the most relevant to healthcare indicators.[7]

Figure 6.6 presents the five control charts that have the most relevance to healthcare indicators. Two of the five charts are used with variables data (the X-bar & S chart and the XmR chart), and three of the charts are used with attributes data (p-chart, c-chart, and u-chart). Each chart is described in detail below. They are organized according to the two basic types of data: variables and attributes.

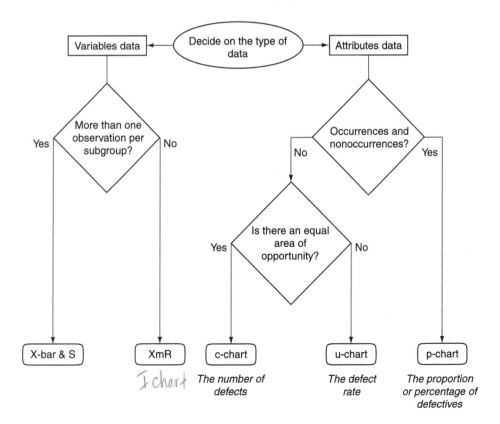

▲ FIGURE 6.6   The control chart decision tree

Variables Charts

X-bar & S chart

This chart is referred to as the average (X-bar) and standard deviation (S) chart. It is the preferred chart when you have multiple *observations* of continuous data that have been organized into *subgroups*. An observation is the actual piece of data that you record or observe (e.g., turnaround time for a lab test or medication order, blood glucose readings for a patient, or time to administer beta blockers to heart attack patients in the emergency department). The vertical axis label defines the units of measurement being applied to the observation (e.g., minutes, hours, or milligrams per deciliter for blood glucose tracking).

The subgroup (Deming referred to these as rational subgroups) usually defines how you have organized your data (usually by a unit of time, such as by hour, day of the week, week, or month). Note that the subgroup could also be a single patient or multiple patients in chronological order. Typically, the subgroups are of equal size, but the X-bar & S chart can be made with an unequal number of observations per subgroup.

When you make an X-bar & S chart, most software programs will give you two charts; one will show the average of the data (the X-bar portion), and the other shows the standard deviation (SD) portion (the S part of the chart). Figure 6.7 provides an example of an X-bar & S chart. In this case the indicator of interest is a patient's systolic blood pressure (the top number in a blood pressure reading). The patient recorded several blood pressure readings each day (a minimum of three and a maximum of seven each day). Note that the control limits are not straight. When limits vary by subgroup, they are referred to as *stair-step control limits*. If the patient had recorded exactly the same number of blood pressure readings (observations) each day (e.g., four), then the UCL and LCL would be straight lines. As we will see in subsequent examples, stair-step control limits also will be found on p-charts and u-charts.

Figure 6.7 reflects a process that is in control (i.e., common cause variation). The upper chart reveals the overall average blood pressure and the average for each day. The lower chart (called the standard deviation chart) shows the overall SD and the SD within each day. Each chart has its own upper and lower control limits.[8]

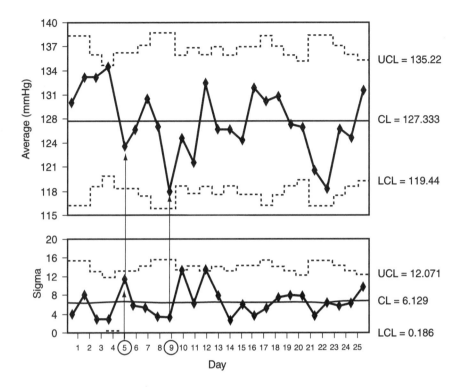

▲ FIGURE 6.7 Example of an X-bar & S chart with a variable subgroup size (systolic blood pressure is the indicator)

The top chart is considered to be the primary chart. It has three main components: (1) the centerline (CL) or average, (2) the UCL, and (3) the LCL. These three pieces define the capability of the process. The average systolic blood pressure for this patient is 127. (Note that the decimal places can be ignored in this case, because this is entirely too finite of a reading for blood pressure results. The degree to which you can control the decimal places on a chart will depend on the software being used.) The UCL is 135 and the LCL is 119. The way to describe this chart is as follows: "On the average this patient's systolic blood pressure is 127. It could have gone up to 136 on any given day or down to 119, and that is the natural rhythm of this patient's systolic process."

The lower chart is the S-chart. This chart has two primary purposes. First, it helps you to understand the variation that exists within each subgroup. For example, the SD for day 5 is around 12, and the average systolic blood pressure for this day is about 123. In comparison, the SD for day 9 is about 4 with an average of about 118. This shows us that not only were the average systolic pressures higher on day 5 but also that the SD was 12. This means that on day 5 the patient had an average of 123 plus or minus 12 points (135 to 111). In contrast, day 9 shows an average of 118 with an SD of only 3. The second purpose of the S chart is that the average SD (the center-line) is used in the calculation of the control limits for the average (upper) chart. In this case, the average systolic blood pressure (i.e., centerline) is 127.

I do not intend to elaborate on the formulae for the calculation of the control limits. These issues are addressed thoroughly in Wheeler (1995) and Wheeler and Chambers (1992) and Western Electric (1985). What is important to realize, however, is that if the SD chart reveals wide variation, then the average SD will be large. Because the average SD is used to compute the UCL and LCL of the average chart, a large SD will contribute to making the control limits of the top chart (the average chart) wider. The relationship of the two charts must be understood together.

XmR chart or the I-chart

The XmR chart is also known as the Individuals chart because each subgroup contains one and only one individual observation. Like the X-bar & S chart, you will typically get two charts when you request this type of chart from your SPC software. The X chart reports the average of all the individual data points and the mR chart documents the "moving range." This chart is typically used when you are interested in answering questions such as "How many surgeries do we do each week?" "What is the average cost per discharge each month?", or "How many home care visits do we conduct each week?" These are essentially accounting questions. You are not interested in finding out how many surgeries started late (this would be classified as a defective, which would require an attributes chart); you merely want to know how many are done in the course of a week. In this case, the week becomes the subgroup and the total number of surgeries completed becomes the individual observation for that week. In short, the XmR chart is designed to help you understand questions related to volume or accounting for the frequency of an activity without asking if the outcome is acceptable or not.

Figure 6.8 provides an example of an XmR chart. Note that like the X-bar & S chart, there are two charts. In this particular example, the indicator is the total number of dollars saved each month as a result of implementing a new transcription system for radiology. The top portion of the chart provides a plot of the individual data points along with the average of all the data points and the UCL and LCL. This chart also has the *zones* identified. These are the dashed lines that divide the chart into three areas above and below the CL. The zones are used to assist in identification of special causes, which will be described in the next section.

The bottom chart is referred to as the *moving range chart*. The moving range is derived by calculating the simple difference between each successive data point on the Individuals chart and then plotting this difference on the mR chart. These steps are shown in Figure 6.8 and highlighted by the circles drawn around each neighboring data point and the corresponding arrows that point to the mR value on the lower chart. Notice that the first three data points on the mR chart are relatively close together. This is because there are small differences between the first four data points that have been coupled together on the Individuals chart. If you look at data points for August and September 2002, however, you see a very different picture. The difference

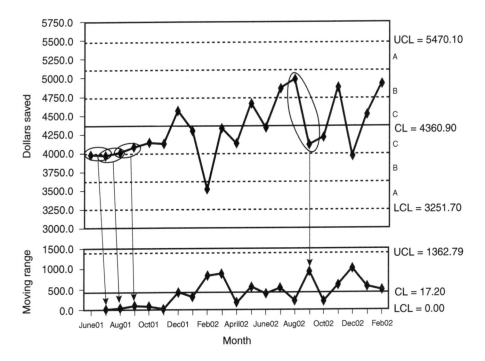

▲ FIGURE 6.8 Example of a XmR chart (transcription savings is the indicator)

(i.e., the range) between these two months is much larger ($938, to be exact) than any of the ranges found when the first four data points were compared. In short, the individual values when coupled together produce the moving ranges. One final thing to note about the XmR chart: The mR chart will always have one less data point on it than the Individuals chart. This is because the first data point (June01) does not have a neighbor for comparison purposes until July's data are posted. Therefore, there is no moving range for June01 on the chart.

Attributes Charts

P-chart

The p-chart derives its name from the fact that either a percentage or a proportion is what you actually plot on the chart. When you make a p-chart, or any other attributes chart, you will get only one chart (unlike the variables charts, which give you two charts). The p-chart is used to monitor defectives when you know the occurrences of the defective product or service and the nonoccurrences. This chart is used frequently in healthcare settings because we track many indicators that look at accuracy, completeness, errors, or the percentage of something done or not done (e.g., C-sections). Figure 6.9 provides an example of a p-chart. In this case, the indicator is the percentage of hospital readmissions for home healthcare patients. The denominators range from a minimum of 326 cases (September 2001) to a maximum of 1041 (October 2002). The numerators range from a low of 75 readmissions (September 2001) to a high of 249 in October 2002. Note that the control limits are not straight lines because the denominators change from month to month, another instance of stair-step control limits. The impact of denominators that keep changing can be seen on Figure 6.9. The third data point (September 2001) has the widest limits because this month has the smallest denominator (326 cases). The tightest limits can be found for September 2002, where the denominator is 1041 cases. It should be noted that if the subgroups were of equal size, the control limits on the p-chart would be straight. But because most health care indicators that are defined as percentages differ from one time period to another (e.g., we do not have the same number of deliveries each month, produce the same number of food trays each day, or have the same number of patients visit a clinic each day), we

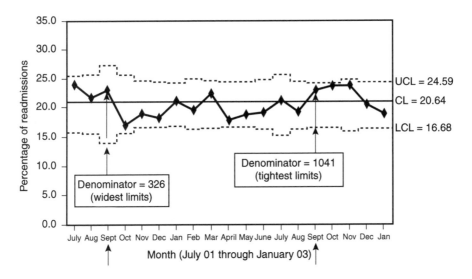

▲ FIGURE 6.9   Example of a p-chart (percentage of home care patients readmitted to the hospital is the indicator)

rarely have equal subgroups when calculating percentages or proportions. Therefore, the p-charts will almost always have stair-step control limits.

C-chart

The c-chart and the u-chart are the charts used to track *defects*. The c-chart is the chart of preference when you have an *equal area of opportunity* for a defect to occur. An area of opportunity has the following characteristics:

- It applies to all attributes or count charts (c, u, and p)
- It defines the frame or area in which a nonconforming unit (defective) or a nonconformity (defect) can occur
- It can be of equal or unequal sizes

A manufacturing example may help clarify this concept. Imagine that you worked on a paint line at an automobile manufacturing plant. If you were assigned to paint the hoods of a single model of a car (e.g., a Ford Taurus), there would be an equal area of opportunity for a paint blemish because all Ford Taurus hoods are the same size. In this case, we would make a c-chart and plot the total number of paint blemishes (defects) on each hood you paint.

The challenge now becomes determining when this equal area of opportunity condition exists in healthcare settings. One of the more frequently used examples of how this might occur is with monitoring patient falls. If you conclude that there is basically an equal opportunity for a patient to fall each day at your hospital, rehabilitation facility, or long-term care facility, then you would merely count the number of falls occurring each day, week, or month and make a c-chart. Other indicators that could be placed on a c-chart if the equal area of opportunity assumption was met include the number of:

- Patient restraints
- Lawsuits
- Patient complaints
- Needle sticks
- Medication errors
- Central line infections

Figure 6.5 was used to show the elements of a control chart. It also provides an example of a c-chart. In this example, the customer service manager of a large medical group is interested in charting the total number of patient complaints it receives each week at its 25 sites. Because each patient could complain more than once, complaints are viewed as defects. The alternative, considering the registration of a complaint as a defective, is not selected because this would preclude counting more than one complaint from a patient. Remember that defectives are based on the binomial distribution (i.e., the patient complained or did not complain). If you approached this indicator as a defective, you would not be concerned with the magnitude of the complaint problem (i.e., the total number of complaints) but rather with the fact that a patient complained or did not complain. Measuring complaints as a defective, therefore, would produce a percentage of patients who complained (a p-chart). As a defect, however, we are concerned with the magnitude of the problem, so we count the total number of complaints, including multiple complaints from the same patient. Finally, note that making a p-chart is not feasible because the manager does not know the number of nonoccurrences (i.e., the people who did not complain) and therefore does not have a denominator to figure the percentage of patients who complained.

The c-chart is selected because the volume of patients seen remains fairly constant each week and the number of sites included in the study does not change. These two conditions allow the manager to assume an equal area of opportunity for a complaint to occur. She merely counts the total number of complaints received each week and plots that number on a c-chart. The chart produces an CL, an UCL, and an LCL that define the capability of the process.

The major problem with using the c-chart for healthcare applications is that there are very few indicators that have equal areas of opportunity. The severity of patients can change easily, the census can show fluctuations, the volume of orders may change rapidly, and the ED may have to go on bypass because there are no more inpatient beds available. So if the assumption of an equal area of opportunity is violated, what do we do next? The answer is simple—make a u-chart.

U-chart

This chart is used frequently in healthcare, especially now that there has been a more concentrated effort to track patient safety indicators. The u-chart, like the c-chart, is used to track defects. The difference is that the u-chart is selected when you conclude that there is not an equal area of opportunity for the defect to occur. Let us return to the paint line at the Ford plant for a moment. Although you have historically painted one model of car at a time, today you have been told that the line will have a mixture of cars and a mixture of hood sizes. So how do you count the paint blemishes on the hoods of a Ford Escort, a Taurus, a Mustang, and a Crown Victoria? Each hood has a different number of square inches, takes a different volume of paint to cover the surface of the hood, and has a varying probability of experiencing a paint blemish. The u-chart takes care of this problem very quickly by computing a defect *rate*. The number of paint blemishes are used as the numerator, and the number of square inches of the hood's surface is used as the denominator. The resultant ratio provides the number of blemishes per so many square inches of hood area. The rate essentially normalizes the differences in denominator size.

Now, back to healthcare. Because it is extremely rare to have the same number of medication orders each week, the same exact patient census, or the same number of central line days in the ICU, the u-chart can be applied to many more situations than the c-chart. Furthermore, since epidemiologists frequently produce rate-based statistics (e.g., the neonatal death rate or the ventilator-associated pneumonia rate), the use of terms associated with the u-chart should sound familiar to healthcare professionals. Because the u-chart looks basically like the p-chart (with a CL and stair-step control limits), an example of the u-chart will not be provided at this time. The u-chart is demonstrated in Chapter 7.

Table 6.2 provides an overview of the five charts just described and offers examples of indicators that could be placed on each type of chart. Other useful tables that summarize how charts should be set up and their various uses can be found in *Statistical Quality Control Handbook* (Western Electric 1985:191) and Benneyan (2001:8).[9] Readers wishing to gain additional insights about the selection of control charts should consult Duncan (1986), Ishikawa (1989), Pyzdek (1990), Montgomery (1991), Wheeler (1995), Wheeler and Chambers (1992), Carey and Lloyd (2001), and Carey (2003).

▼ TABLE 6.2   Control chart summary

Type of control chart	Type of data and data collection issues	Examples of indicators used on this type of chart
X-bar & S chart This is known as the average (X-bar) and standard deviation (S) chart. Most SPC software programs will give you two charts when you select this chart: one for the X-bar portion and one for the S portion. This is considered to be the most statistically powerful of all the charts.	**Continuous data** The X-bar & S chart usually involves drawing a small sample of observations that are organized into rational subgroups. The statistical principles behind this chart are based on the assumptions of the normal (Gaussian) bell-shaped distribution.	• Actual turnaround time for 5 lab tests or 3 pharmacy orders each day • Blood pressure readings (e.g., 3 per day) • Diabetes monitoring (mg/dl) • Anesthesia time for selected procedures • Patient satisfaction scores
XmR chart This chart is known as the Individual values and moving range chart. Sometimes it will be referred to as the Individuals or I-chart. It does not have the statistical rigor or power of the X-bar & S chart. This chart is used to answer questions related to volume: "How many surgeries did we do this week?" The XmR chart does not address the question of whether these surgeries were started on time (this would require a p-chart). Instead, the XmR chart is answering a neutral question: "How many?"	**Continuous data** The XmR chart is used when you have a single observation for each subgroup. Sampling typically is not done but might be if the process being monitored has an extremely large volume. Because this chart frequently uses aggregates as the plotted number (e.g., days in accounts receivable this month), it is important to make sure that the data are consistently collected from one time period to the next. This chart is used to evaluate questions related to process outcomes (volumes), with no concern as to whether the outcomes of the process are acceptable or not acceptable.	• Patient wait time to see the physician or to be seen in the ED • The number of days to mail a patient bill after discharge • The number of calls coming into a clinic each day • Average length of stay by week for a particular DRG • The number of surgeries done each week • Operating margin by month • Pounds of laundry each day • Average turnaround time by day • The number of food trays produced

▼ TABLE 6.2 Control chart summary *(continued)*

Type of control chart	Type of data and data collection issues	Examples of indicators used on this type of chart
p-chart The p-chart is used frequently in healthcare to compute the percentage (or proportion) of defective products or services. The p-chart requires being able to count both the occurrences and the non-occurrences.	**Attributes data** These data are classified as defectives or nonconforming units because they reflect the percentage (or proportion) of undesirable outcomes (the numerators). The denominators usually (but not always) are of varying sizes, which produce stair-step control limits. Data of this type reflect the binomial distribution. The denominators need to be sufficiently large (e.g., greater than 12) to enable a reasonable percentage to be calculated, yet not too large (e.g., over 300).	• Percentage of C-sections • Percentage of late food trays • Percentage of incomplete charts • Percentage of late surgery starts • Percentage of bills that are inaccurate • Percentage of mortality • Percentage of RN turnover • Percentage of patients responding "Very Good" to a survey question
c-chart The c-chart is used to count the number of defects that occur within an equal area of opportunity when the nondefects are unknown. In this case, each observed unit (e.g., a patient) can have multiple defects (e.g., falls). Generally speaking, these are considered to be "rare events."	**Attributes data** The key to using a c-chart is that there must be an equal opportunity for a defect to occur. This condition frequently makes it difficult to use this chart in healthcare because the conditions under which we provide care do not always remain constant. These data are based on the Poisson distribution.	• The number of falls • The number of restraints • The number of needle sticks • The number of lawsuits filed • The number of ventilator-associated pneumonias • The number of nosocomial infections • The number of medication errors • The number of returns to surgery
u-chart The u-chart is used to track defects when the area of opportunity is not equal. For this reason, the u-chart is used more often in healthcare than the c-chart. This chart is based on rates rather than simple counts.	**Attributes data** The Poisson distribution is also used as the frame of reference for this chart. The u-chart presents rates (e.g., so many falls per 1000 patient days). Knowledge of how to collect data to form rates is essential.	• Medication errors per 100 admissions • Ventilator-associated pneumonias per 1000 vent days • Total falls per 1000 patient days • Total readmits per 1000 discharges

Deciding If a Special Cause Is Present

The beauty of the Shewhart control chart lies in its simplicity. It requires little data (about 20 data points to construct a reliable chart), is easy to read, and allows you to determine very quickly if special cause variation is present in your data. Control charts, according to Pyzdek (1990:90), "are an operational definition of a special cause."

For decades the Western Electric *Statistical Quality Control Handbook* (1985) has served as the standard reference for the special cause tests. In fact, the tests are usually referred to as the "Western Electric tests for detecting special cause." Although there are dozens of tests to detect special causes, most experts in the field of SPC maintain that only a few of the tests are essential for a basic understanding of what the chart is trying to tell you. Consider the following passage from Wheeler (1995) on this issue:

> Shewhart used Detection Rule One.
>
> David Chambers often remarked that "No data set could stand up to the scrutiny of all of the detection rules in the Western Electric Handbook."
>
> Irving Burr recommended the use of no more than Detection Rules One and Four. Ellis Ott essentially recommended the use of Detection Rules One, Two and Four. Lloyd Nelson recommends the routine use of Detection Rules One and Four, along with his Test 3 (trends) and Test 4 (sawtooths). (139)

Note that the "Detection Rules" referenced in this passage refer to the four classic Western Electric Zone Tests for special cause variation. These terms and the specific tests are described later in this section.

The application of the tests to a control chart begins by dividing the chart into zones. The area between the CL and the UCL is divided into three equal areas or zones. Because the control limits are referred to as *sigma limits,* each zone is the equivalent of one sigma.[10] The area from the CL to the LCL is divided in a similar manner. These zones are labeled C, B, and A, respectively, and emanate outward from the CL. Figure 6.10 provides an example of how a control chart is divided into zones. The creation of zones is a very simple manipulation that can be achieved easily with any of the existing SPC software programs.

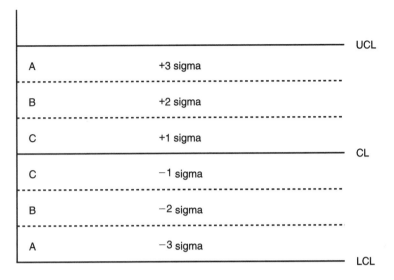

▲ **FIGURE 6.10** Dividing a control chart into zones

All the tests to detect special causes are organized under the general heading of "tests for unnatural patterns." This phrase is referring to the fact that when data points do not represent a random array of data, then the unnatural patterns will reveal special causes that have basically knocked the process out of whack and made it unstable and unpredictable. A natural pattern of data, for example, will include the following three characteristics:

- Most of the data points are near the solid centerline

- A few of the data points spread out and approach the control limits

- None of the data points (or at least only a very rare and occasional point) exceeds the control limits (Western Electric 1985:24)

A natural pattern of data will have these three characteristics simultaneously. One of the first signals that a process has special causes, therefore, is the absence of any one of these characteristics.

The specific tests for special causes are typically divided into two categories: (1) tests for instability, and (2) tests for other unnatural patterns (Western Electric, 1985:23–31). There are eight basic tests for special causes that are typically discussed in most textbooks on SPC. Although some of these tests are not found frequently in healthcare situations, I believe it is helpful to at least be aware of the range of special causes that could arise. After reviewing the tests, I will identify a smaller subset that I have found to be most useful.

Tests for Instability

The tests for instability include:

- **Test #1: A single data point that exceeds the upper or lower control limit** (Figure 6.11). This is usually referred to as a 3-sigma violation and is the most easily recognized of all the tests. This is the only test that Shewhart used to identify special causes and the reason why Wheeler (1995) stated that "Shewhart used Detection Rule One." Some texts refer to a single data point that exceeds 3-sigma as a "freak" point. Irrespective of the term being used, this is a clear signal that the variation of this single point is very different from the variation demonstrated by the rest of the data points on the chart.

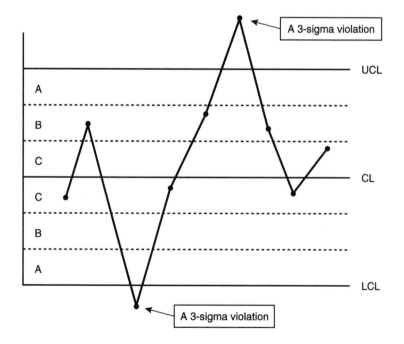

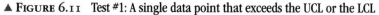

▲ Figure 6.11   Test #1: A single data point that exceeds the UCL or the LCL

- **Test #2: Two out of three consecutive data points that fall in Zone A or beyond** (Figure 6.12). In this particular case, the data point not in Zone A can be anywhere on the chart. The deciding criterion is whether two out of the three data points are Zone A or beyond on the same side of the centerline.

- **Test #3: Four out of five consecutive data points that fall in Zone B or beyond** (Figure 6.12). Like Test #2, the data point not in Zone B can be anywhere on the chart. The key is having four of the points in Zone B or beyond on the same side of the centerline.

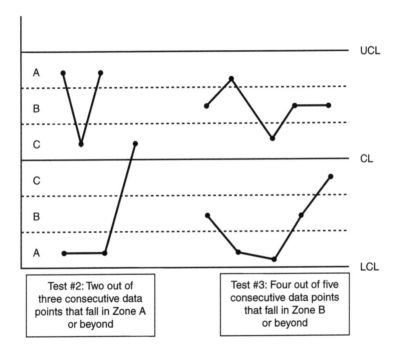

▲ **FIGURE 6.12** Test #2 and Test #3 for special causes

- **Test #4: Eight or more consecutive data points that fall in Zone C or beyond** (Figure 6.13). Most writers refer to this as "eight consecutive data points on the same side of the centerline." When such a pattern is observed, it usually signals that there has been a shift in the process. This test is a variation on run chart Test #2.

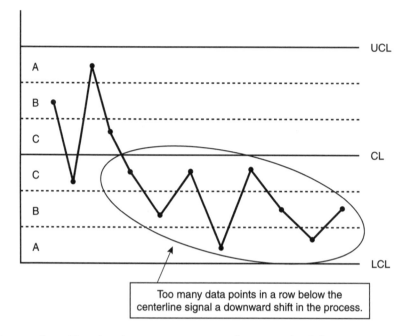

▲ FIGURE 6.13 Test #4: Eight or more consecutive data points that fall in Zone C or beyond

Tests for Other Unnatural Patterns

In addition to the tests for instability, there are a number of other tests designed to detect what the Western Electric handbook calls other unnatural patterns. These tests are applied to the entire chart:

- **Test #5: Stratification occurs when 15 or more consecutive data points falls in Zone C, either above or below the centerline** (Figure 6.14). This test is not found very often in healthcare. When it does occur, however, it is a very clear indication that the process has too little variation. A pattern of stratification is also known as "hugging the centerline" because there is a run of 15 or more data points within one sigma of the centerline (i.e., in Zone C). Stratification occurs most often because the data collection plan was flawed. For example, you will find a stratification pattern when two separate distributions of data have been collected (e.g., day shift turnaround time was combined with night shift turnaround time) or the sample of data points was drawn from two different distributions of data. The principles behind this test are the same ones that apply to run chart Test #4.

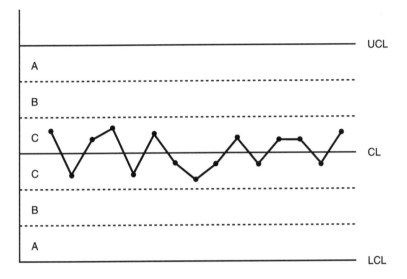

▲ **FIGURE 6.14** Test #5: Stratification occurs when 15 or more consecutive data points fall in Zone C, either above or below the centerline

- **Test #6: Eight or more consecutive data points on both sides of the centerline with none of the points in Zone C** (Figure 6.15). This test is classified as a "mixture." It is identified when the data points avoid the centerline and have a tendency to cluster close to the control limits. In this case the data do not form a bell-shaped curve but rather tend to create a bimodal distribution. This test identifies conditions that are just the opposite situation from Test #5.

- **Test #7: Systematic variation will be observed when a long series of data points (usually 14 or more) are high, then low, then high, then low, without any interruption in this regular pattern** (Figure 6.16). A random process will not have systematic variation. The very nature of a random process requires that it not be systematic or repeating. A systematic pattern of any kind indicates the presence of a systematic variable in either the process or the data (Western Electric 1985:175). This special cause produces the "sawtooth" pattern that Nelson (1985) favors as a principal test of special cause. Most authors define "a long series of data points" as 14 or more consecutive up and down points. The thing to remember with this test is that the data points can fall anywhere on the chart as long as it is point-to-point fluctuation (i.e., up, down, up, down, up, down, and so on).

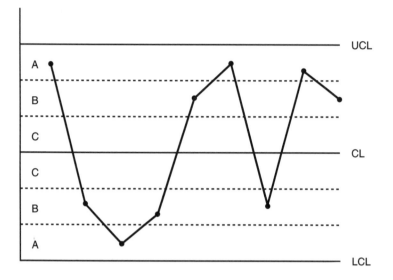

▲ FIGURE 6.15 Test #6: Eight or more consecutive data points on both sides of the centerline with none of the points in Zone C

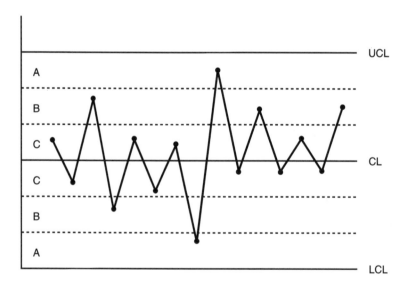

▲ FIGURE 6.16 Test #7: Systematic variation will be observed when a long series of data points are high, then low, then high, then low, without any interruption in this regular pattern

- **Test #8: A trend exists when there is a constantly increasing or decreasing series of data points** (Figure 6.17). The Western Electric handbook does not specify how many data points are needed to identify a trend. They merely indicate that a trend is detected when there are "consecutive data points without a change in direction." Most definitions of a trend use 6 data points constantly increasing or decreasing if you have fewer than 20 data points on your chart. If you have 20 or more data points on your chart, a trend is defined as 7 or more data points constantly going up or down (Pyzdek 1990). When deciding if a trend exists, duplicate points (i.e., repeating values) should be ignored.

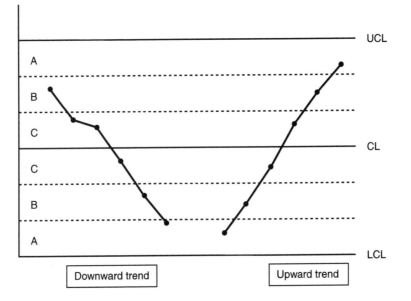

▲ **FIGURE 6.17**   Test #8: A trend exists whenever there is a series of consecutive data points without a change in direction

Although these eight tests are widely used in industry and manufacturing settings, I typically find that a subset of these tests is quite adequate for most healthcare applications.[11] From my experience, I have found that the eight tests described above can be grouped into three categories for healthcare applications:

Category 1: Tests that occur most often in healthcare applications

- Test #1: A single data point that exceeds the upper or lower control limit.
- Test #4: Eight or more consecutive data points that fall in Zone C or beyond.
- Test #8: A trend exists when there is a constantly increasing or decreasing series of data points.

Category 2: Tests occurring with less frequency in healthcare applications

- Test #2: Two out of three consecutive data points that fall in Zone A or beyond.
- Test #3: Four out of five consecutive data points that fall in Zone B or beyond.

Category 3: Tests that do not occur very often in healthcare applications

- Test #5: Stratification occurs when 15 or more consecutive data points fall in Zone C, either above or below the centerline.
- Test #6: Eight or more consecutive data points on both sides of the centerline with none of the points in Zone C, which is known as "mixture."
- Test #7: Systematic variation will be observed when a long series of data points (usually 14 or more) are high, then low, then high, then low, without any interruption in this regular pattern.

Now that you have familiarity with the basic ideas behind the control charts, the next step is to apply this knowledge to your own indicators. The study questions in Figure 6.18 will serve as a quick overview of some of the central issues related to control chart development and as a test of your current knowledge. If you struggle with some of the questions, you can review the material presented in this chapter and then explore some of the listed references for additional explanations. In learning about control charts I have found it very useful to read how different authors have described the charts and their use. Another way to enhance your knowledge base is to attend workshops on SPC. The ASQ, for example, offers public seminars on SPC. You may want to check with your local ASQ chapter to see when such courses will be offered. Finally, if you have the opportunity to attend a local or national quality conference, make sure that you sit in on sessions that are discussing control charts and SPC. Hearing about control charts from multiple sources will be very beneficial.

1. When is it appropriate to use control charts? Should I use them in place of descriptive statistics? What is the relationship between control charts and tests of significance?

2. How many data points do I need to make a chart? What do I do if I do not have enough data?

3. Which is better, attributes or variables data?

4. What is a subgroup? Do I have to have one to make a control chart? Can I make a chart with only single data points?

5. Do my subgroups have to be equal when I make X-bar & R or X-bar & S charts?

6. Much of the data I get are not dated. Does it really matter if the data points are not in chronological order?

7. I still don't get this distinction between a standard deviation and a sigma limit. Why aren't they the same? Does it really matter? My spreadsheet software will give me a standard deviation. Why can't I just multiply this number by 3 and then add and subtract this product from the mean to get the control limits?

8. Why do I have to use 3 sigma control limits? Why can't I use 2, or maybe 1.5 sigma limits?

9. Do defects add up to make defectives or is it the other way around?

10. When I make a p-chart, does the size of the denominator make a difference? Can I have, for example, 4 or 5 in my denominator?

11. What is the difference between a proportion, a percentage, and a rate?

12. Should I view common cause variation as "good" variation and special cause variation as "bad" variation?

13. Do I really have to investigate a special cause? Can't I just remove the data point from the chart and get on with making changes?

14. Are you serious about calling a trend 6 or 7 data points constantly increasing or decreasing? I can't afford to wait until 6 or 7 patients die in surgery before taking action.

15. What do I do when I am looking at relatively rare events? In these cases, I do not have enough data to plot a continuous variable because the occurrence of the event (e.g., sternal wound infections or maternal death after a C-section) is discontinuous and rather rare.

16. It is impractical to make these charts by hand. What software is out there to help us through the drudgery of chart construction and which one works best?

▲ FIGURE 6.18   Control chart study questions

You can also test your knowledge of the various charts by completing the control chart self-test presented in Figure 6.19. When I teach my one and two day classes on control chart applications, I give the participants this exercise

Subgroup	Type of data	Situation	Chart
_____	_____	You know the number of late dietary trays each day and the total number of trays produced each day.	_____
_____	_____	The clinic receptionist notes the time of check-in for each patient. Physicians note the time when they first see the patient in the exam room. An analyst compiles the data daily and reports total patients and the number who had to wait more than 30 minutes.	_____
_____	_____	An analyst pulls a sample of 50 orthopedic surgery charts per week and counts all discrepancies from standard documentation practice.	_____
_____	_____	Each medication order is checked against five potential types of errors. You also have the total number of orders placed each week.	_____
_____	_____	You have data on average length of stay by week for a particular DRG.	_____
_____	_____	A manager wishes to analyze the total number of surgeries done each week in the OR suites.	_____
_____	_____	You are interested in the average time patients spend in your waiting room, so every day a student randomly selects 8 patients (throughout the day) and measures their actual waiting time.	_____
_____	_____	ER has data on turnaround time for 20 lab orders each day.	_____
_____	_____	You know the number of people who come to the ER complaining of chest pain each week and the number who are actually diagnosed with an MI or unstable angina.	_____

▲ FIGURE 6.19 You make the call!

to complete in class. It gives them a chance to "make the call" and test their knowledge of control charts. The situations listed in this table are taken from actual teams I have had the opportunity to facilitate or advise. Start the exercise by determining the subgroup. Remember that the subgroup is the label for the horizontal axis and reflects how you have organized your data (e.g., by day or week). Next, decide if you have variables or attributes data. Finally, on the far right of the page, list the chart you think is most appropriate for this situation. You may want to refer to the control chart decision tree shown in Figure 6.6 to assist you in thinking through the chart options.[12]

Making the Appropriate Management Decisions

At some point after reading various control chart books and listening to others explain control chart theory, you will all of a sudden proclaim in a clear voice, "I think I get it!" Once you reach this point, it is time to start applying this knowledge to actual improvement opportunities. But be careful. I have seen some people become so enthusiastic about the control charts that they start making graphs on any process that produces data. It is at this stage that I remember an old adage—if you give a child a hammer, the whole world looks like a nail. Control charts play a valuable and central role in all quality improvement efforts. It is important to realize, however, what they can and cannot do.

First, appreciate the fact that the control charts do not answer the following questions:

- What is the reason for a special cause?
- Should a common cause process be improved?
- What should I do to improve the process?

The answers to these questions do not come from the charts or statistics. They come from the will, ideas, and knowledge of the team that owns the process being measured. I have seen too many teams feel that once they have created a control chart, their work is finished. I think that this occurs because the chart is a tangible thing that can be pointed to and shown to others. Improvement strategies, on the other hand, are not as finite or discrete. Developing improvement strategies is actually much more difficult than mastering control chart theory and construction because you are dealing with people and behaviors, not numbers.

Second, after you make a chart and decide if the process exhibits common or special cause variation, you then need to decide how you are going to approach the variation you have identified. All improvement strategies emanate from an understanding of variation. If the process exhibits special cause variation, the appropriate decision is to investigate the special cause(s) and determine why they have made the process unstable and unpredictable. Just as we would investigate a patient safety event (i.e., a sentinel event) by conducting a root cause analysis, we also need to do the same thing with a special cause on the control chart. Ignoring a special cause will guarantee that it will rear its ugly head at some point in the future. We cannot predict exactly when a special cause will occur, but you can be sure that it will pop up again if you choose to ignore it.[13]

The other aspect of a special cause is that every special cause is not negative and undesirable. Remember that special causes are not inherently bad. The key point is that special causes make a process *unstable* and *unpredictable*. It is very likely that you will observe a special cause that you want to emulate—for example, when lab turnaround time is much faster than it has been for the past 15 days. In this case, you want to investigate why the process worked so well on these days and see if these conditions can be replicated.

Common causes, on the other hand, are not inherently good. Common cause variation merely means that the process is stable and predictable (i.e., predictable within the boundaries of the UCL and LCL). Just as you can have a special cause that you might want to emulate, you can also have common cause variation that is unacceptable (e.g., when a patient's blood pressure is running at a very high level and staying there, or when the wait time to see the family physician is consistent and predictable but at such a high level that it is unacceptable).

There are two other mistakes people make when confronted with common and special causes of variation. The first is to treat normal variation as if it were special. In this case, there is a tendency to overreact to one or two data points (usually the ones that do not fit the person's view of reality) and then underreact to other data points. This places you in the "good data/bad data" dilemma. When you do this with a common cause process, you end up tampering and increasing variation (see the explanation of the funnel demonstration described earlier in this chapter for additional details on this point). The second mistake people make is to change the process when confronted with a special cause (instead of investigating why it occurred in the first place). For example, if a patient waited 15 hours in the emergency department before they were admitted to an inpatient unit, and it so happens that this person was the mayor's wife, there could be an overreaction to this special cause when the mayor complains vigorously to the hospital CEO. Changing the entire process because of one special cause will waste resources (people's efforts and money).

A classic example of changing a process when confronted with a special cause happened in the summer of 1988 when the Environmental Protection Agency (EPA) overreacted to an event that had never occurred before. Medical waste unexplainably started washing up on the beaches of New Jersey. Beachgoers became very worried about the possibility of contracting AIDS from these materials. The local hospitals in and around New York City were singled out as the sources of the medical waste material. This was clearly a special cause. The press made it sound as though the local hospitals were actually depositing the medical waste on the beach. In reality, this special cause was related more to the trash removal services in the area than to the producers of medical waste. It turns out that once the waste was collected, barge haulers took the material and dumped it in the ocean. For a variety of reasons, the barge haulers did not dump the waste as far out into the ocean as they usually did, and the currents then picked up the debris and washed it up on the New Jersey beaches. Instead of investigating the origin of the problem, however, the EPA changed its regulations relating to the ways in which hospitals collect and dispose of medical waste. Because of this one special cause, all healthcare providers in the United States are now required to dispose of their medical waste in special "red bags." This "red bag waste," as it is known, must be incinerated or microwaved and then augured to make all the material indecipherable. Estimates are that an average hospital spends the equivalent of a CAT scanner each year in complying with the red bag waste regulations. Every day you will read or hear about examples of how someone or some organization changed a process because they failed to investigate the origin of a special cause.

Quality improvement starts with making the correct decision about the variation that lives in the data. Walter Shewhart introduced the control chart and the notions of common and special causes of variation in 1924 (Hare 2003). Since then SPC has become the foundation for all successful quality improvement initiatives. It is a key component of the Baldrige criteria, Six Sigma, and ISO. Without a clear understanding of variation and its causes, however, individuals and organizations will continue to suffer from numerical illiteracy.

Notes

1. I want to acknowledge and thank my good friend and colleague Dr. Ray Carey for finding this example. We have used this story in our public seminars for many years but never placed it in print. It is a wonderful demonstration of the tendency to attribute special cause characteristics to common cause variation. I appreciate Dr. Carey's keen eye for observing examples of variation in everyday life.

2. It is interesting to note that the deficit did demonstrate a special cause in the months following the *Wall Street Journal* article of September 19, 1997. Dr. Carey continued to track the deficit and discovered that the next four months after July 1997 continued upward. When these four data points were combined with the last two data points shown in Figure 6.2, an upward trend was identified (i.e., six data points constantly going up). If the newspaper had taken the time to understand variation and track it properly, they would have had a real story.

3. I worked for an organization a number of years ago that perfected this behavior. The project I was managing would be above the expected budget one month and below it the next. The individual responsible for "leading" our area was probably one of the most numerically illiterate individuals I have ever met. Not only did I have to write a detailed justification for why the project was over the expected monthly average but I also had to sit through a ceremonial tongue-lashing for allowing the expected budget threshold to be breached. I would be told I was a poor manager for allowing this to happen and that it would have a negative impact on my performance review if it continued. I found it curious that I was never praised for being a good manager when the expenses were below the expected monthly average. When this did occur, which was about 6 months out of 12, I was merely told that I was doing

what was expected of me. Well, I got very tired of this numerical illiteracy and decided to prepare six memos that provided different (and very compelling) reasons why the expenses were greater than expected. Every time the breach occurred, which again was about half the year, I would select a memo that had not been used in a while, date it, and send it on to you-know-who. This cut down significantly on the writing process but did not help the tongue-lashing aspect. That component, unfortunately, continued and quickly motivated me to find an organization that had a better understanding of variation.

4. There is frequent confusion over the difference between the mean and the median. They are both measures of central tendency (i.e., they identify where a distribution of data is centered), but they are different. The mean is the arithmetic average (you add up all the numbers and divide by the total number of data points). The median, on the other hand, is the midpoint of a distribution of data points. This is the numerical value that divides the data set exactly in half, the 50th percentile. The run chart uses the median as a center line, but the control chart uses the mean as the center line.

5. When data points fall right on the median, you cannot say if they are above or below this value. It is as if they have not decided which way they want to go. The basic premise of the run chart is that we must know how many data points are *above* the median and how many are *below* the median. Data points *on* the median are of no value in evaluating run charts, so we drop them from the analysis.

6. The traditional statistical use of process capability (C_p) is to indicate whether or not the process can meet the predetermined specifications (Blank 1998). There are numerous variations on the C_p statistic, all of which are designed to help the quality control researcher eliminate special causes and get the process to perform as closely as possible to the expectations of the customer (i.e., the specifications). I have never calculated a C_p statistic on healthcare indicators or clinical outcome measures. Healthcare simply does not function at the same level of specificity as the manufacturing industry. So when I use the term process capability I am using it in a general sense to describe the variation in the process as defined by the mean (center line) and the UCL and

LCL. These numbers define what the process is capable of performing.

7. When Dr. Ray Carey and I first started teaching control chart applications to healthcare professionals in 1992, we taught the traditional list of seven control charts. In 1995 we wrote a book that described these seven charts and their use (Carey and Lloyd 2001). In December 2002 Dr. Carey and I taught a minicourse and two workshops on control charts at the 14th National Forum on Quality Improvement in Health Care sponsored by the IHI. This was the first time in the 12 years that we have been teaching for the IHI that we reduced the number of charts we teach from 7 to 5. The sessions were well received, and the participants found the more simplified approach to be appealing. The two charts we dropped were the X-bar & R chart and the np-chart. Our reasoning for doing this is that the X-bar & S chart can be used in any situation that calls for the X-bar & R chart, and the np-chart (a count of defectives) requires equal subgroups (denominators), which do not happen very often in healthcare settings. The p-chart can be used effectively in any situation that does produce equal denominators. Readers should also consult Dr. Carey's 2003 book to review his discussion on this topic.

8. The control chart examples presented in this chapter have been developed to demonstrate the five different charts. The substantive importance of the charts is not the focus of this chapter. The charts have been developed for heuristic purposes, and the clinical or operational impacts of the indicators presented on the charts are not the primary objective in this chapter. Analysis and interpretation of control charts are addressed in Chapter 7.

9. The idea for creating this table came from Dr. James Benneyan of Northeastern University in Boston. In a paper entitled "Design, Use, and Preferences of Statistical Control Charts for Clinical Process Improvement" (September 16, 2001) he used a table to summarize the various charts. After reading this paper, I realized that the table was something I had not used to summarize the control charts. I believe a table format works nicely to augment the utility of the decision tree shown in Figure 6.6. Dr. Benneyan has written extensively on the topic of control charts in healthcare and I would encourage readers to

review his work. He can be reached at the following address: MIME Department, 334 Snell Engineering Center, Northeastern University, Boston, MA 02115; phone 617-373-2975; email benneyan@coe.neu.edu.

10. The term sigma limit is the proper term for the control limits. They are similar to the concept of the standard deviation of a distribution but are not identical. The sigma limits are basically parameters of a process as it lays itself out over time. The standard deviation, on the other hand, is a statistic of a fixed distribution. These differences are subtle and need to be understood so that the appropriate formulae are used to compute the control limits. For example, if you place your data into a spreadsheet, request the standard deviation, multiply it by three, and add and subtract the result from the mean, you will obtain incorrect control limits. Each control chart has a different set of statistical formulae for computing the control limits (Western Electric 1985; Duncan 1986; Montgomery 1991; Wheeler 1995; Carey and Lloyd 2001). None of these formulae use the classic definition of a standard deviation to create the UCL and LCL. If you do not use the appropriate formula for computing a particular chart's limits, you will produce limits that are too wide or too narrow. This will then lead you to making the wrong decision about the variation in your data (i.e., you will see special causes when they do not exist and miss them when they are actually present).

11. In an earlier work (Carey and Lloyd 2001) we identified seven tests from the Western Electric listing that we thought would be useful. As Dr. Carey and I have used these charts over the years, however, we have found that several of the tests were not very relevant to healthcare situations. In Dr. Carey's 2003 book he reduced the initial list of seven tests to the following four: (1) a single data point exceeding either the UCL or LCL (i.e., a 3-sigma violation), (2) two out of three successive data points in zone A or beyond, (3) eight successive data points in a row on the same side of the centerline, and (4) six or more data points constantly increasing or decreasing (i.e., a trend). I agree with Dr. Carey that these represent a minimum core set of decision rules. I have presented the four additional tests in this book in order to acquaint the

reader with the eight basic tests described in most of the classic books on SPC (Duncan 1986; Western Electric, 1985; Wheeler and Chambers, 1992; Montgomery, 1991; Pyzdek, 1990; Wheeler, 1995). I have then grouped the tests into three categories in terms of their utilization in healthcare applications: (1) frequently used tests, (2) tests used rather often, and (3) tests that are not used very often in healthcare applications.

12. The answers to this exercise are as follows:

Subgroup	Type of data	Situation	Chart
Day	Attributes	Late food trays	p-chart
Day	Attributes	Wait time to see the physician	p-chart
Week	Attributes	Orthopedic chart reviews	c-chart
Week	Attributes	Medication errors	u-chart
Week	Variables	Length of stay for a particular DRG	XmR chart (a.k.a. the I-chart)
Week	Variables	Number of surgeries	XmR
Day	Variables	Wait time	X-bar & S
Day	Variables	Turnaround time	X-bar & S
Week	Attributes	Diagnosis of an MI	p-chart

13. There are many good examples of how people have ignored special causes when they first occurred and then decided to deal with them when they popped up again. The terrorist attacks on our nation on September 11 provide a classic example. Several years ago the World Trade Center was bombed by terrorists. Although this seemed to draw the nation's attention for a while, interest in this special cause soon faded into the "old news" category. The September 11 special cause, however, generated a completely different reaction. Our nation mobilized not only to investigate the special cause but also take steps to literally eliminate the origin of the special cause. Now our nation is in a very different state of awareness and vigilance because of this special cause.

References

Benneyan, J. "Design, Use and Performance of Statistical Control Charts for Clinical Process Improvement." Unpublished paper, Northeastern University, September 2001.

Benneyan, J., R Lloyd, and P. Plsek. "Statistical Process Control as a Tool for Research and Health Care Improvement." *Journal of Quality and Safety in Healthcare*, 12:6 (December 2003):458–464.

Blank, R. *The SPC Troubleshooting Guide.* New York: Quality Resources, 1998.

Carey, R. Improving Healthcare with Control Charts. Milwaukee: Quality Press, 2003.

Carey, R., and R. Lloyd. *Measuring Quality Improvement in Healthcare: A Guide to Statistical Process Control Applications.* Milwaukee: Quality Press, 2001.

Deming, W. E. *Out of the Crisis.* Cambridge, Mass.: Massachusetts Institute of Technology Center for Advanced Engineering Study, eighteenth printing, 1992.

Duncan, A. J. *Quality Control and Industrial Statistics.* Homewood, Ill.: Irwin Press, 1986.

Hare, L. "SPC: From Chaos to Wiping the Floor." *Quality Progress* (July 2003): 58–63.

Ishikawa, K. *Guide to Quality Control.* White Plains, N.Y.: Quality Resources, 1989.

Montgomery, D. C. *Introduction to Statistical Quality Control,* (2nd ed.). New York: John Wiley & Sons, 1991.

Nelson, L. "Interpreting Shewhart Average Control Charts." *Journal of Quality Technology* 17 (April 1985):114–116.

Pyzdek, T. *Pyzdek's Guide to SPC. Volume 1: Fundamentals.* Milwaukee: Quality Press, 1990.

Schultz, L. *Profiles in Quality.* New York: Quality Resources, 1994.

Shewhart, W. *Economic Control of Quality of Manufactured Product.* New York: D. Van Nostrand, 1931. Reprint, Milwaukee: Quality Press, 1980.

Western Electric Company. *Statistical Quality Control Handbook.* Indianapolis: AT&T Technologies, Inc., 1985.

Wheeler, D., and D. Chambers. *Understanding Statistical Process Control.* Knoxville, Tenn.: SPC Press, 1992.

Wheeler, D. *Understanding Variation: The Key to Managing Chaos.* Knoxville, Tenn.: SPC Press, 1993.

———. *Advanced Topics in Statistical Process Control.* Knoxville, Tenn.: SPC Press, 1995.

Chapter 7

Applying Quality Measurement Principles

This chapter provides case studies that demonstrate the quality measurement concepts and principles discussed in previous chapters. The intent is to show brief practical applications of these ideas. Some of the case studies are short and address issues related to indicator identification, operational definitions, stratification, and sampling. All of the examples discussed are based on real-life situations that I have encountered with teams. Teams that have given me permission to show their actual data are noted. I have adjusted the data of those who have asked that their actual data not be disclosed. In those instances when a team did not want to have their actual data reported, I asked if I could at least recognize the team members for their creativity and hard work. In nearly all cases the teams agreed to be recognized. There were a few teams that preferred to remain anonymous. I have respected these requests.

Each case study is divided into two sections. First, the quality measurement challenge is described in the situation section. This is followed by a discussion section in which options for remedying the situation are presented. In some cases the discussion section is fairly brief (e.g., if the challenge is to clarify an operational definition). In other cases (e.g., the control chart case studies) the discussion section will go into a little more depth, because the example involves the actual presentation, analysis, and interpretation of data. Finally, note that there is no particular order or clustering of the case studies.

Case Study #1: Predicting a Cardiovascular Event[1]

Situation

The medical director of a 165-member medical group decides to evaluate how well his nuclear medicine–trained cardiologist predicts the need for cardiac catheterization compared to the nuclear medicine–trained radiologists. Inappropriate cardiac catheterization not only place patients at unnecessary levels of risk but also waste valuable resources and physician time that could be directed more appropriately to other patients. The total number of cases referred for possible cardiovascular (CV) concerns constitutes the patient population. From this population, a subset of patients is actually referred for a nuclear medicine thalium treadmill stress test. Once the films are read, a certain number of patients are identified as "high risk" for coronary artery disease. These "high risk" patients are recommended to the cardiologist for cardiac catheterization, a procedure to confirm/refute the initial conclusions obtained from the stress test exam. The research question is "What is the accuracy of the nuclear-trained cardiologist compared to the nuclear-trained radiologists in predicting a cardiac catheterization that shows significant (greater than 50% occlusion) coronary artery disease?" The literature is not definitive on this issue, but the general belief is that the predictive percentage (i.e., true positives) should be somewhere between 70% and 90%.

There are 7 physicians who read the thalium stress tests and make recommendations to proceed or not proceed with a cardiac catheterization. Over the past 18 months, the 7 physicians read a total of 505 films, of which 303 were done in an outpatient setting, with the remaining 202 performed in an inpatient setting. The data for the 7 physicians are presented in Table 7.1. The control chart is presented in Figure 7.1.

▼ TABLE 7.1 Proportion of appropriate catheterizations (CATHS) found to be appropriate by physician

Physician	Films read that were referred for a CATH	CATHS initially thought to be appropriate	CATHS determined to be appropriate after procedure	Proportion of CATHS found to be appropriate
1	77	50	30	0.60
2	69	59	44	0.75
3	85	49	30	0.61
4	58	35	28	0.80
5	63	56	23	0.41
6	81	57	32	0.56
7	72	41	34	0.83
Totals	505	347	221	0.64

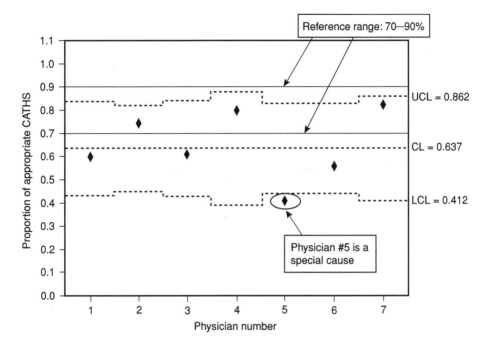

▲ FIGURE 7.1   Proportion of appropriate catheterizations by physician (p-chart)

Discussion

- When looking at an outcome that is either correct or not correct, what type of data have we collected, attributes or variables?

  Indicators that are based on only two possible outcomes (correct, not correct) form a binomial distribution, which is a form of attributes data.

- Do we have equal or unequal subgroups?

  The subgroups are of unequal size because each physician reviewed a different number of films each month.

- What is the preferred chart for these data?

  The preferred chart for this type of data is the p-chart. This chart requires a numerator and a denominator and produces a percentage or proportion. In this case, the numerator is the number of catheterizations that were determined to be appropriate (i.e., the cardiologist confirmed greater than 50% stenosis). The denominator is the number of catheterizations performed. The objective is to be as close to 100% as possible, which means that every catheterization that was done was required and determined to be appropriate by the cardiologist. Every time a catheterization is performed and it is discovered after the procedure that the patient did not need the catheterization, this is considered to be a defective, which is the appropriate concept for a p-chart.

- Why are the dots not connected by a line?

  The dots are not connected because the seven physicians do not represent a process displayed over time. Most control chart examples show some unit of time (e.g., day, month, or patients in chronological order) displayed along the horizontal axis. This is the traditional format for a control chart. In this example, the horizontal axis displays the individual physician numbered 1–7. This p-chart is known, therefore, as a "comparative chart" because it is comparing each physician's percentage of correctly interpreted films at a fixed point in time. Prior to making this comparative chart, a p-chart for each physician's performance over the last 18 months should have been prepared. These physician-specific charts (not shown) should all reflect common cause variation before proceeding to make the aggregated comparative chart shown in Figure 7.1. If one or more of the physician-specific charts contained special causes, then the comparative p-chart should not be constructed. The reasoning behind this decision is straightforward: if the constituent parts (i.e., the individual physicians) reflect special cause variation, then the aggregated comparative chart will similarly reflect an unstable process. For additional applications of the comparative chart see Carey (2003).

- Is there any value in knowing the numbers of films done on an outpatient and an inpatient basis? How could these data be used to further our understanding of the accuracy of the reading process?

  The data in Table 7.1 show the total films and procedures associated with each physician. Once the overall pattern has been analyzed, the next step would be to see if there are any notable differences between the accuracy percentages for inpatient and outpatient settings. Stopping any analysis after analyzing only the totals can be a big mistake. Stratification (discussed in Chapter 3) enables you to drill down to the constituent parts of a process. In this case, there could be differences between the inpatient and outpatient settings because of differences in the severity of the patients.

- What do you conclude about the seven physicians who read the films? Do they form a common cause system or are there special causes present?

  Figure 7.1 does demonstrate a special cause. The positive predictive percentage for Physician #5 is below the LCL. The remaining six physicians' percentages all fall between their UCL and LCL. Note that because this is a p-chart, each dot (which represents a physician) has its own control limits. The width of these limits is based on each physician's denominator (total number of films read that were initially thought to be appropriate for a catheterization). The more films read, the tighter the control limits, while the smaller the denominator, the wider the limits. Physician #4, for example, had the widest limits because he had only 35 films as a denominator. On the other hand, Physician #2 had the largest denominator with 59. Even though Physician #5 falls below the LCL, this does not mean that this physician's performance is "bad" and that of the other six physicians is "good." Good and bad are not appropriate concepts for interpreting control charts. The more appropriate terms are stable and predictable (common cause variation) versus unstable and unpredictable (special cause variation). With one physician falling below the LCL, therefore, the primary interpretation of this chart is that when it comes to the percentage of positive predictive outcomes, this group of physicians does not exhibit common cause variation. The secondary interpretation is that one physician's performance (i.e., Physician #5) is notably different from the rest (i.e., this physician is a special cause). Why he or she is different or if this difference is clinically meaningful remains to be seen. Remember that control charts do not tell you the reasons why a process is unstable or not performing in an acceptable manner. The control chart only tells you (1) if the process is stable and predictable and (2) what impact an intervention had on the performance of the process.

- Of what value is the reference range for positive predictive percentage accuracy (70–90%)?

  The reference range provides an opportunity to see how well this process is performing against an established norm. These numbers also can be viewed as the lower specification limit (LSL = 70%) and upper specification limit (USL = 90%) for the process. In this case, if the UCL and

LCL coincide with the USL and LSL, then the process would be performing in line with the expectations for the process. When the control limits are wider than the specification limits, then the process is not performing in line with the expectations for the process. Conversely, if the process control limits are less than the specification limits, then the process is functioning better than expected. As you can see from Figure 7.1, only three physicians are performing within the reference range of 70–90%. The remaining four are performing below the lower specification limit of 70%, and one of these has fallen below the LCL. The challenge in this case is deciding whether the specification limits (i.e., 70–90%) are clinically appropriate. For example, this range allows for 10% error because 90% is the upper specification limit. Why would we not expect this process to function in the range of 70–100%? Why was 70% selected as the minimum acceptable standard? When a team starts to discuss these questions, then they have moved into the issues discussed in Chapter 4 (i.e., setting targets and goals). The control chart does not necessarily answer all the questions, but it should certainly serve as a foundation for raising questions.

Case Study #2: Sampling Central Line Infections[2]

Situation

The director of infection control is interested in getting a clear understanding of the central line infections occurring within your hospital, so each day she and her staff review the charts that have central lines, looking for any sign of infection. Pathology then cultures any suspicious lines to see if an infection is present. Each day the patient has a line in place is counted as 1 central line day. Because this is a very time-consuming task, they have been considering doing a sample of the central lines but are concerned that they might miss something. After attending a national infection control conference, the director of infection control tells her staff what she heard about sampling at one of the conference's workshops. The presenter told the group that the easiest method of sampling for central line infections is to take a sample of 5 random days during the month and then review all the central lines on these 5 days. Then take the total number of central line infections found in these 5 days and multiple this number by 6 to get the estimated number of central line infections for the month (the reasoning being that 5 days $\times$ 6 = 30 days in the month). The total number of central line days could be estimated in a similar manner. Does this seem like a reasonable approach to sampling?

Discussion

Although I do not disagree with the idea of possibly applying sampling to this indicator, I do not think that taking a random sample of days is the correct path to follow. The unit of analysis is the patient, not the day of the week. So if we have 15 patients with central lines this week, we could randomly pick a sample of these 15 to track each day (e.g., 3–5 randomly picked patients each day). The thing I really disagree with is multiplying the number of central line infections obtained through a sample by a number (e.g., 6, as the speaker at the conference suggested) to get the estimated monthly number of central line infections. This could produce a very misleading estimate. I believe you would be better off by just picking a random sample of patients (possibly stratified) and then applying the review criteria for central line infections to this sample of patients. Finally, given the seriousness of central line infections, it might be advisable not to apply sampling to this indicator. This may be more time consuming but will produce more valid and reliable results.

Case Study #3: Sampling Medicare Insurance Audits[3]

Situation

As manager of performance improvement, you receive a call from a woman in registration asking how many Medicare insurance audits she should do in a month to feel confident about having 95% accuracy. In a single day there are almost 200 new cases that are eligible for an audit. You think this seems like one of those questions that you really cannot answer with a single number. You remember reading in a statistics book that a "reasonable" sampling distribution starts to form somewhere between 25 and 30 observations. So you suggest this as a starting point for a monthly sample but add that she should pull as many as time permits when weighed against her other responsibilities.

Discussion

Her goal to be at "95% accuracy" is not really the issue here. People often confuse accuracy, reliability, and significance. I am not sure what the woman in registration means when she says she wants 95% accuracy, but she is probably thinking something to the effect that if she pulled repeated samples, they would be "representative" of the entire population 95% of the time. At any rate, the manager of performance improvement needs to help this person understand what sampling can and cannot do. His initial statement of 25–30 out of the 200 is a very good starting recommendation. The manager was also correct in asking what is practical. There is no magic number here. Sampling should be structured around a very simple guideline—pull as much as you must and as little as you dare. I also think that stratification would be a good addition to this discussion. Are all the charts the same? They are not all the same, so let us look at how to divide them into more relevant buckets (e.g., medical versus surgical; male versus female; age splits; complications; or total costs). The registration staff should also be asked what it is that they are trying to measure. All too often, people want to start collecting data without a clear picture of what it is they expect the data to do for them. What is the specific indicator or indicators that are being assessed? The identification of the objective for conducting the audit might play a critical role in setting up the sample design. Most of the time, questions about sampling are more about logic than statistics.

Case Study #4: Tracking Patient Falls

Situation

In February 2003 your facility introduced a new program to reduce the number of patient falls. As risk manager, the question you have been asked repeatedly is "Did this new program have the desired impact?" To answer this question, you decide to take advantage of the knowledge and experience of the team that created the new program. They have been working on this process since February 2001 and have (1) developed a standardized operational definition of a patient fall (which was probably a major accomplishment in and of itself), (2) developed and implemented an ongoing data collection plan, (3) established a baseline, and (4) prepared the c-charts shown in Figures 7.2 and 7.3. Did the falls prevention program make a difference? If you think it did, how did you arrive at this conclusion?

Discussion

Each data point on the chart represents the total number of falls occurring within the facility each month. Notice that both charts show the number of falls both *before* (the historical baseline) and after the falls prevention program. Finally, note that the mean and control limits on Figure 7.2 are based on the 24-month period from February 2001 through January 2003. The remaining 8 weeks of data are being compared to the centerline and control limits for the baseline period. This is known as "freezing" the control limits. This was done in order to compare the preprogram falls with the number of falls after the program was introduced.

The left side of Figure 7.2 represents the baseline or history of the falls process prior to implementation of the prevention program (February 2001 through January 2003). During this period the process was stable and predictable (common cause variation) with a mean (C-bar) of 53, an UCL of 75, and an LCL of 31. This means the process can be expected to produce, on the average, roughly 53 falls each month, though it is capable of producing as few as 31 or as many as 75 falls each month because of normal variation in the process.

The right side of Figure 7.2 demonstrates the impact of the falls prevention program on the falls process. During each month after the falls prevention program was introduced (February 2003 through September 2003), the process produced fewer falls than the mean number of falls during the baseline period. These eight data points below the centerline constitute a special cause (i.e., a signal that there has been a downward shift in the process). But in this case it was a desirable special cause since the falls prevention program was expected to reduce the number of falls.

Now that the process has shifted to a more acceptable level of performance (i.e., a lower number of falls each month), we can compute control limits just for the new process. Figure 7.3 shows what are called historical control limits. In this case, we have two sets of control limits: one for the old process and one for the new process. The new process also shows us that the mean is lower (45 falls per month) and that the control limits are a little closer together (UCL = 65.6 and LCL = 25.2).

The information presented on this control chart does not tell the team whether or not it should continue its efforts to reduce the number of patient falls. It merely tells the team that the initial efforts have been successful, and that the current process produces fewer falls per month than the baseline

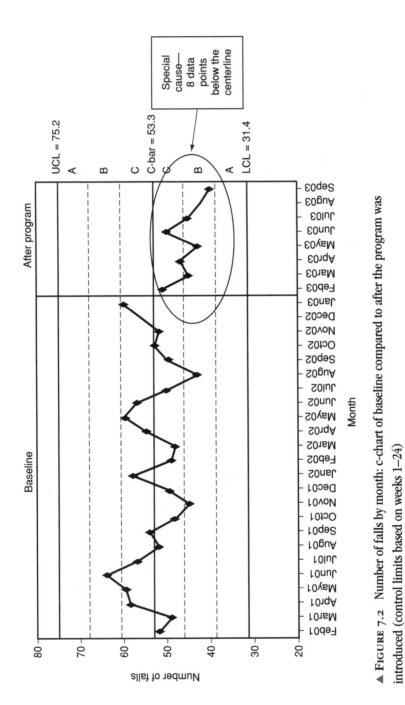

▲ FIGURE 7.2   Number of falls by month: c-chart of baseline compared to after the program was introduced (control limits based on weeks 1–24)

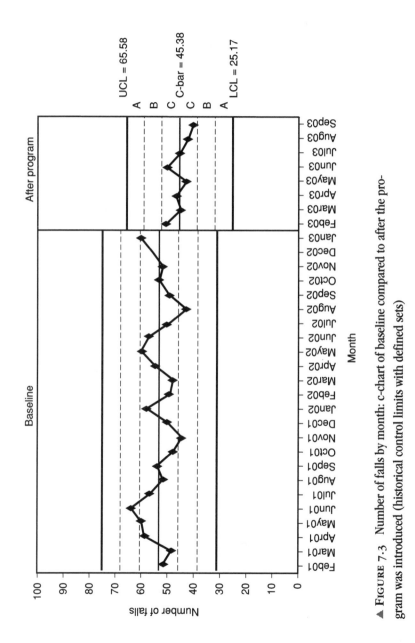

▲ **FIGURE 7.3** Number of falls by month: c-chart of baseline compared to after the program was introduced (historical control limits with defined sets)

process. Should the team decide to introduce another intervention to further reduce the number of falls? The answer to this question lies with the team. As owners of the process, they need to decide if the process is capable of further improvement and if the resources are available to support this work. If the facility is part of a system, for example, maybe they can obtain comparative reference data (norms) and see how their performance compares to that of the other facilities in the system. If such data do exist, then there is an opportunity for internal benchmarking. The team would also be well advised to continue monitoring the number of patient falls over the coming months, even if they decided not to introduce any further improvement efforts. The reason is that the team should be responsible for the performance of the process and confident that the observed improvement is maintained during future months. The control chart provides the conceptual and statistical foundation for doing this.

Case Study #5: Pressure Ulcer Prevention[4]

Situation

You are the director of care management at a 250-bed hospital and have become curious about the incidence and prevalence of pressure ulcers within the hospital. Pressure ulcers seem to be one of those topics that everyone takes for granted. It is not unusual, for example, to hear staff say, "They will occur and there is not a lot we can do about it." You believe, however, that there are some things that can be done to improve clinical outcomes and save the hospital money. You begin by preparing a brief summary of the two types of pressure ulcers. The first is nosocomial or hospital-acquired pressure ulcers (incidence). The second is known as community-acquired pressure ulcers (prevalence). This summary is distributed to the inpatient nursing staff, the physical therapists, and the staff at your skilled nursing facility to increase awareness and start a dialogue on this topic. Next you develop a measurement plan. The primary outcome measure is the percentage of patients that develop nosocomial pressure ulcers during their admission (the incidence indicator).

The CQI team created to work on reducing hospital-acquired pressure ulcers decides that it will introduce a new type of mattress with a pressure-relieving surface and a downward-slanted heel slope. They also begin working on developing a new protocol for assessing patients and preventing pressure ulcers before they develop. Based upon a national comparative norm of 7%, you set off to establish a baseline for the incidence of nosocomial pressure ulcers. After establishing a baseline, you will implement the improvement strategies and see if they have the desired impact. Figure 7.4 shows the baseline data, and Figure 7.5 shows the baseline and the process after the two interventions (the new mattresses and the pressure ulcer prevention protocol) were introduced. What conclusions do you make about the effectiveness of these two interventions? Did one work better than the other?

Discussion

Figure 7.4 shows the baseline for the incidence of nosocomial pressure ulcers. Note that this is presented as a proportion, not as a percentage.[5] The p-chart reflects common cause variation with a process average of 0.24 or 24%. The process could operate as high as the UCL (or .449 or 45%) or as low as 0.033 (3.3%). Because the process exhibits common cause variation, we can expect the process to continue to perform within these parameters unless (1) an unexpected special cause enters the picture and knocks the process out of whack, or (2) we plan an intervention to move the process to a new level of performance.

Because the team chose to follow the second option (i.e., the improvement route), we are now curious to see if the interventions did have a positive impact on nosocomial pressure ulcer prevention. Figure 7.5 provides the answer to this question. This chart displays the baseline data shown in the previous chart (i.e., weeks 1–17) and the proportion of nosocomial pressure ulcers after the team introduced the interventions during week 18. The UCL, LCL, and CL are all computed on the baseline period (note that the averages in Figure 7.4 and Figure 7.5 are the same). When you use the UCL, LCL, and CL from the baseline period and extend them into the future for comparison against the new data (weeks 18–28), this is known as "freezing" the control limits. It is quite clear that the process has shifted to a new level of performance. This is confirmed by having 8 or more data points below the CL (there were actually 13 weeks in a row that the proportion of nosocomial pressure ulcers was below the baseline average).

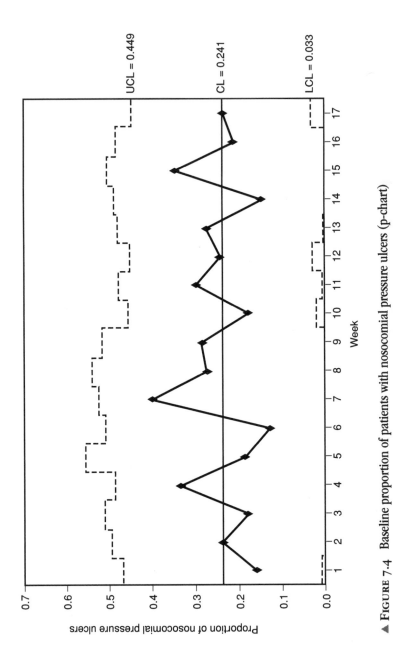

▲ FIGURE 7.4 Baseline proportion of patients with nosocomial pressure ulcers (p-chart)

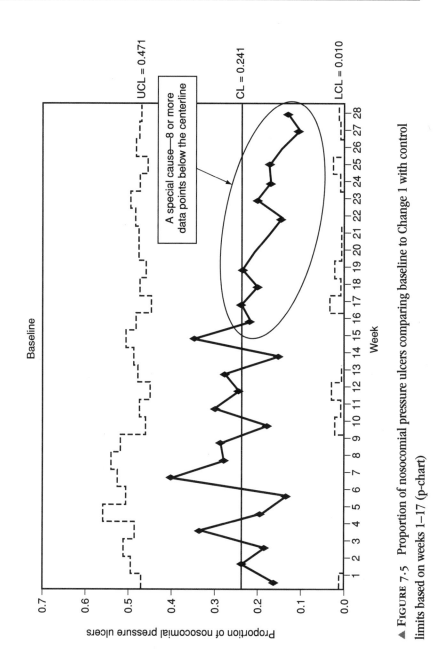

▲ FIGURE 7.5 Proportion of nosocomial pressure ulcers comparing baseline to Change 1 with control limits based on weeks 1–17 (p-chart)

Figure 7.6 displays the final step in presenting the data for this case study. Notice that this chart has two sets of control limits. The left side of the chart is the same baseline we observed in the previous chart. The right side of the chart (labeled Change 1) reveals what happened to the process after the interventions were implemented. Not only did the control limits narrow but we also notice that the centerline or process average has dropped to 0.17 or 17%. Both sides of the chart display common cause variation.

The team has just cause to celebrate its success. But when you compare the new process average to the national comparative norm of 7%, you realize that there is still considerable work to be done. The next steps would be to continue to educate staff on the new protocol for detecting and preventing pressure ulcers. Because it is easier to change mattresses than it is to change the behaviors of individuals, it might be that the impact of the protocol training will take longer to have an influence on the process average. The control chart methodology provides, however, a very easy and simple way to track the interventions as the team progresses.

Case Study #6: Evaluating Staffing Effectiveness

Situation

In 2001 JCAHO established a new staffing effectiveness requirement for all hospitals. This requirement is designed to test relationships between two sets of indicators: human resources indicators and clinical/service indicators. The basic assumption driving this new requirement is that changes in the human resources indicators may have impacts on clinical, patient safety, and service outcomes.

The specific JCAHO standards (JCAHO 2003) and requirements related to staffing effectiveness include:

- **HR 2.1**

  "The hospital uses data on clinical/service screening indicators in combination with human resource screening indicators to assess staffing effectiveness."

- **Intent of HR 2.1**

  Multiple screening indicators that relate to patient outcomes, including clinical/service and human resources screening indicators, looked at in combination, may correlate with staffing effectiveness.

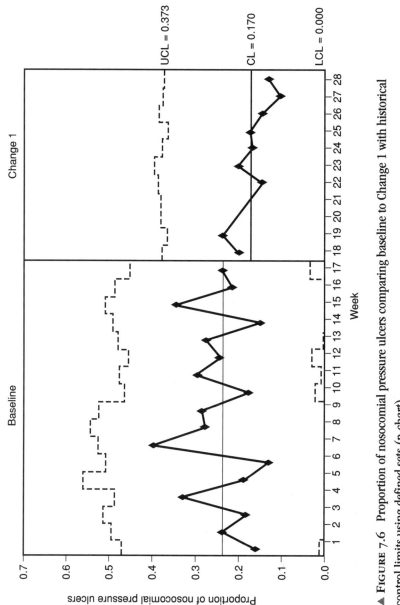

▲ FIGURE 7.6 Proportion of nosocomial pressure ulcers comparing baseline to Change 1 with historical control limits using defined sets (p-chart)

- **A minimum of four staffing effectiveness indicators,** two clinical/service and two human resource indicators, are selected (see the list that follows later in this section). The focus is on the relationship between human resource and clinical/service screening indicators, with the clear understanding that no one indicator in and of itself can directly correlate with staffing effectiveness.

- **At least one of the human resource and one of the clinical/service screening indicators** are selected from a list of JCAHO-identified screening indicators.

- **Additional screening indicators are identified by the hospital** to recognize the hospital's unique characteristics, specialties, and services. Rationale for screening indicator selection is determined by the hospital.

- **Both direct and indirect caregivers are included in the human resources screening indicators.** Hospitals define which caregivers are included in the human resource screening indicators based upon what impact, if any, the absence of such caregivers is expected to have on patient outcomes. The data collected and analyzed from the selected screening indicators are used to identify potential staffing effectiveness issues.

- A process is established to analyze screening indicator data over time per measure (for example, target ranges, trends over time, stability of process, external comparison data) and then in combination with other screening indicators (such as matrix report, spider diagram, radar diagram, and/or statistical correlation).

- Screening indicators are analyzed at the level most effective for planning staffing needs in the hospital and in collaboration with other areas in the hospital, as needed.

- **The hospital reports at least annually to the leaders (of the hospital and its board) on the aggregation and analysis of data related to the effectiveness of staffing (PI.3.1.1)** and any actions taken to improve staffing. There is evidence of action taken, as appropriate, in response to analyzed data.

JCAHO has not mandated specific indicators for this analysis. In their seminars on this topic, however, they have used the following indicator sets as examples:

- Human resource indicators
  - Overtime
  - Staff vacancy rates
  - Staff satisfaction
  - Staff turnover rates
  - Nursing hours per patient day
  - Staff injuries
  - On-call per diem use
  - Sick time utilization rates

- Clinical/service indicators
  - Patient complaints
  - Family/caregiver complaints
  - Patient satisfaction
  - Patient falls
  - Adverse drug events
  - Patient injuries
  - Skin breakdowns
  - Pneumonia rates
  - Urinary tract infections
  - Shock/cardiac arrest
  - Length of stay

These lists are not seen as being definitive. Hospitals are encouraged to identify additional indicators within each set.

One of the main challenges with these two lists is that JCAHO has not offered specific operational definitions for any of the indicators. Each hospital must decide, therefore, how they will define terms such as vacancy, turnover, patient injuries, skin breakdowns, or staff satisfaction.

Discussion

Each hospital is expected to match *one human resources indicator* with *one clinical/service indicator* and then test the relationship between these two measures. Whenever two measures are matched in this way, the objective is to determine if there is a *causal connection* between the two measures. In this case, the human resources indicator (e.g., number of nursing vacancies) is considered to be the *cause,* and the patient safety indicator (e.g., the number of patient falls) is viewed as the *effect* or outcome. Stated differently, if you decided to compare the number of nurse vacancies with the number of patient falls, one possible hypothesis that JCAHO would expect you to explore is as follows: As the number of nursing vacancies increases, we expect patient falls also to increase.

Depending on the indicators selected, the expected relationship between the two will have one of the following outcomes:

- There is a *positive relationship* between the two indicators (i.e., as one indicator increases, the other indicator also increases).

- There is a *negative relationship* between the two indicators (i.e., as one indicator increases, the other indicator decreases).

- There is *no relationship* between the two indicators.

Once you have selected the indicators, the following steps should be taken to test the relationships between the indicators:

Step #1: Organize the Data

In order to make sure that the conclusion about the relationship between the two indicators is (reasonably) true, you need to have an adequate amount of data. Ideally, the indicators would be based, at a minimum, on monthly data. Some indicators may even be available on a weekly basis. The least desirable time frame for any indicator is quarterly. Quarterly data will produce only 4 data points for the entire year, which is too little data to successfully test the relationship between the 2 indicators. A minimum of 12 observations (e.g., 12 months of patient fall data) should be obtained for each indicator.

Step #2: Prepare Control Charts

A control chart should be prepared for each indicator. If an indicator exhibits special cause variation, then the special causes need to be addressed before the indicator is matched up with the second indicator. If both of the selected indicators exhibit special causes, then the conclusion about the relationship between the two indicators will be suspect because both indicators are unpredictable, and you basically have little understanding of what the process is capable of producing.

If special causes are present, the first thing to do is to review the data collection procedures. Inconsistent data collection procedures can produce special causes that are a result of:

- Operational definitions that keep changing
- Changes in the patient population (e.g., a more severely ill patient population emerged midway through the year)
- Improvement strategies implemented by a team during the data collection period
- New employees who did not understand the data collection procedures

Any or all of these factors can create special causes in your data.

As an alternative to preparing control charts, you can develop a histogram for each indicator to see if the data are reasonably close to forming a normal distribution. Histograms can be made very easily in most statistical software packages.

Step #3: Develop Line Graphs

There are two basic approaches for testing the relationship between the matched indicators. The first approach is to make a simple line graph with both indicators plotted on the same graph. The second approach is to develop scatter diagrams, which are discussed in Step #4.

Figure 7.7 shows the relationship between the number of nursing vacancies and the number of falls each month. Notice that the two lines have different amplitudes but basically follow the same path over time. This indicates that the two indicators are related and follow a similar course (i.e., as one goes up the other goes up, and when one goes down the other also goes down). This is the simplest way to show a relationship between two indicators. Figure 7.8 shows that the two indicators are not related. As one goes up the other goes down. For these two indicators, however, the hypothesis was stated as a positive relationship: *As the number of nursing vacancies increases, we expect patient falls also to increase.* Simple line graphs provide the first level of analysis, but they do not allow you to evaluate the strength of the relationship between the two indicators. To do this you need to move to scatter diagrams.

Step #4: Develop Scatter Diagrams

A scatter diagram (also called a scatter plot, a scattergram, or an XY plot) is a graph of data points based on two variables, where the one variable defines the horizontal (or x) axis and the other defines the vertical (or y) axis. These graphs enable you to test for possible cause and effect relationships. Note that scatter diagrams do not *prove* that one variable causes the other. Instead they allow you to determine if a relationship exists and the possible strength of that relationship.

The data for scatter diagrams must be *variables data* that is measured along a continuous scale. Attributes data (e.g., categories such C-section delivery versus vaginal delivery) cannot be placed on a scatter diagram. The values of the two indicators are arranged as pairs of coordinates (i.e., the x-axis is the independent variable or cause and the y-axis is the dependent variable or effect). These coordinates are then plotted as dots on the graph.

If the dots are clustered close together, the relationship between the two indicators is considered to be stronger than if the dots are spread farther apart. The more the clustering of dots looks like a straight line, the stronger the correlation is between the two indicators.

Figure 7.9 shows a strong positive relationship (correlation) between the number of falls (the y-axis) and the number of RN vacancies (the x-axis). Figure 7.10, on the other hand, shows a positive but weak relationship between falls and RN vacancies (the dots are not clustered in a tight pattern). Note that when the two indicators are positively related, the pattern of the dots will rise from the lower left to the upper right. In this case, as one indicator increases the other one also increases.

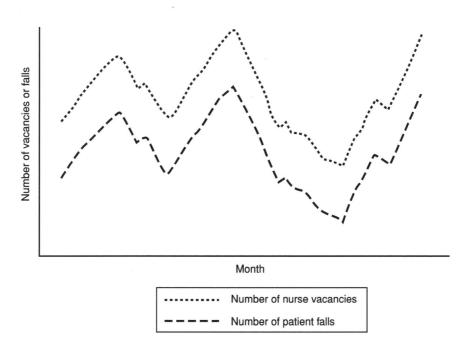

▲ FIGURE 7.7   A simple line graph showing two indicators that are related

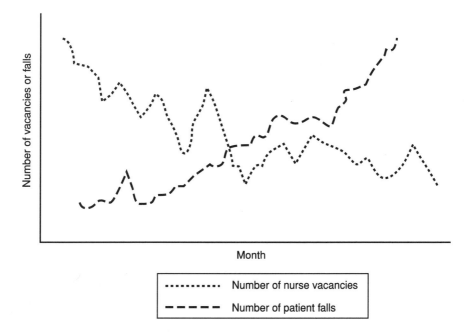

▲ FIGURE 7.8   A simple line graph showing two indicators that are not related

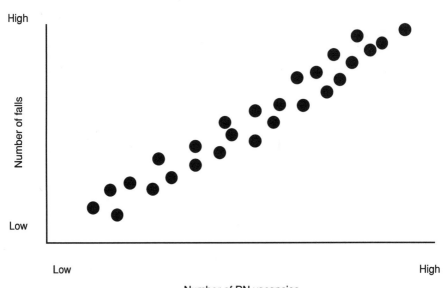

▲ FIGURE 7.9 A strong positive relationship between the two variables

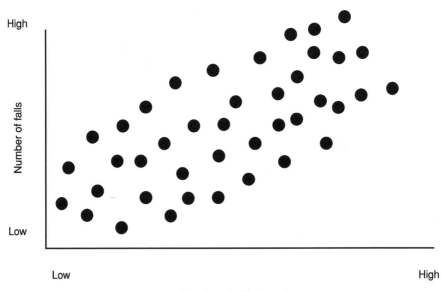

▲ FIGURE 7.10 A weak positive relationship between the two variables

In contrast, negative relationships present patterns that are similar to those shown in Figures 7.11 and 7.12. In Figure 7.11 we note, for example, that when the number of vacancies was high, the number of falls was low. When the number of falls was high, however, the RN vacancies were low. If you detect negative relationships, one indicator's values will increase while the other indicator's values will decrease. Again, the stronger the relationship, the tighter the pattern of the dots.

The final outcome of a scatter diagram might be that you discover no relationship between the indicators. This is shown in Figure 7.13. When this happens the dots are randomly scattered on the graph with no discernable pattern emerging.

Note that if you really want to maximize the use of a scatter diagram, you should also produce a correlation coefficient. This is a single value that tells you the actual strength of the relationship between the two indicators. The correlation coefficient (usually designated as r) will range from -1.0 to $+1.0$.

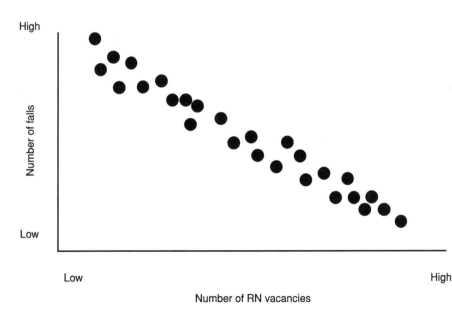

▲ FIGURE 7.11   A strong negative relationship between the two variables

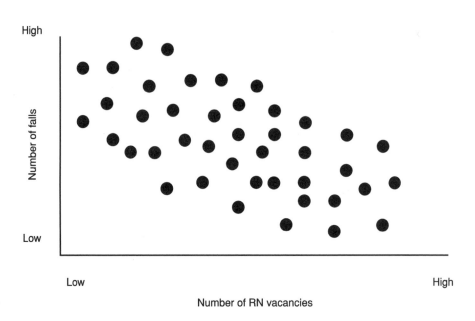

▲ FIGURE 7.12   A weak negative relationship between the two variables

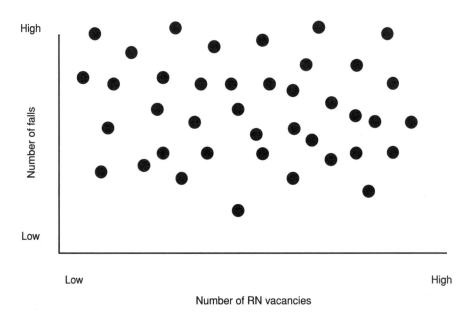

▲ FIGURE 7.13   No relationship between the two variables

In summary, JCAHO is interested in knowing if you can detect relationships between pairs of indicators. This means that you have to:

1. Select pairs of indicators representing human resource and clinical/service activities.

2. Develop theories about the possible relationships between the indicator pairs that you have selected. For example, if you select *staff satisfaction* as the human resource indicator and *patient satisfaction* as the clinical service indicator, what theories or hypotheses do you have about the possible relationship between these two indicators? Do you think there will be a positive or negative relationship?

3. Do a quick analysis of the data to see if it has been collected with consistent operational definitions and if the time periods for the indicators all match.

4. Create a control chart for each indicator to determine if the data represent common or special causes of variation. If special causes are present, investigate them and try to determine why they are present in your data. Indicators that reflect special cause variation will create problems for you when you try to interpret the line graphs and/or scatter diagrams.

5. Place both indicators on the same line graph and determine if the lines track in a similar or dissimilar fashion.

6. Create scatter diagrams to analyze the pattern of the dots and decide if there is a positive relationship, a negative relationship, or no relationship between the indicators.

7. Determine the strength of the relationship. You can do this by merely using common sense (the tighter the pattern, the stronger the relationship), or if you are comfortable with correlation coefficients, you can request this statistic from the software program you used to create the scatter diagram.

Finally, note that during the first year of this new staffing effectiveness requirement, JCAHO *will not*:

- Specify the exact indicators you must use
- Require that four indicators are from the lists JCAHO has presented at various workshops
- Score for failure to cover the entire patient population with indicators

- Judge the validity or reliability of the indicators you have selected
- Score or debate your operational definitions applied to the indicators
- Challenge the expected outcomes of your indicators, the benchmarks you use, or the range of expected performance for the individual indicators
- Look negatively on your analysis if you find no relationship between the two indicators being tested

What this does mean, however, is that JCAHO expects you to:

- Think through the logic of your analysis
- Develop plausible theories about the relationships
- Make sure your data are valid and reliable
- Be ready to drill down in the data to explore alternative analyses when you do not find a relationship between the indicators

Case Study #7: To Flash or Not to Flash— That Is the Question[6]

Situation

You are the director of surgical services at a 180-bed hospital. Recently during lunch with one of your friends, who just happens to be hospital's director of infection control, you mention that you have noticed an increase in the hospital's surgical infection rate. Your friend suggests that one possible area that could be contributing to this increase is the use of flash sterilization (FS). When you first started working at the hospital, FS was used only in emergency situations (e.g., when an instrument was dropped during surgery). Now it seems to have become a rather routine procedure. Not only does FS have a serious potential impact on infection rates but it has also become a concern of JCAHO. In fact, two other hospitals in your area have actually received citations from JCAHO for excessive use of FS.

You decide to begin by looking at the FS rate and how it has varied over time. You consult with the hospital's measurement expert and prepare Figures 7.14 and 7.15.

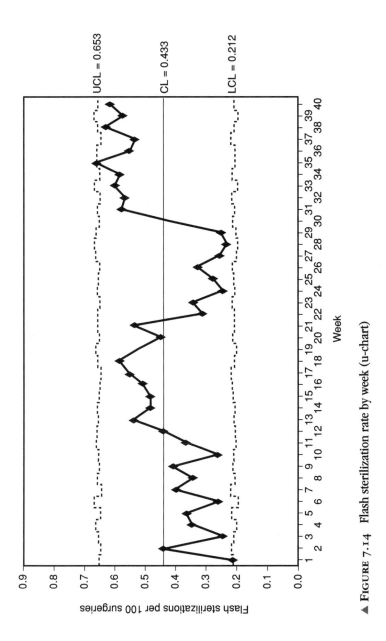

▲ **Figure 7.14** Flash sterilization rate by week (u-chart)

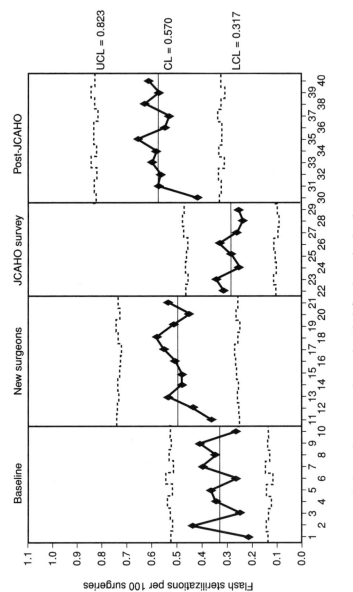

▲ FIGURE 7.15 Flash sterilization rate by week with defined sets (u-chart)

Discussion

The data are plotted weekly (the subgroup) on u-charts. The FS rates are calculated as follows:

$$\text{FS rate} = \frac{\text{Total number of FSs done each week}}{\text{Total number of surgeries done each week}}$$

- Why do you think a u-chart was used instead of a c-chart or a p-chart?

  The u-chart is the chart of preference because each surgery case could have more than one FS. Each time an FS occurs it is viewed as a defect. A c-chart would not be used because the c-chart requires that the subgroups for counting the defects (which are weeks in this case study) have an equal opportunity for a defect to occur. Because there are a different number of surgeries performed each week, this constitutes an unequal subgroup, which requires the use of the u-chart. A p-chart would be used only if the measurement question was as follows: "Was FS used during this surgical case?" The answer to this question is simply yes or no. It is not a count of the actual number of FSs occurring. The p-chart does not address the issue of multiple occurrences of an FS. If a surgical case had 1 FS or 100 FSs, it would merely be recorded as a "Yes" on a p-chart because the frequency of the event does not matter. The p-chart is used to measure the percentage or proportion of defectives, but the u- and c-charts are used to count defects.

- Do you detect any special causes in the charts? If so, what are they and what do they tell you?

  Figure 7.14 reveals numerous special causes due to shifts in the process. As you look at the patterns in the data, you notice that there seems to be a cyclical nature to the data. The dots form a cluster in the lower left side of the chart, then they jump up to a higher FS utilization rate. After running for a few weeks at a fairly high level, the data drop dramatically to a lower level. Finally, in the last part of the chart the process shifts again to a higher level (actually the highest level so far). What could be causing these shifts in the data? The statistician supporting this initiative suggests that it might be useful to partition the data into sets. Not quite sure what he is suggesting, you follow his lead and agree. After a few quick strokes on the keyboard, he produces the chart shown in Figure 7.15. In this chart all the special causes have disappeared, and there are four distinct phases that form common cause sets of data. As you ponder this chart, you notice the dates associated with the four segments. All of a sudden the light bulb goes on. You identify the four phases as (1) the baseline—that is, when you started tracking the FS rate, (2) when a new group of surgeons came on board, (3) when the hospital was gearing up for the JCAHO survey, and (4) the period after the JCAHO survey was completed. This is a very clear demonstration of how organizational conditions can have rather dramatic impacts on a process. The addition of new surgeons created an entirely new process. Why these new surgeons had such an impact is unknown at this point but certainly merits further study. The impact of the pending JCAHO survey had another dramatic impact on the process. Even the new surgeons seemed to have changed their behaviors with respect to FS during this time. But after the JCAHO survey ended, the use of FS not only increased but also moved to an all-time average high of 57 FSs per 100 surgeries.

- How will you know if a planned change improves the current process?

  If there is serious concern over the FS rate, then the last time period (weeks 30–40) should serve as the new baseline. If the objective is to lower the FS rate, then the creation of a team would be advisable. The team should continue to track the FS rate and begin to gain a better understanding of why FS is used. In this case the creation of a Pareto diagram documenting the reasons for flashing an instrument or surgical item would help to identify the vital few. The team might also consider finding out what the FS rates are at other hospitals in the area. If the hospital is part of a system, then getting this same indicator from other hospitals in the system sets up the opportunity for internal benchmarking. As the team develops improvement strategies they can partition the data on the control chart and see if the interventions are able to reduce the FS rate.

Case Study #8: Clarifying the Operational Definition of Readmission

Situation

A home healthcare agency is interested in tracking the percentage of its patients that are readmitted to the hospital. So they set about collecting data only to find out that the numbers seem to vary rather dramatically from what they expected. Do you (1) assume that the data are the true reality and that the agency staff has been missing something, or (2) do you go back to square one and check on the accuracy of the data?

Discussion

Whenever data seem to be at odds with what you think they should be telling you, the first thing to do is to check the data before you jump to a conclusion about the results. Three key questions should be explored: (1) Is the operational definition clear? (2) Is everyone interpreting the operational definition in the same way? and (3) Have the data collectors gathered the data in the same way? Based on my experience in developing indicators, the most common problem is that the operational definition is not clear. A good operational definition should be clear and unambiguous; it should define the decision criteria to be applied when collecting the data and the methods to follow when actually collecting the data. Basically, if you have developed your operational definition correctly, all three questions will be answered simultaneously. Now let us consider the issues related to defining a readmission. The major issue I have encountered is first determining if the readmission is for the same diagnosis or any diagnosis. Most of the time the team's interest is in determining if the patient was readmitted for the same diagnosis. But it is surprising how many times I have found teams in conflict over this issue. Although the team members usually reach consensus on the fact that readmission for the same diagnosis makes the most sense, the people pulling the data are often not told to eliminate all readmissions for a different reason. For example, if a congestive heart failure (CHF) patient was admitted to the hospital for a CHF-related problem and then readmitted within 30 days for a broken arm, would this be considered a readmission? Most staff would conclude that this is not a readmission because the patient was not admitted for a CHF-related problem. I have seen teams debate this conclusion because some think that the CHF caused the patient to stagger and then fall on his arm. Therefore, the patient's CHF was the causal factor leading to the readmission. The other issue that I have seen enter into discussions of readmission is whether the team was considering a 30-, 60-, or 90-day readmission. It seems obvious, but I have seen teams waste considerable time and effort because they did not specify the time frame for a readmission.

Case Study #9: Managing a Breast Cancer Patient's Clotting Levels

Situation

A breast cancer patient decides to have a mediport inserted into her chest to aid in the delivery of chemotherapy drugs. The insertion of the port goes without incident, but about a month after it is in place, the patient develops a deep vein thrombosis (DVT) in her left arm. She is hospitalized for several days on heparin, sent home on a brief regimen of enoxaparin injections and then begins oral doses of warafin sodium. During each visit to a local outpatient clinic (which takes about 15 minutes), a small amount of blood is extracted via a finger stick and analyzed, and adjustments are made on the spot. The patient assists the pharmacist by keeping track of her daily intake of vitamin K (inconsistent intake of vitamin K can have a dramatic impact on the effect of warafin sodium). The challenge with managing a patient on this particular drug is that there is a very narrow specification limit for the drug. When the patient exceeds the USL, there is a risk of bleeding. Conversely, when the patient falls below the recommended therapeutic limit, there is a risk of clotting. The pharmacist creates control charts to assist in managing the patient's progress on warafin sodium (Figure 7.16 and Figure 7.17).

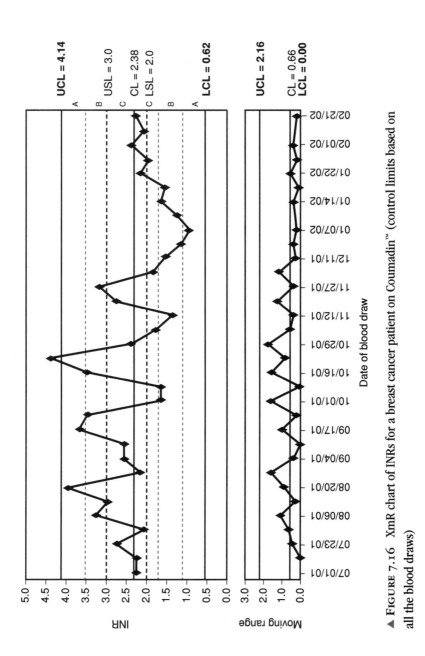

▲ FIGURE 7.16 XmR chart of INRs for a breast cancer patient on Coumadin™ (control limits based on all the blood draws)

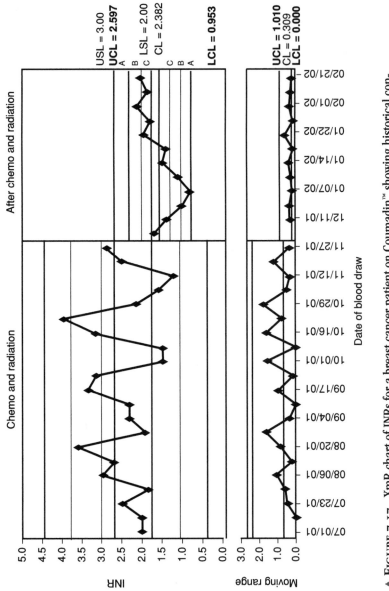

▲ FIGURE 7.17 XmR chart of INRs for a breast cancer patient on Coumadin™ showing historical control limits (during and after chemo and radiation therapy)

Discussion

- What chart did the pharmacist make for this patient? Why do you think she used this chart? Is there another chart that she could have used?

   Because the indicator used to measure the effect of warafin sodium is a continuous measure, the pharmacist has a choice of making the X-bar & S chart or the XmR chart. The chart of preference in this case is the XmR chart (a.k.a. the Individuals or I-chart) because there is only one observation per subgroup (i.e., each time the patient visits the clinic, which is weekly, the pharmacist takes one blood draw for analysis). If multiple blood draws were taken each week, the pharmacist could make the X-bar & S chart. Because multiple blood draws each week are not necessary, the appropriate chart is the XmR chart.

- Is this patient's process in control or out of control?

   The patient's process is not in control. There are two special causes in Figure 7.16. One occurs at the blood draw on October 22, and the other one occurs after chemo was terminated on November 27 (i.e., the process stayed below the centerline for more than eight data points in a row, signaling a shift in the process).

- What do we learn by looking at the moving range chart?

   The moving range chart (the bottom chart of Figure 7.16) depicts the variation from one data point to the next. If there are large swings from one data point to the next, then this chart will have wide control limits. The moving range chart exhibits wider variation during the period when the patient was receiving chemo and radiation. After these treatments were ended, the moving range does not show as much fluctuation.

- Note that the chart shows the USL and LSL. Of what value are these lines? How do they differ from the UCL and LCL?

   Not too many clinical measures actually have specification limits. The ones that typically have specification limits are those that relate to physiological measures (e.g., hemoglobin levels, white blood counts, or platelets). Warafin sodium levels are measured in terms of clotting times. The standard measure is known as the INR (international normalized ratio) value. The therapeutic range for the INR value is 3.0 to 2.0. These values can be used as the USL and LSL for the drug. When the patient's control limits do not coincide with these specification limits, then the patient is at risk. The principal difference between specification limits and control limits is that the specification limits represent the desired levels of performance, but the control limits capture the actual levels of performance. From a clinical perspective, note that the number of INRs that fell beyond the specification limits during treatment (10 of them) exceeded the number that fell within the therapeutic limits (only 11 of them).

- Figure 7.17 partitions the data points into two segments. The first part covers the chemo/radiation period (7/1 through 11/27/2001). The second period is after all chemo and radiation treatments were completed. Why do you think the pharmacist divided the chart into two parts? Does it help understand the patient's process? What could be causing the shift in the INRs?

  The pharmacist knew, from experience, that once a patient completes the chemo and radiation treatments, the management of warafin sodium usually moves into a new phase. Specifically, without the influence of chemo and radiation, the patient's body begins to exhibit its true response to warafin sodium. So the pharmacist divided the control chart into a treatment data set (blood draws 1–21) and an after-treatment data set (blood draws 22–33). Consistent with previous patients, this patient exhibited a dramatic drop in the INRs after treatment was terminated. This was followed by a gradual increase to a more stable period that coincided (for the first time) with the specification limits. It is important to note that the moving range chart also shows extreme stability after the treatments were stopped.

- What other patient conditions can you think of that could be monitored with control charts?

Control charts have great utility for tracking blood pressure, blood glucose levels, the daily intake of fat, sodium, and cholesterol, or the impact of physical therapy treatments.

Case Study #10: Group B Streptococcus in Pregnant Women

Situation

A team of nurses at Advocate Good Samaritan Hospital (Downers Grove, Illinois) was interested in studying the administration of antibiotics to pregnant women who present for delivery with a positive culture for group B streptococcus (GBS).[7] According to the Centers for Disease Control and Prevention, about 20–30% of all women have GBS naturally in their bodies. Although GBS is benign to the woman, the transference of GBS to the newborn during delivery can have extremely negative consequences for the baby, including death (approximately 1 death per 1000 deliveries). Women should be tested for the presence of GBS during weeks 35–37 of pregnancy. If they test positive for the flora, they should be administered antibiotics for at least four hours prior to delivery in order to minimize the potential of transferring the GBS to the newborn and thereby causing sepsis.

Discussion

Carol Burke, the nurse manager for labor and delivery at Advocate Good Samaritan Hospital, was somewhat dismayed when she called me because she thought the percentage of women receiving the appropriate antibiotics was not improving. She said that she thought the problem was the result of an increase in the number of women presenting with a positive GBS who were under the four-hour threshold. Because you cannot tell a pregnant woman, "We're going to wait three more hours to deliver your baby so we can administer antibiotics," these women receive less than the recommended regimen of antibiotics. I asked Ms. Burke if they were combining all cases (i.e., women presenting four hours or more before delivery and women presenting less than four hours prior to delivery) in their data analysis. She said that they were. I asked if they could stratify the cases into these two categories, and she said that they could. The issue here is that the increased volume of women presenting four hours before delivery is something the hospital cannot control. The application of the antibiotic protocol should only be applied to the women who present at least four hours before they deliver. These are the women that can experience positive results from the application of prophylactic antibiotics. Those who present less than four hours prior to delivery should be placed in a separate category (stratum).[8] Figure 7.18 depicts the

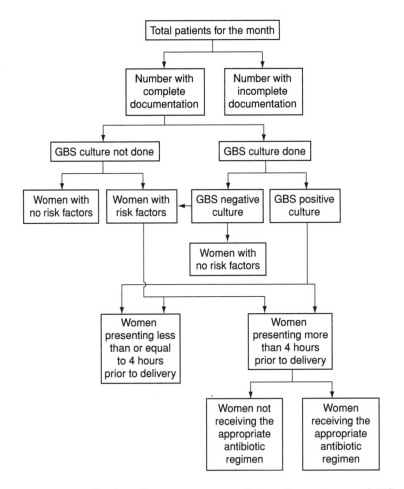

▲ FIGURE 7.18 Stratification of pregnant women with group b streptococcus (GBS)

various levels of stratification we developed for this team. Note that the decision tree places patients into categories or buckets that are mutually exclusive. In this way the team can decide which categories it wishes to measure and which are not particularly relevant to their intended objectives. The team has to decide what is important. Stratification is an aid in making these decisions because it can assist them in determining if the data need to be broken down into smaller and more relevant comparison groups.

Prior to developing Figure 7.18, the team had prepared a control chart to show the percentage of women that received antibiotics within the prescribed time period. Because they had adopted the national average of 89% as their goal, the hospital's average of 72% (recorded for March 2003) was somewhat disappointing. After applying the stratification decision tree shown in Figure 7.18, however, the team discovered that the true percentage of patients receiving intrapartum antibiotic prophylaxis (IAP) was actually 88%, not 72%. Since we met to discuss more appropriate ways to stratify and organize their data, there has been a positive shift in the percentages of women receiving IAP (see Figure 7.19), which reflects the true performance of the process. Now the team is challenged to move this new average as close to 100% as possible. The team's current improvement strategies include:

- Revising their data collection instruments and procedures to make sure they are all using the logic shown in Figure 7.18

- Continuing education for the nursing staff on the importance of understanding that IAP should be initiated for women with GBS within 30 minutes of admission

- Enhance collaboration between nursing and clinical management to make sure pitocin inducement is delayed for women with GBS

- Increasing the number of nurses involved with the data collection efforts

- Adding GBS status to the mother/infant record and prenatal record

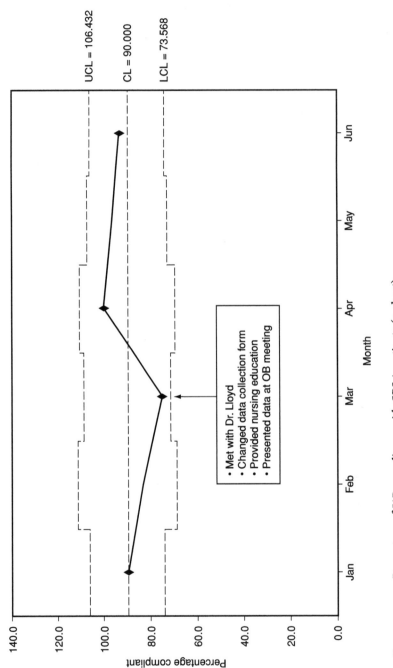

▲ FIGURE 7.19   Percentage of IAP compliance with GBS+ patients (p-chart)

Case Study #11: Emergency Department Fast Track[9]

Situation

An emergency department (ED) has proudly announced to the community that it now has a "fast track" in place for emergency visits that are not life threatening. Brochures have been developed and a banner has been placed across the ED proclaiming that "Fast Track is here!" The ED team set a goal of 75 minutes from ED registration to discharge from the fast track area. They did not use data to establish this goal; it "just felt right." Besides, one of the staff had read that a hospital in New York City was able to get people in and out of its fast track service in 60 minutes. If an urban city hospital could achieve 60 minutes or less, then surely a suburban hospital should be able to do it in 75 minutes. Unfortunately, after a month of operation the only problem seems to be numerous complaints from patients in the "fast track" that things do not move quite as fast as they think they should.

Discussion

The first thing the team needs to do is to gather patient wait times in the ED fast track and determine how much time it actually takes to get a patient through the process. Then they can see how far they are from the goal of 75 minutes. The team consults with their internal CQI measurement expert, and she advises them that they do not need to record the wait times of every patient. A random or stratified random sample should be sufficient. After she explains the differences between the two sampling approaches, the team thinks it would be best to draw a stratified random sample. In this case two stratification levels will be used: (1) day versus afternoon shift (the fast track process does not operate during the night shift) and (2) type of injury (i.e., visible blood versus no blood). A sampling plan is laid out, log sheets are created, and a date is selected to start collecting patient wait times. The subgroup (i.e., how they will organize their data) is day. Each day they select a predetermined number of patients using the established stratification criteria. They attempt to get the same number of patients each day (5), but some days they get more patients and other days they get less. They are concerned that this variable subgroup size will affect the analysis of the data. The CQI expert assures them that this will not be a problem, because the control chart she will be preparing for the team (the X-bar & S chart) can handle varying subgroup sizes. They collect data for 20 days, all the while trying to get patients through in 75 minutes. The baseline data for the day shift and patients with no observable blood are presented in Figure 7.20. What does this chart tell you about the fast track process?

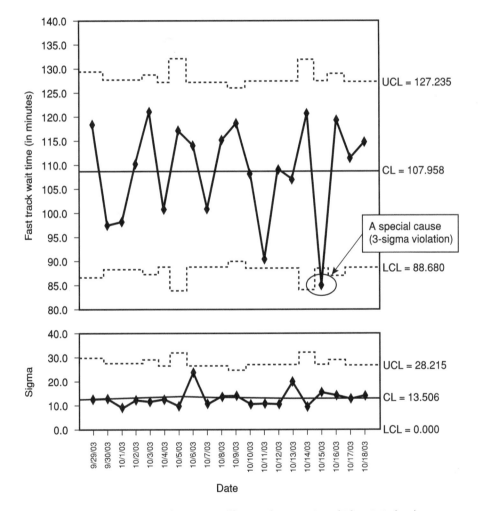

▲ FIGURE 7.20 Emergency department "fast track" wait time (X-bar & S chart)

The first thing that you observe is that a special cause occurred on 10/15/03. This is a 3-sigma violation because the average for the day (84.4 minutes) fell below the LCL. This is actually a special cause that the team would like to see repeated, because it is the lowest wait time during the entire study period. The team should investigate why the process worked so well on this day. Were the patients presenting with less critical problems? Was the regular ED slow so that staff came over to assist on the fast track side? Could it be that there was a data-recording mistake on this day and someone transposed a number? Why was this day different from the other 19 days? There are lessons to be learned with every special cause.

The second thing you should notice is that the control limits are not straight. These are called stair-step control limits. They are found on any chart that does not have a consistent subgroup size. Stair-step control limits are seen most of the time on the p- and u-charts, but you will find them on an X-bar & S chart when the sample being pulled is not consistent over time. In the present example, the subgroups ranged from three to seven.

Finally, you do not need a degree in statistics to see that this process is not operating anywhere near the desired goal of 75 minutes. Despite the fact that there is a special cause present, which basically makes the process unstable and unpredictable, you can still apply the "interocular test of significance" to the data (the old eyeball test) and see that the average is 108 minutes. The complaints of the patients seem to be justified—particularly if word got out that this process was going to get people in and out in 75 minutes or less.

So what should the team do? One of the staff suggests taking down the banner that proclaims that "Fast Track is here!" This idea is considered but then discarded; the banner stays up. The next idea is to see if the baseline data for the afternoon shift differ from that of the day shift and whether the presence of blood has an impact on the process. The CQI expert suggests that there also may be difference based on the hour of the day and the volume of patients coming to the ED. In conjunction with the additional data work, they also decide to develop a flowchart on the process and see if they can identify any bottlenecks in the process.

The final thing the team does is to take time to engage in a dialogue about the nature of the concept of the "fast track." They begin to wonder if everyone has the same operational definition of this concept. How fast can the ED fast track process be expected to go? What does the public think about when they see a sign that tells them there is a fast track process in place? Part of this team's problem is simply managing the customers' expectations. It is a classic example of creating an expectation in the customer's mind, publicizing the idea, and then unleashing a process that is not capable of even meeting expectations, let alone exceeding them. Quality does not happen merely because you have good intentions and a colorful banner across the entrance to the ED. It happens when you understand the VOC and the VOP and then take action to make sure that the process can at least meet minimum expectations. In this case study, it is not surprising that the fast track team was not near their goal. They did not start out with an understanding of the capability of the process. Their good intentions were detoured by poor planning.

Case Study #12: Tracking Patient Complaints

Situation

A group practice clinic decides to change the processes for registering patients and scheduling follow-up visits. Within the center are the following subspecialties: family practice, internal medicine, and obstetrics/gynecology. In addition, there is an outpatient laboratory, a pharmacy, and a durable medical equipment service. In the past, each of the medical subspecialties had their own areas for registration, scheduling follow-up visits, and payment (billing/insurance questions, etc). Driven primarily by financial factors, the managers of the various subspecialties agree in September 2002 to consolidate all the administrative functions. As a result, they decide to have one area to handle the three functions of registration, scheduling follow-up visits, and handling billing questions. They also decide to physically rearrange the floor space and the way in which the patients move within the facility. Figures 7.21 and 7.22 show the impact of these changes on the number of patient complaints received each month.

Discussion

- What type of control chart should be used with this indicator?

  Complaints are typically seen as defects (i.e., attributes data). In this case, the charting options are the c-chart and the u-chart. The c-chart provides a count of defects (complaints) when there is an equal area of opportunity for a complaint to occur. The u-chart, on the other hand, is reserved for counting defects when there is an unequal area of opportunity for a defect (complaint) to occur. The c-chart was used because the daily number of visits to the various subspecialties showed very little fluctuation and the types of patients visiting the clinic remained reasonably constant. If either or both of these assumptions were to change, however, the chart of preference would be the u-chart.[10]

* What conclusions do you make about the changes that were put in place? Did they have a positive or negative impact?

Figure 7.21 clearly shows that something has happened to the complaint process. The overall pattern of the data suggests that there has been a shift in the process. Furthermore, there are numerous special causes on this chart. If this chart were used in a presentation, however, it would be very misleading.

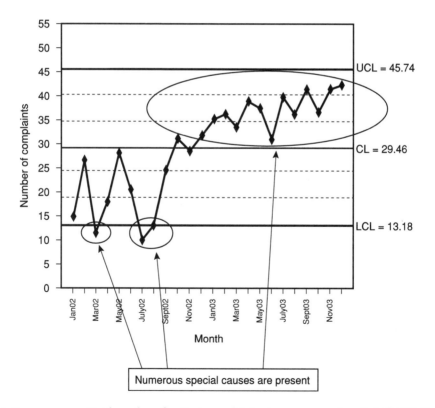

▲ **FIGURE 7.21** Total number of patient complaints at a group practice clinic (c-chart)

- Is there a better way to present the data in Figure 7.21?

  In the overview of this case study, it was noted that the changes the administrative team made to the administrative functions occurred in September 2002. After this point the process for registering, scheduling follow-up visits, and answering questions about billing and insurance changed. Therefore, the team should have partitioned the data set into two segments—the old setup and the new setup. This division of the data is shown in Figure 7.22. Now it becomes very clear that there are really two processes. One occurred under the old arrangement and another with the new process. Under the old arrangement the process produced around 18 complaints each month. After the changes were made, the complaints jumped up to an average of 36. You can see from Figure 7.22 that the original process and the new process are both stable and reflect common cause variation. This means that they are both predictable. The problem is that the new process is predictably bad.

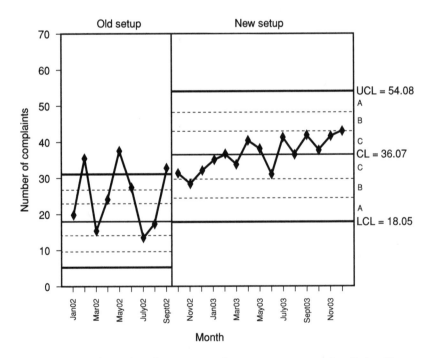

▲ **FIGURE 7.22**   Total number of patient complaints at a group practice clinic with historical control limits (c-chart)

- Given these results, what are the next steps?

Because there has clearly been a shift in the process, the management team needs to have a serious discussion about the tradeoffs between cost and quality. If the desire is to cut costs by consolidating the administrative functions and cutting staff, then the customer satisfaction consequences of these changes need to be evaluated. If the complaints continue to increase, it is very likely that patients may start to look elsewhere for medical care. Although patients typically have strong allegiances to their physicians, there comes a point when the administrative functions serve as a catalyst to push patients away from their current providers. This clinic staff needs to conduct further data analysis and develop a Pareto diagram on the reasons for the complaints. If they do not gain a better understanding of why patients are complaining, then they will flounder around in the dark, cursing the ever growing number of complaints but not understanding which ones are the major problems.

Case Study #13: Reducing Ventilator-Associated Pneumonia[11]

Situation

In the fall of 1999 an article published in the *American Journal of Critical Care* highlighted the importance of an oral care protocol to improve the oral health of patients in the ICU (Fitch *et al.* 1999). Based on that article, ICU nursing staff at Advocate Good Shepherd Hospital (Barrington, Illinois) concluded that current policy and practice did not designate a consistent oral care procedure for unconscious or ventilated patients. Therefore, a CQI project was initiated to investigate alternative protocols to improve the quality of oral care. During this process, the nurses discovered that implementing a new oral care policy and procedures may have had a positive impact on the occurrence of ventilator-associated pneumonia (VAP).

Discussion

Bonnie Schleder, a critical care–clinical nurse specialist, and Kathleen Stott, an ICU registered nurse, at Advocate Good Shepherd Hospital partnered to revise the hospital's policy and procedures for the performance of oral care for all adult mechanically ventilated patients in a 10-bed medical/surgical

ICU. Current literature was reviewed to identify recommendations for comprehensive oral care on ventilated patients. The following best practices were identified:

- A daily assessment should be performed to evaluate the level of oral dysfunction and provide the most appropriate care to keep the patient comfortable and prevent complications.
- Brushing a patient's teeth should occur at a frequency of every two to four hours and as needed to prevent the formation of plaque, which can be a reservoir for respiratory pathogens.
- Alcohol-free, antiseptic oral rinse should be used to prevent bacterial colonization of the oropharyngeal area.
- Suctioning of oral secretions in both the oral cavity and the subglottic area (above the cuff) should be performed to prevent the aspiration of microorganisms.
- Application of a water-based mouth moisturizer should be used to maintain the integrity of the oral mucosa.

The nursing staff reviewed new oral hygiene products on the market. After a thorough review of several new products, one was selected and an implementation plan was developed. Once the new policy and procedure statement was finalized, copies were distributed to ICU nursing staff. Group education on the rationale for the changes and instructions on proper product usage were provided by the manufacturer. The manufacturer also provided posters, evaluation forms, and follow-up to further clarify, troubleshoot, and educate staff. The presence of a "champion" for this process change (in this case a registered nurse from the ICU) provided leadership, accountability, and support to ensure a successful transition to the new process and products.

The specific indicator selected for analysis was the VAP rate. This indicator had been tracked at Good Shepherd Hospital since 1996, so there was a good baseline for comparison. The VAP rate is operationally defined as the number of pneumonia occurrences per 1000 ventilator days. The specific components of the VAP rate are:

- Numerator—Total number of inpatient ICU occurrences of VAP
- Denominator—Total number of days ICU patients spent on a ventilator

This value is then multiplied by a constant of 1000, so the rate can be compared with national data.

Data were collected manually on a monthly basis and then reported to Lori Pinzon in the quality improvement department for tabulation and analysis. The chart she selected for analysis of the VAP rate calculations was the u-chart, because this is the chart of preference for the presentation of all types of rates (e.g., fall rate, medication error rate, nosocomial infection rate, or neonatal death rate). Initially, the data were going to be analyzed on a monthly basis. Because there were a disproportionate number of months with no VAP occurrences, however, a decision was made to group the data by quarter rather than by month.

To determine if the new oral hygiene products and procedures had an effect on the VAP rates, a pre/post comparison was made. The VAP rates prior to implementing the new oral hygiene protocol were compared to the rates after the process was changed. If the VAP rate declined after the protocol was introduced, then the u-chart would document the nature and extent of the change.

Figure 7.23 shows the u-chart comparing preprotocol VAP rates with those after the new oral hygiene equipment and protocol were introduced. Eight quarters of data form the baseline or preprotocol period.[12] All the data

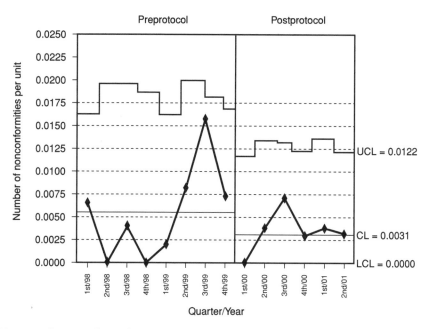

*Because there are fewer than 20 data points in each segment of the control chart, the control limits should be considered to be "trial" control limits. As more data points are obtained in the postprotocal period, these limits will become more stable and reliable.

▲ **Figure 7.23** Ventilator-associated pneumonia rate, January 1998–June 2001 (u-chart)

points fall between the UCL and LCL, and there are no abnormal data patterns occurring between them (e.g., a trend or a shift in the process). In short, the preprotocol period reflects common cause variation.

The new oral hygiene protocol was introduced at the end of the 4th quarter of 1999. A vertical line has been drawn on the control chart to identify this point. The data after this point reflect a shift in the process. Not only are the control limits closer together, but the centerline has also dropped. The VAP rate during the baseline period was slightly greater than 5 VAPs per 1000 ventilator days. After the protocol was introduced, the rate dropped to 3.1 per 1000 ventilator days. The comparative reference mean from the National Nosocomial Infections Surveillance (NNIS) System database is 8.9 per 1000 patient days. If the VAP rate at Good Shepherd Hospital starts to migrate back toward the higher preprotocol average, then it would appear that the new oral care procedure had only a temporary impact on staff behaviors and/or other untested factors influenced the decline in the postprotocol rates. Conversely, if the postprotocol VAP rates continue to be below the preprotocol average for several more quarters, then a shift in the process will have occurred.

Although there are fewer data points used in this chart than desired, the preliminary results suggest that the new oral care procedure may be playing a key role in reducing the VAP rate at Good Shepherd Hospital. Further study is clearly warranted to validate these results. Currently within the Advocate system we have established a multisite research design that is testing the new products and protocols with different groups of patients to see if the same results are obtained.

Case Study #14: Pain Management for Hip and Knee Replacement Patients[13]

Situation

Delnor-Community Hospital (Geneva, Illinois), known for its high inpatient satisfaction survey results, noted a less than desired overall score with the following survey question: "How well was your pain controlled?" The nursing staff from the orthopedic department investigated pain control on their particular unit by drilling down further into the data. Through data analysis they determined that hip/knee replacement patients would be an ideal target group for improved pain management. Two nurses who worked regularly with these patients decided to investigate the possible causes of dissatisfaction. They enlisted the assistance of an internal quality measurement consultant and decided to start tracking the effectiveness of the pain management process. They designed a study to determine if pain was being controlled effectively <u>after</u> the postsurgical epidural and/or patient-controlled analgesia (PCA) pump were removed. Their concern was that once these more automated systems for the administration of pain medication were removed, gaps were occurring in the manual administration of pain medications. They believed that these gaps led to (1) lengthy delays in the administration of pain medications, (2) the undesirable "peak and trough" pain management cycle, and (3) increased dissatisfaction on the part of patients.

Discussion

The first thing the team did was to randomly pull 50 hip and knee replacement charts and evaluate the pain medication administration process. For all 50 patients the times that they were administered pain medications were recorded, and a bar graph showing the number of medications given by hour of the day was prepared (Figure 7.24). This bar graph reveals that the most popular time for administering pain medications was between 9 and 10 A.M. Note that there is a ramping-up effect from midnight to 9 A.M. then there is a decline in the frequency with spikes at 2 P.M. and 10 P.M. The diagram reinforced the nurses' beliefs that there was considerable variation in the amount of time between medication administration and that some patients were experiencing unacceptable delays in receiving pain medications. This suggested that the unit took a patient-reactive approach to pain management rather than a desired nursing-proactive approach.

The next thing they did was to develop an indicator to evaluate the effectiveness of the pain management program. They used a modified version of the Indicator Development Form© described in Chapter 3 to specify the indicator and the measurement plan (Figure 7.25). Using the universal pain scale, the nurses asked the patients to evaluate their levels of pain two times during the day and evening shifts and at least one time during the night shift.

Even though the universal pain scale is based on a 0–10 evaluation, the data are basically attributes in nature, not variables. This is because there are not equal-appearing intervals between each number on the scale. The pain scale is a very subjective scale that basically produces a rank order distribution rather than a true interval scale like a ruler. Therefore, the appropriate way to analyze these data is by computing a percentage. The only decision that needs to be made is where to divide the scale in order to compute the percentages. The nurses reached consensus that an unacceptable pain level would be any evaluation that was above 4 on the universal pain scale.

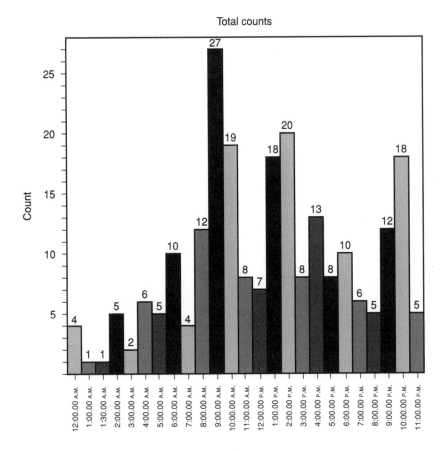

▲ FIGURE 7.24 Number of pain medications administered by hour of the day

Unit/Department: 2 North Completed by: Sue Herrmann, Marjie Schoolfield	
1) What key quality characteristic (KQC), process, outcome, or safety does this indicator measure? (i.e., turnaround time, answering telephones within three rings, etc.) Prompt relief from pain. Maintain low level of pain. Acknowledgment of pain.	2) What is the specific name of this indicator? (i.e., radiology turnaround time: procedure to dictation time) "Quality of pain control in postop patients"

3) What is the rationale for this indicator? (Why has this indicator been selected? What is the purpose of the indicator?) Keeping pain levels low is an obvious benefit to the patient. Low levels of pain will also increase the patients' satisfaction with their treatment at Delnor-Community and will be demonstrated by increased scores on pain question on Press-Ganey Patient Satisfaction surveys. Observations have also indicated the lack of a standardized approach to the dispensing of oral pain medications to postop patients. Often times patients have to complain of pain, then wait for medication, and finally wait for medication to take effect. This often results in dramatic shifts of pain levels.

4) Data source collection method: ☐ Medical record ■ Patient satisfaction reports ☐ Data logs ☐ System reports, please specify ■ Other: recording of pain level on laminated form by nursing staff	**Collection frequency and duration:** **Collected:** ■ Daily ☐ Weekly ☐ Monthly **Reported:** after baseline and after intervention **Duration:** 07/08/02 to 15–20 patients

5) **Operational definition:** Remember: Include full definition with all inclusions and exclusions, specify all required data elements (i.e., patient types, financial class, data dictionary elements, DRGs, codes, clinical specialty, etc. Given a solid operational definition, 10 different people measuring the same thing should arrive at identical results.)

Using a population of total hip/knee replacement patients concurrently, nursing will use the universal pain scale to record patient's pain number two (2) times per shift (standard shift is 7–3, 3–11) and at least one (1) time per noc shift (11–7). RN on each shift will record on laminated collection tool the actual time and pain number when assessed utilizing the universal pain scale (0–10). At the end of noc shift, start a new form each day. Place completed form in 2 North office.

Marjie Schoolfield and Sue Herrmann will be accountable for entering data from the laminated sheets and compiling additional information.

Bill Peters will be responsible for generating control charts. Order on control charts will be based on admit dates (date of surgery). P-charts will be used along with a Pareto chart.

6) **Numerator statement:** (if applicable, i.e., number of C-sections) number of pain measurements over 4	7) **Denominator statement:** (if applicable, i.e., number of births) number of pain measurements

8) **What is this indicator measuring?** ☐ Rate ☐ Days ☐ Time ■ Percentage ☐ Other _____	9) **Baseline:** *see attached charts	10) **Goal:** a reduction in pain level responses over 4 as demonstrated by control chart mean and upper and lower control limits (see charts)

11) **This indicator will satisfy the following objective(s):**		
☐ Physician partnership	■ Customer satisfaction	☐ Regulatory requirement
☐ Culture transformation	■ Clinical excellence	☐ Risk management
☐ Value enhancement	☐ Operational excellence	☐ Patient safety
☐ Market development	☐ Cost reduction	

12) **Which of our 5 Pillars does this indicator affect?**
■ Service ☐ Financial ☐ Growth ■ Quality ☐ People

▲ **FIGURE 7.25** Indicator development worksheet (pain management team at Delnor-Community Hospital)

The baseline data are shown in Figure 7.26. Not only does the baseline contain several special causes (patients #1 and #9) but there is a fair amount of variation from patient to patient. This process is basically unstable and unpredictable. This essentially confirmed what the nurses thought was occurring with this process. The data also reinforced their belief that improvements needed to be made. After evaluating the baseline data, the team:

- Conducted several in-service sessions for the nursing staff to reacquaint them with the importance of pain management and the hospital's commitment to managing it consistently and effectively.

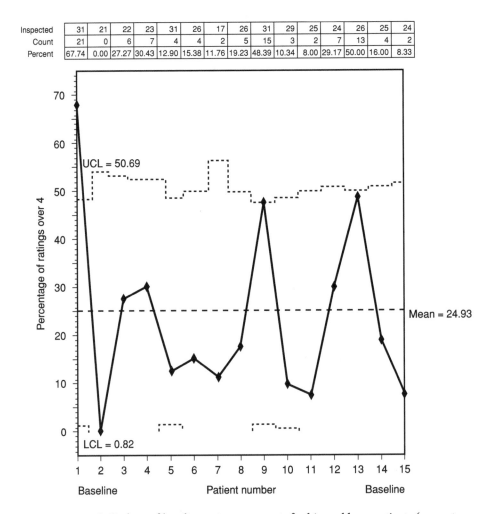

▲ **FIGURE 7.26** P-chart of baseline pain assessments for hip and knee patients (percentage of patients indicating that pain was greater than 4 on a scale of 0–10)

- Introduced pain management concepts in their established presurgical education program for hip and knee patients. This consisted of a presurgery orientation program as well as bedside education after the surgery. The content of these sessions helped the patients understand the different methods for managing pain and the different routes for the delivery of medications (e.g., epidural, PCA, oral medications, and injections).

- Created posters that were placed on the units informing the public of the hospital's commitment to effective pain management practices and outcomes.

- Instituted a pain interventions contract with the nurses (Figure 7.27). This was a direct effort to get the nurses to not only think about the pain management process and its components but also emphasize the importance of making a personal commitment to "change my practice in relation to pain control, specifically in the total joint patients." Each nurse on the unit was asked to sign the contract as a demonstration of their endorsement of this initiative.

PAIN INTERVENTIONS CONTRACT

Pain control is very important to our patients and a quality goal that is very important to the 2 North nursing staff. Therefore, as an RN on the 2 North team, I agree to change my practice in relation to pain control, specifically in the total joint patients.

1. **Pain assessment** will be done on my patients at least every four hours.
2. I will be **proactive** regarding pain—asking about pain levels on hourly checks and offering pain medications before the patient has to ask.
3. Total joint patients will **receive pain meds around the clock** (at a minimum, at bedtime, and at awaking in the morning) so that therapy and pain control can be obtained.
4. P.M. staff **will medicate for pain at the hour of sleep.** P.M. staff will also **script** "Would you like to be woken during the night when your next dose of pain medication is due?" If patient does not receive pain meds during the night, pain meds will be given when awaking in the morning or, at the very, with latest breakfast. This practice will increase the ability of our patients to be able to participate in physical therapy.
5. **Education** regarding around-the-clock pain meds administration will be done with my patients.

Signature of RN

Date

▲ FIGURE 7.27 Pain interventions contract

Once the interventions were in place and operational, additional data were collected to see if the percentage of patients indicating that their pain levels were over 4 had declined. Figure 7.28 shows the baseline period (patients 1–15) and the patient assessments of pain after the intervention (data points 16–41). The control limits for the baseline period were "frozen" and extended across the postintervention period. This was done in order to see if the intervention was able to produce a special cause (e.g., a downward trend or possibly a shift in the process). Figure 7.28 does not reveal that the process has changed, but there are two special causes (3-sigma violations) that need to be addressed (patients #29 and #34). Whenever there are data points that are markedly different from the rest of the data, it is useful to ask:

- Was there a data entry error?
- Is this a stratification problem (i.e., are these two patients different from the rest of the patients in the study)?

The team did not uncover any data entry errors. What the nurses did discover, however, was that these two patients were unlike the rest of the patients.[14] These two patients, therefore, were removed from the analysis and the p-chart was recalculated. The result is shown in Figure 7.29. Notice that in this figure there is a period after the intervention when the percentage of patients who indicated that their pain was greater than 4 is very similar to the baseline (i.e., compare patients 1–15 with patients 16–28 and you will see similar patterns of variation). Then an interesting thing happens. A special cause is detected from patient #29 to #39. This is a signal that there has been a shift in the process because 11 data points are below the centerline. You would not expect to see this many data points below the centerline if this was merely a random process.

Why did it take the process so long to respond to the interventions? Is this potentially another data entry problem, or could it be that the last 11 patients did not fit the profile of the previous patients? As the team discussed these questions, they arrived at several conclusions:

- The data were clean and the patients were very similar to those in the previous time periods.

- They had instituted four new interventions simultaneously (see discussion earlier in this section). Typically you would introduce one change at a time and evaluate the impact of that single improvement

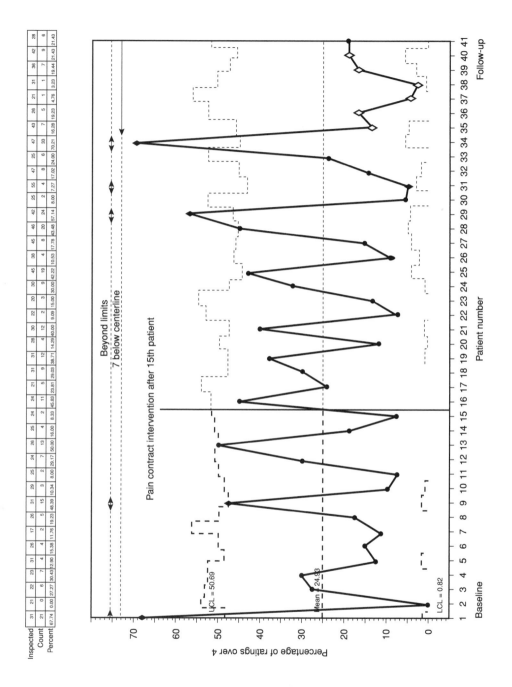

▲ FIGURE 7.28 P-chart of pain assessments for hip and knee patients before and after the intervention (control limits are based on data points 1–15, the baseline period)

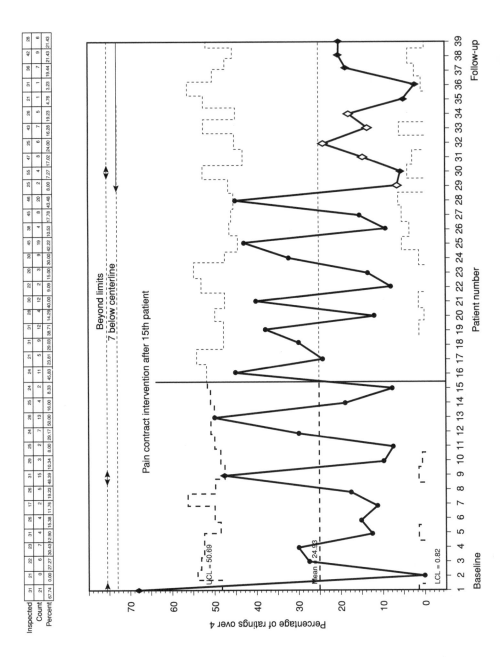

▲ FIGURE 7.29 P-chart of pain assessments for hip and knee patients before and after the intervention and removing patient #29 and patient #34 (control limits are based on data points 1–15, the baseline period)

strategy. This is the nature of the PDSA cycle. When you implement several changes simultaneously, however, it is hard to determine which intervention or combination of interventions caused the change in the process.[15]

- Several of the changes required behavioral adjustments on the part of the nurses and the patients. Because behavioral changes do not happen instantaneously, there is probably a lag effect when it comes to observing the impact of the interventions.

- Data points 16 through 28 represent a "learning curve" and therefore a transition phase after the intervention for both the patients and the nursing staff.

- The chart should be partitioned into three segments to reflect the baseline, the transition period, and the current process.

Figure 7.30 shows the process segmented into three defined sets of data. The left side of the chart (patients 1–15) shows the baseline with an average of about 25% of the patients reporting pain levels greater than 4. The middle section of the chart (patients 16–28) reflects the transition or learning period. The control limits during this period are not very different from the baseline, and the centerline is actually a little higher (26%) than the baseline. This is not uncommon for a period of transition, because people are adapting to new ways of behaving, which has a tendency to create more variation rather than less. These conditions are compounded when multiple interventions are implemented simultaneously. In this case, staff and patients are not sure of the expected behaviors. During periods of uncertainty and new learning, the process will typically display increased variation and/or instability.

Finally, the right side of Figure 7.30 (patients 29–39) reveals how the process has shifted to a new (and better) level of performance after the transition. During this phase the patients and staff appear to be settling into the new process. The real test of improvement will be if the average percentage of patients evaluating their pain levels greater than 4 stays at or below the new process average of about 15%.

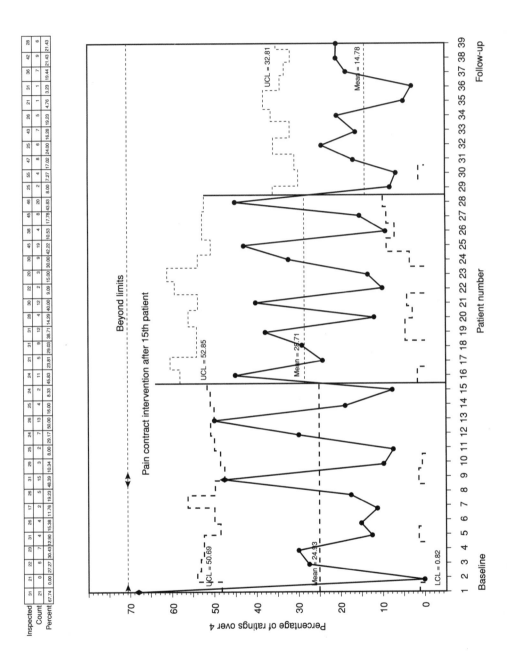

▲ **Figure 7.30** P-chart of pain assessments for hip and knee patients before and after the intervention and removing patient #29 and patient #34 (baseline [patients 1–15], after interventions [patients 16–28], and follow-up [patients 29–39] all have separate control limits)

Postscript

This case study encompasses nearly all the principles that I have been discussing in previous chapters. It started out with a concern for the VOC, specifically that staff observed dissatisfaction with the pain management questions on a patient satisfaction survey. It then moved to defining an indicator that would capture the VOC and a data collection plan. Once the data were collected, they proceeded to analyze the patient assessments on a p-chart (which was the correct chart for this indicator) and interpret the charts for common and special causes of variation. Finally, they tested their improvement strategies against a baseline to see if their interventions made a difference. At first they were a little discouraged because the improvement did not happen right away. But they soon realized that behavioral change does not occur overnight. The team is to be commended for applying the PDSA cycle, having constancy of purpose, and using data to make the right decisions.

Notes

1. Dr. Charles Derus, medical director of the Advocate Dreyer Medical Clinic, provided the idea and background for this case study and offered invaluable advice on the clinical steps involved in determining the need for a catheterization.

2. I want to thank Dawn M. Johnson, RN, BSN, performance improvement coordinator at Advocate Christ Medical Center (Oak Lawn, Illinois), for giving me the idea for this case study.

3. Bill Peters, manager of decision support at Delnor Hospital (Geneva, Illinois), called one day and posed this question. I thank him for the idea.

4. Connie Cutler, director of clinical excellence at Advocate Health Care's corporate office, took time to explain the background and history of this important topic and was kind enough to review an initial draft of this case study. As an aside, it should be noted that Advocate is actually working on this initiative and will be implementing improvement strategies before the year is over. The measurement plan will parallel what is described in this example.

5. Most control charting software will provide you with the option for presenting the data as a proportion or as a percentage. Remember, to convert a proportion to a percentage you merely multiply the proportion by 100. Thus the average proportion of nosocomial pressure ulcers in this figure is .241, which translates to 24.1% (.241 × 100).

6. I want to thank my good friend Connie Cutler for tutoring me on the subtleties of flash sterilization. She provided me with background reading on the subject and suggested guidelines for the frequency of occurrence of flashing instruments in the operating rooms. Like many aspects of healthcare, this is one of those topics that most people do not think about on a regular basis. It can have profound implications not only for process efficiency and resource allocation but also, and most importantly, for patient safety.

7. I want to thank Carol Burke, RN, Nancy Longino, RN, and Julie Marre, RN, from Advocate Good Samaritan Hospital in Downers Grove, Illinois, for sharing this case study with me and helping to develop the measurement plan and indicators. The potential seriousness of this situation requires a passion and commitment to break down barriers and make improvements. These women have met this challenge with great energy and spirit. They have spent numerous hours with me thinking through the logic of how the levels of stratification influence the various outcomes and spent after-work hours assembling data, analyzing control charts, and developing improvement strategies. I thank them for their dedication and willingness to share their story.

8. I also suggested to Carol Burke, RN, that she should consider tracking a new indicator—the percentage of pregnant women with positive GBS who deliver in less than four hours after arriving at the hospital. This indicator will help her understand if the volume of women who do not meet the criteria is actually increasing and potentially influencing the overall performance of this process. The last recommendation I had was that they should develop a Pareto diagram to document the reasons why the antibiotics were not delivered according to the protocol for those women arriving at the hospital four or more hours prior to delivery. The Pareto diagram will enable the team to focus in on the major reason(s) why the protocol is not working for the targeted population.

9. I want to express my thanks to Jeanne Dore, RN, from Advocate Good Samaritan Hospital (Downers Grove, Illinois) for the idea to prepare this example. Jeanne and her team are working on improving their own fast track process. She was very helpful in providing background information on this topic. The data do not come from Good Samaritan's fast track. I created these data for heuristic purposes.

10. If the conditions creating an equal area of opportunity for a complaint changed (i.e., there were wide swings in the daily volume of patients and/or the severity and mix of patients changed constantly), then the chart of preference would be the u-chart. The u-chart would provide a complaint rate where we would have the number of complaints as the numerator and the number of visits as the denominator. This would produce a complaint rate (i.e., the number of complaints per 100 or 1000 patient visits).

11. I had the pleasure of working with Bonnie Schleder, critical care–clinical nurse specialist, and K. Stott, intensive care unit registered nurse, on this project. Our preliminary findings were presented in the *Journal of Advocate Health Care* 4, no. 1 (Spring/Summer 2002): 27–30. Because this journal is an internal publication, copies of the detailed report can be obtained from Bonnie Schleder at Advocate Good Shepherd Hospital (847-381-9600). An updated version of this initial research will be published in *Nursing Management* in the fall of 2003. I also want to thank the ICU staff for their support of this initiative and Eileen Yaeger, clinical epidemiologist, and Lori Pinzon, quality improvement specialist, for data analysis and technical support.

12. Regrouping the data by quarter was necessary in order to provide a sufficient number of occurrences to legitimately construct a control chart. Because it is preferable to have about 20 data points for a control chart, this regrouping produces a chart with fewer data points than desired. When a chart is made with fewer than 20 data points, the control limits are referred to as "trial control limits." As more data become available, the limits will become more reliable and predictability will be increased.

13. I want to thank Susan Herrmann, RN, MS, clinical specialist, medical/surgical unit, Marjie Schoolfield, RN, BSN, OCN, and William

Peters, MA, health care data analyst at Delnor-Community Hospital (Geneva, Illinois) for this case study. They have been very vigilant in applying quality measurement principles and tools to this initiative. They have also been generous in devoting time to explain to me the steps they have taken to track their indicators, interpret the charts, and make improvements. Bill Peters did a very good job of constructing the charts and partitioning the data to demonstrate the points I wanted to make with this case study. Congratulations to all of you for a job well done.

14. Because these are individual patients I am not revealing the specific factors that each patient possessed.

15. There are methods to test the simultaneous effects of multiple variables on a process. The technique is known as design of experiments (DOE) and is frequently used in manufacturing (Sloane 1997). Other approaches involve the development of causal models (Blalock 1971) and multiple regression models (Kerlinger and Pedhazur 1973; Namboodiri, *et al.* 1975). These methods have a great deal of utility in addressing healthcare issues.

References

Blalock, H. (ed.). *Causal Models in the Social Sciences.* Chicago: Aldine, 1971.

Fitch, J. A., C. Munro, C. Glass, and J. Pellegrini. "Oral Care in the Adult Intensive Care Unit." *American Journal of Critical Care* 8, no. 5 (September 1999): 314–318.

Joint Commission on the Accreditation of Healthcare Organizations. *Comprehensive Accreditation Manual for Hospitals: The Official Handbook.* Oak Brook Terrace, IL: 2003.

Kerlinger, F., and E. Pedhazur. *Multiple Regression in Behavioral Research.* New York: Holt, Rinehart and Winston, 1973.

Namboodiri, N., L. Carter, and H. Blalock. *Applied Multivariate Analysis and Experimental Designs.* New York: McGraw-Hill, 1975.

Sloan, D. *Using Designed Experiments to Shrink Health Care Costs.* Milwaukee: Quality Press, 1997.

Chapter 8

Connecting the Dots

"Transformation is required to move out of the present state, metamorphosis, not mere patchwork on the present state of management."
W. Edwards Deming

Most children like to engage in the connect-the-dots activity. It is a great way to help a child see the relationship of apparently disparate dots and the image that can emerge if they connect the dots correctly. Organizational success is not unlike this popular childhood activity. If individuals and organizations take time to deliberately think about the various factors (the dots) that affect their futures and then make the linkages between these factors, they will not only be able to adapt to change but they will also be able to proactively harness the changes and manage them to their benefit.

From my perspective the dominant changes facing the healthcare industry will be centered on the following key topics:

- More public scrutiny of the healthcare profession by people who are not trained as clinicians
- Increased demand on the part of patients to become more involved in making decisions about their care and treatment
- Declining trust in the medical community
- Less autonomy and income for physicians
- Increased pressure to create safe environments for the delivery of medical services
- Greater demand for the release of data related to cost, quality, service, access, and safety
- Renewed focus on containing healthcare costs

But how does an industry that seems to be characterized more by fragmentation than integration connect all the factors related to these pressing changes? It seems to me that there are several rather straightforward strategies that we can take. First, connecting the dots requires an understanding of the forces that have brought us to this point in time. These issues were summarized in Chapter 1 and will not be reviewed further in this chapter.[1] Second, healthcare providers need to move away from the old fragmented ways of thinking about quality and begin to see quality as a central operating strategy.[2]

Understanding the Dots

Deming provided an extremely valuable framework for not only understanding the dots but also describing how they should be connected. Deming's system of profound knowledge (Schultz 1994; Langley *et al.* 1996) defined four components that form the basis of CQI and organizational transformation:

- Systems thinking (how all the parts fit together)
- Theory of knowledge
- Understanding variation
- Psychology (human behavior)[3]

He made it very clear that all four components need to be in place in order to have quality permeate the entire organization. Proficiency in one or even two of the components will not transform an organization. Although this book has focused primarily on one aspect of profound knowledge, understanding variation, skill in making control charts and being able to explain the technical aspects of performance measurement will not achieve excellence unless this knowledge is integrated with the other three components.

Peter Senge, in laying out the components of a "learning organization," has developed a framework that is very similar to what Deming has defined as profound knowledge. Senge's classic work *The Fifth Discipline* (1990) and the companion book *The Fifth Discipline Fieldbook* (Senge *et al.* 1994) explore the interrelationships between the following disciplines:

- Systems thinking
- Personal mastery
- Mental models
- Building shared vision
- Team learning

Senge wastes no time in stating his basic premise. On page 4 of *The Fifth Discipline* he writes: "The organizations that will truly excel in the future will be the organizations that discover how to tap people's commitment and capacity to learn at <u>all</u> levels in an organization." The fact that organizations have historically not approached learning in this way has been a major reason, according to Senge, that most organizations die before they reach the age of 40.

Although neither Deming nor Senge specifically addresses how their conceptual frameworks can be applied to healthcare, the implications are obvious and direct. They can be of tremendous assistance in understanding the dots. How the dots get connected is up to you. I believe that three levels of transformation are needed in order to make healthcare organizations more like the ones described by Deming and Senge. These include personal, organizational, and societal transformation.

Personal Transformation

Despite what many might say or think, organizations do not change. They have no inherent life of their own. What changes within an organization are individuals who in turn create the collective intent (energy) that allows the entity known as the organization to adapt (or not adapt) to internal and external factors. All change begins and ends with the individuals within the organization. Deming's notion of psychology or human behavior and Senge's discipline of personal mastery are central to personal transformation. Personal mastery, according to Senge, is the discipline of continually clarifying and deepening our personal vision, of focusing our energies, of developing patience, and of seeing reality objectively (Senge 1990:7). The specific components of personal mastery are very similar to what Covey refers to as *The Seven Habits of Highly Effective People* (1989).

But how do we motivate people to excel, change, or take pride in their work? There are basically two lines of thinking around this question. One camp would argue that individuals respond to extrinsic motivation, and the other would argue that intrinsic motivation is the key. The extrinsic motivational group is grounded in the theories and work of Pavlov and Skinner (see Chapter 2). It relies on the basic notions of behavior modification. Simply stated, the underlying assumption of extrinsic motivation is that you can get people to change their behaviors through a series of rewards, bonuses, or incentives. Similar to what Pavlov discovered with his salivating dog, this approach assumes that people will be motivated by what Alfie Kohn calls "rewards, gold stars, incentive plans, A's, praise and other bribes" (1993).

In sharp contrast to the extrinsic camp are those who believe that the workers are intrinsically motivated to achieve excellence (Peter and Hull 1970; Kohn 1986, 1993; Covey 1989; Senge 1990; Deming 1992; Briskin 1998). Proponents of this approach (including this author) maintain that it is management's responsibility to create an environment in which individuals can become self-actualized and engage in personal mastery. If such an environment does not occur, then it reflects a problem with management and the vision that management has for the employees and the organization.

Where do you find yourself on this continuum between extrinsic and intrinsic motivation? Do you believe that your employees are intrinsically motivated and will strive for excellence on their own? Or do you think that the workers must be watched and directed by management? How much micromanagement occurs within your organization? Are the employees coming to work and enjoying each day, or do they dread putting on their clothes and coming to work? Do you offer incentives and rewards for doing what is expected? Finally, have you set up structures and processes that enable the workers to:

- Take pride in what they do?
- Have independence in making decisions about their work?
- Grow and have new experiences?
- Know that they are part of a larger system of events?

Figure 8.1 provides a little self-test on the subject of motivation. There are 15 factors listed that are frequently identified as possible motivators. This list contains both extrinsic and intrinsic motivators. Select 10 of these items that are important to you. Then rank order the 10 items you selected with 1 being the most important motivator and 10 being the least motivating.[4] What factors did you rank as being most important? What was the #1 factor? According to Key (2003), most employee surveys rank extrinsic motivators (coming from outside the worker) as inferior to intrinsic ones (i.e., doing something for the sheer pleasure of it). Hertzberg (1987) refers to the extrinsic motivators as "hygiene" factors (e.g., working conditions, salary, status, supervision, and working relationships) and intrinsic factors as true "motivation" factors (e.g., achievement, recognition, responsibility, and the nature of the work). He classifies the hygiene factors as "satisfiers," which would cause worker dissatisfaction if they were absent. This would be similar to not being offered a chair, silverware, and water when you go to a restaurant. These factors can be viewed as basic expectations. The real motivational factors are those that fuel the intrinsic desire to strive for excellence.

From this list of potential motivating factors select the 10 statements that are most important to you. Then rank order these 10 factors with 1 being the highest motivator for you personally and 10 being the least motivating factor.

____ Recognition

____ The opportunity to contribute, to serve, to produce quality

____ Status/title

____ A paycheck

____ Feeling part of a team

____ The opportunity to learn, advance, and grow

____ The opportunity to get an annual bonus or incentive check

____ Benefits

____ Self-esteem

____ Managing a large number of employees

____ Freedom for creative expression

____ Feeling that your work is important

____ A manager who does not micromanage your work

____ Being told that you make a difference

▲ FIGURE 8.1   A self-test of motivating factors in the workplace

Peter and Hull (1970) described very clearly what happens to people when they are not motivated and fully integrated into the organization—they suffer from the Peter Principle. This principles states that "In a hierarchy every employee tends to rise to his level of incompetence" (1970:7). Peter and Hull follow with a related principle: "Work is accomplished by those employees who have not yet reached their level of incompetence" (10). They continue in the analysis of the employee–organization relationship by stating that "in most cases of incompetence, there appears to be a definite wish to be productive. The employee would be competent if he could. Most incompetents realize, however dimly, that the collapse of the organization would leave them jobless, so they try to keep the hierarchy going" (89). The type of organizational environment described by Peter and Hull is very different from the one envisioned by Deming and Senge.

Deming frequently talked about finding "pride in work." Several of his 14 points of management address these issues (Scherkenbach 1990, 1991). Roberts and Sergesketter (1993) build on Deming's ideas by laying a foundation for personal transformation and total quality management. In their book *Quality Is Personal,* they state: "Quality as practiced by the individual is the foundation on which Total Quality management is built. Quality is based on the actions of people. Total Quality management cannot exist without people in an organization understanding and practicing the principles of quality at a personal level" (1993:xiii).

As a demonstration of how such thinking can be incorporated into an organization's vision, Roberts and Sergesketter reference Bob Glavin, former CEO of Motorola, in an address to the Economic Club of Chicago:

> We have operated very substantially under the rubric of quality control. Our institutions, our companies have had quality departments. And the old testament was that quality is a company, a department, and an institutional responsibility. The new truth is radically different. Quality is a very personal obligation. If you can't talk about quality in the first person . . . then you have not moved to the level of involvement of quality that is absolutely essential. You must be a believer that quality is a very personal responsibility. (1993: xiii)

Roberts and Sergesketter describe the use of personal quality checklists as a way to start taking stock of the role that quality plays in your own life.

They even provide examples of how they have initiated their own checklists to improve the following quality behaviors:

- Showing up for meetings on time
- Finding misplaced items
- Returning phone calls or responding to letters in a timely manner
- Getting rid of junk mail
- Unnecessary inspection of daily activities
- Blood pressure management

The authors skillfully connect personal quality to the identification of key indicators (see Chapter 3), the practice of benchmarking (see Chapter 4), and the use of control charts (see Chapter 6). I believe everyone interested in enhancing their own understanding of quality needs to add *Quality Is Personal* to their reading list. Roberts and Sergesketter not only set the context for defining quality but also provide a very clear argument as to why personal transformation lies at the very heart of all quality improvement.

Personal transformation in the area of performance measurement has been the focus of this book. The best way to improve your skills and knowledge in this arena is to apply the concepts and tools described in this book on a regular basis. To assist you in developing your own learning plan, I have developed a measurement self-assessment tool (Figure 8.2). This self-assessment is designed to help you gain a better understanding of where you *personally* stand with respect to explaining or demonstrating various performance measurement topics and tools. What would your reaction be if you had to explain enumerative versus analytic studies? Can you construct a run or control chart and interpret it? You may not be asked to do all of the things listed in Figure 8.2 today or even next week. But whether you are leading, facilitating, or a member of a quality improvement team, sooner or later these questions will be posed. How will you deal with them? The place to start is to be honest with yourself and see how much you know about measurement. Once you have had this period of self-reflection, you will be ready to develop a learning plan for self-improvement and advancement. The measurement issues listed in Figure 8.2 cover two major categories: theoretical topics and tools/techniques. Because you need to be able to blend theory and technique together to be truly successful at measurement, I have not divided the items into categories. The order of the items follows the steps you would

Topic/Tool	Response
Scale	
1 I could teach this topic to others	
2 I could do this by myself right now but would not want to teach it	
3 I could do this but I would have to study first	
4 I could do this with a little help from my friends	
5 I'm not sure I could do this	
6 I'd have to call in an outside expert	
Explain the "quality measurement journey" (i.e., when does measurement begin and when does it end?)	1 2 3 4 5 6
What are quality characteristics (QCs) and why should I be concerned about them?	1 2 3 4 5 6
What is the difference between the voice of the customer and the voice of the process?	
How are they related?	1 2 3 4 5 6
How do I select one key quality characteristic (KQC) out of all possible QCs?	1 2 3 4 5 6
Construct and explain a Pareto chart	1 2 3 4 5 6
Can you make and explain a detailed flow chart?	1 2 3 4 5 6
How are you at critiquing a detailed flow chart?	1 2 3 4 5 6
What are the major components of a data collection plan?	1 2 3 4 5 6
Explain the difference between a simple random sample and a stratified random sample	1 2 3 4 5 6
How do you use a random number table?	1 2 3 4 5 6
Make a presentation on understanding variation	1 2 3 4 5 6
Who cares about the difference between enumerative and analytic studies? Do I care?	1 2 3 4 5 6
So what's wrong with collecting data for a day and using this to understand the variation in a process?	1 2 3 4 5 6

▲ FIGURE 8.2 Measurement self-assessment tool

Topic/Tool	Response
Scale	
1 — I could teach this topic to others	
2 — I could do this by myself right now but would not want to teach it	
3 — I could do this but I would have to study first	
4 — I could do this with a little help from my friends	
5 — I'm not sure I could do this	
6 — I'd have to call in an outside expert	
Show a team how to construct a run chart	1 2 3 4 5 6
Where do the four run tests come from?	1 2 3 4 5 6
Why do 6 data points constantly increasing (or decreasing) constitute a trend? This seems like a lot of data to me. Why not 3 or 4 data points in a row?	1 2 3 4 5 6
Can you explain the difference between common and special causes of variation? Give examples?	1 2 3 4 5 6
Why can't I improve a process that contains special causes? Aren't we supposed to make things better? Now you tell me I can't until I get rid of these special causes!	1 2 3 4 5 6
CQI, SPC, UCL, LCL, CL — it all sounds like alphabet soup to me! Who cares and why are you being so compulsive about making me follow this "quality roadmap"? I can tell you what is wrong with the process. Why do I need to go through all of this? It is wasting time!	1 2 3 4 5 6
How do you know when to use a control chart?	1 2 3 4 5 6
What is the difference between variables and attributes data?	1 2 3 4 5 6
What is a subgroup and how would I know one if I tripped over it?	1 2 3 4 5 6
When do I use a u-chart? A c-chart?	1 2 3 4 5 6
What is a "sigma" anyway? And how does it differ from a standard deviation?	1 2 3 4 5 6
Why do we use 3-sigma limits? Why not 2 or 2.75 sigma units?	1 2 3 4 5 6
Can you determine when data are normally distributed? If the data are not normally distributed, can you proceed with making a control chart?	1 2 3 4 5 6
Can you explain why you can (or cannot) make a control chart on an individual employee's performance?	1 2 3 4 5 6

▲ FIGURE 8.2 continued

typically take in conducting any improvement initiative. For each item listed, use the scale shown at the top of the page to record your responses. Although some of the items do have right or wrong answers, many of them are open to interpretation. What you have to do is to determine the level of expertise you wish to have in the measurement area, figure out which topics/tools you need to understand more thoroughly, and then outline a plan for how you will reach this goal.

In addition to honing your measurement skills, I also believe that presentation skills are important. At some point in the quality journey you will be asked to present the results of your CQI initiative. Although being comfortable with standing up in front of people and actually making a presentation is a skill that comes with experience, there are a number of simple tips that can enhance your presentations. Figures 8.3 through 8.7 provide examples of graphics that are clearly labeled and annotated. Figure 8.8 provides tips that I have found useful in actually making presentations before groups. Whenever I am at a conference or attending a seminar, I am listening for content and observing the presenters. You can learn a great deal by watching others present and teach. The trick is to evaluate what you think they did well and what they could have improved. The other central point about making presentations is that you have to find your own rhythm, tempo, and style. I have seen numerous people try to copy the presentation style of someone else and fail gloriously. Learn from others but present in a fashion that is true to your own style. A good reference on this topic is Frederick Mosteller's article "Classroom and Platform Performance" (1980).

For those of you who are genuinely interested in furthering your skills in this area, I would strongly recommend the work of Edward Tufte, a professor at Yale University who teaches classes in statistics, graphic design, and political economy. I first attended one of his public seminars in 1993. I enjoyed it so much that I attended another one in 2000. His books, *The Visual Display of Quantitative Information* (1983), *Envisioning Information* (1990), and *Visual Explanations* (2000) are not only extremely rich in content but also three of the best-designed and formatted books I have ever seen. Tufte provides a historical review of how numbers have played a central role in human development. He provides examples that range from Charles Joseph Minard's classic depiction of Napoleon's ill-fated march to Moscow in 1812 (which Tufte claims may well be the best statistical graphic ever drawn) to graphical tables that were used successfully to get John Gotti acquitted in 1987. One of Tufte's most famous examples of how data were statistically and graphically misinterpreted involves his analysis of the space shuttle Challenger. He clearly shows how NASA and Morton-Thyokol had all the data to show beyond a shadow of a doubt that the O-rings would fail under the conditions that prevailed on launch day. The problem was that the engineers and scientists never looked at the data in the correct way. To use Tufte's terms, they never "envisioned" what the data were trying to tell them.

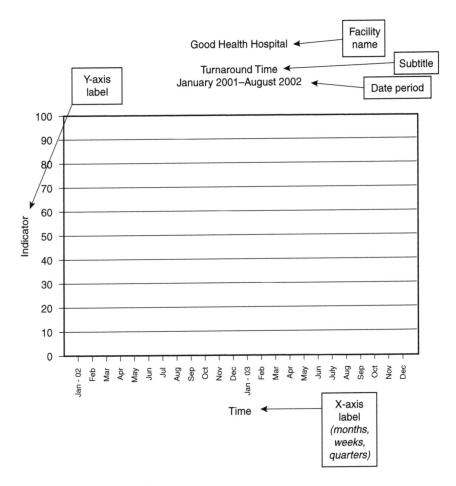

▲ FIGURE 8.3 Tips for labeling a chart

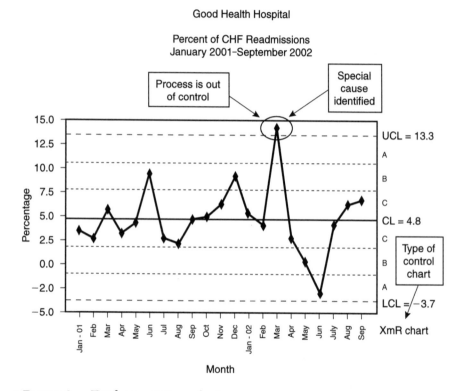

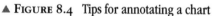

▲ FIGURE 8.4 Tips for annotating a chart

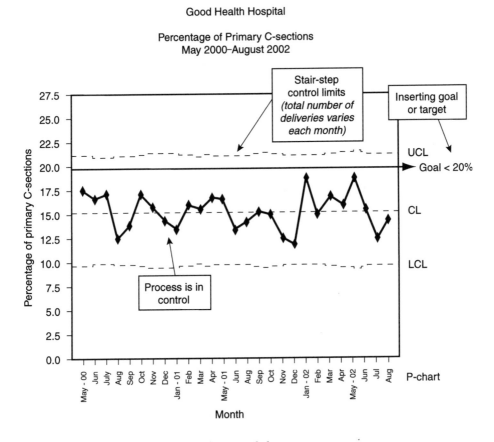

▲ FIGURE 8.5 Tips for interpreting the control chart

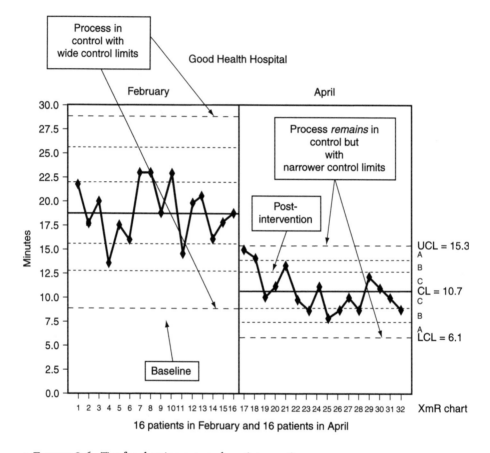

▲ FIGURE 8.6 Tips for showing pre- and postintervention

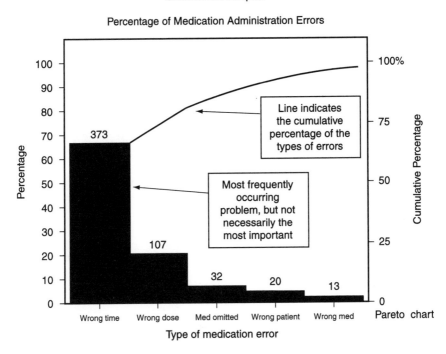

▲ FIGURE 8.7   Tips for presenting a Pareto diagram

- Be prepared (know your material and be ready for "showtime")
- You will succeed or fail on the integrity of your message and content
- Show up early to check out the room and meet people as they drift in
- Don't read your overheads or slides—your audience knows how to read
- Tell people how you have organized your presentation and any ground rules for questions and group participation
- Never apologize to your audience!
- Respect your audience (they are the reason you exist)
- Listen to questions and encourage discussion (if time permits)
- Be truthful ("I don't know, but I'll look into that" is preferable over some contrived half-truth)
- Use humor to highlight your content but be sensitive to what the audience will tolerate (you are not a stand-up comic)
- Drink plenty of water (avoid a lot of coffee)
- If you are giving a half day or day-long presentation, plan several breaks
- Take the first morning break between 60 and 75 minutes (morning coffee)
- Be alive—demonstrate energy and passion for your subject matter
- Don't stand in front of the overhead or block it with your shoulder
- Never leave the overhead on without a transparency on it (it's blinding)
- Dress appropriately for the audience and the circumstances
- Maintain a verbal flow without using "and ahh," "you know, like," etc.
- Change your tempo to emphasize key points or lessons
- Listen to yourself on tape or watch a video of your presentation
- Work the audience and get as close to them as you can (avoid podiums)
- End early

▲ FIGURE 8.8 Tips for making good presentations

Organizational Transformation

Personal transformation is the starting point for organizational transformation. As individuals adopt new ways of thinking, they create the potential for change. The role of leadership is to harness this potential and direct it for the benefit of the entire organization. This is essentially what the Baldrige criteria are designed to capture. The amount of literature on organizational change and leadership is legion. I do not intend to review what others have addressed at length.[5] My purpose in this section is to review several of the key organizational factors that I believe help an organization transform from the old ways of thinking about quality to the new ways described in this book.

Creating a "quality" organization requires more than merely establishing process improvement teams and developing control charts. Research has suggested, for example, that management, not technology, is the key to developing a quality culture and organization. Figure 8.9 provides a starting point for evaluating the priority that your organization places on quality. This checklist identifies a number of issues that senior management needs to address if they are serious about promoting and fostering quality throughout the entire organization. Two evaluations are required in this exercise. The first is an assessment of the current status of each item, and the second is the future priority assigned to each issue. Your responses to this organizational self-assessment should provide the basis for a dialogue on where quality currently stands within your organization and the future needs for enhancing your strategic view on quality. The next step after completing this brief exercise would be to engage in a more formal self-assessment. Participating in your state's quality award process or conducting a Baldrige self-assessment will provide a fairly rigorous assessment of your organization's quality readiness.

In Chapter 1 I identified a number of organizational ingredients needed to foster quality. These points are revisited in more detail below. They should serve as a guide to assist the organization in moving from a strategic view of quality to a more tactical focus.

- A commitment to quality starting with the board and senior management (e.g., a quality committee of the board and a chief quality officer who is a member of the senior management team)
- A strategically defined role for quality (a role that is equally as important as the other major organizational functions such as finance, human resources, business development, information systems, and clinical care)

For each item, you should make two responses. First, indicate the **current status** of each item within your organization by marking one of the following responses:

- Completed (C)
- In process (IP)
- Not started (NS)

Then assign what you believe will be your **priority** for each item over the coming twelve months by marking one of the following responses:

- High (H)
- Moderate (M)
- Low (L)

Issue	Current status			Future priority		
	C	IP	NS	H	M	L
1. Evaluating your organization's mission, vision, and values to make sure that they are consistent with CQI principles.						
2. Educating the following groups in the theory and tools of CQI: • The board • Managers • Physicians						
3. Restructuring your performance evaluation system so that it supports your efforts in continuous improvement.						
4. Working with suppliers to establish long-term partnerships that are based on collaborative efforts to improve quality.						
5. Providing employees with the support and resources they need to measure and improve quality.						
6. Setting up process improvement teams.						
7. Creating a process to set priorities for selecting quality improvement initiatives.						
8. Developing performance indicators of quality improvement initiatives.						
9. Preparing communication tools that share information on quality goals and initiatives with all associates.						

▲ FIGURE 8.9 Issues and priorities for healthcare leaders

- A model upon which to build (e.g., profound knowledge and the PDSA cycle)
- A plan for CQI deployment throughout the entire organization (it will not happen by chance or good intentions)
- CQI education and training (formal and informal opportunities to create what Senge (1990) calls a learning organization)
- A measurement philosophy and the related tools needed to track performance
- Procedures and structures for managing quality teams (e.g., a quality council to charter teams, review progress, and sponsor quality initiatives)
- Internal quality resources and consultants (e.g., dedicated staff trained in quality theory, methods, tools, and facilitation techniques as well as resource materials such as reference books, training films, and quality journals)
- A formal mechanism designed to celebrate quality and excellence (e.g., an annual quality day celebration, a "quality corner" in the organization's news magazine, or a designated site on the organization's intranet that provides information on quality-related activities)

When the strategic and tactical components are brought together, quality simply becomes the way an organization does its daily work. Figure 8.10 provides a template to help an organization move from strategy to implementation tactics. It is what I call laying the groundwork. This template is a combination of the Indicator Development Form© (Chapter 3) and the control chart applications discussed in Chapter 6. All the milestones you will encounter along your quality measurement journey are identified on this form. It also serves as a checklist to see if the team has been able to successfully progress through the various stages of process improvement.

One of the hospitals in my system provides a very good example of how an organization can combine strategy and tactics to deploy quality throughout the organization. Advocate Good Samaritan Hospital (Downers Grove, Illinois) has developed what they refer to as the Performance Improvement (PI) Showcase. Each month the CEO and the management team, along with directors and managers, gather for three hours to review recent improvement initiatives. The objectives of the PI Showcase include:

Instructions

Central to the success of any continuous quality improvement (CQI) initiative is a team's ability to integrate quality measurement principles and practices into an overall plan of action. This exercise is designed to assist you in this process. Specifically, you are asked to think about the material presented in this book and then outline how you would apply the principles and techniques to an improvement opportunity within your organization. Try to be as specific as possible when answering the questions.

1. Please identify the *process* that needs to be improved. Be as specific as possible. Remember that the more specific you are, the greater the chances of demonstrating actual improvement. Frequently teams select processes that are entirely too broad or too complex. When this happens, the teams usually become frustrated because they are either not making progress or they are unable to demonstrate tangible improvements. Also identify the *boundaries of the process* (i.e., when it begins and when it ends). If you cannot agree on the boundaries, it will be extremely hard to move forward.

   - The *process* to be improved is . . .

   - This process *begins* when . . .

   - And *ends* when . . .

▲ FIGURE 8.10 Laying the groundwork

2. Who is the *primary customer* of this process? This is the person or group that receives the output of the process. The primary customer is typically the patient. But the primary customer can also be the physicians, nurses, or other employees. The answer to this question is not always readily apparent. Sometimes it is helpful to identify not only the primary customer but also the *secondary customers*.

   - Identify the *primary customer(s)* . . .

   - Secondary *customers* include . . .

3. What does the primary customer value most about this process? What aspect of this process does the primary customer use to judge quality? The answers to these questions should enable a team to list the customer's *key quality characteristics* (KQCs).

   What are the *KQCs of the customer(s)?*

   - _____
   - _____
   - _____
   - _____

4. Many different indicators can measure a KQC. For example, if you selected "reducing medication errors" as your KQC and the patients are your primary customers, what would you measure about medication errors? For example, you could count the *number* of medication errors or the *percentage* of medication errors, or you could compute a medication error *rate*. All three of these possibilities measure different concepts. Deciding upon the specific indicator to measure is the first major step in the quality measurement journey.

   What is the specific *name* of your indicator?

   _____

▲ FIGURE 8.10 continued

5. Now that you have selected an indicator, the next major challenge is to develop an *operational definition*. If we return to the medication error example, we would need to specify exactly what constitutes a medication error. Is it wrong dose, wrong patient, wrong time, wrong route, dose omitted, and/or dose repeated? Or is it some other combination of criteria? Poorly constructed or vague operational definitions are one of the major reasons measurement efforts frequently fail. Remember to include a full definition of the indicator with all inclusions and exclusions. Specify the numerator and denominator of a percentage and the components of any indicator based on a rate. Finally, specify all the required data elements (e.g., patient types, financial classes, types of drugs or tests, data dictionary elements, DRGs, medical record codes, or clinical specialties to be included).

Our indicator (name the indicator)_____
is operationally defined as . . .

6. Once an indicator is operationally defined, the next step is to outline the *data collection plan*. In this case, you need to answer the following questions:

   - **What type of data did we just define?**
     Attributes data _____   or   Variables data _____

   - **Who will be responsible for actually collecting the data?** All too often there are assumptions made about who is responsible for collecting the data but there is no definite plan that specifies the individuals involved.

▲ FIGURE 8.10 continued

- **What will be the frequency of data collection?** That is, how often will the data be collected (e.g., every hour, every day, or once a week)?

- **What is the duration of data collection?** In this case, you need to think about when data collection will be initiated and when it will end (i.e., how long will you collect data?).

- **What are the primary data sources for these data?** Name the sources of data and where these data sources can be found.

- **What method will be used to collect the data?** Method refers to the procedures or processes that will be used to collect the data. Another way to think of this step is to consider the plan for gathering the actual data. If you were collecting turnaround time for lab tests, for example, would you use the data collector's wristwatch for the time, the clock on the lab wall, or the automated clock that records the time when the order is entered into the computer? All three methods could produce different turnaround times.

▲ FIGURE 8.10 continued

- **Will you employ a sampling plan?** If so, what type of sampling design will you use? Will you use a simple random sample? A stratified random sample? Or possibly a judgment sample? Will it require replacement sampling? Identify the type of sampling plan you will use and the specific components of the plan.

  The sampling plan will include (mark as many as appropriate):
  _____ Convenience sampling
  _____ Quota sampling
  _____ Mechanical sampling
  _____ Simple random sampling
  _____ Stratified random sampling
  _____ Proportional, stratified random sampling
  _____ Judgment sampling
  _____ Replacement sampling

7. Is there a current *baseline* for this indicator?
   Yes _____ No _____
   (Remember that a baseline represents the actual *current* measure of the indicator. It is not what you want it to be or what you expect the process to produce. It is simply what the process currently produces.)

   If yes, what is the time period from which the baseline is obtained?

   _____

   What is the actual baseline value?

   _____

8. Is there a *target* or *goal* for this indicator?
   Yes _____ No _____

   If yes, is this target or goal:
   Internally developed _____ or *Externally* required _____?
   In either case, specify the actual values associated with the target or goal:

   _____

▲ FIGURE 8.10 continued

9. Groups often get so involved with the data collection phase of indicator development that they forget to spend time discussing what they plan on doing with the data once they have collected it (i.e., develop an analysis plan). Initially, it might be useful to analyze the data with *descriptive statistics* to determine how closely the data reflect a normal distribution. This is particularly helpful if you have collected a sample and you are curious to see if the sample adequately represents the larger population. Once you have looked at measures of central tendency and measures of dispersion, you are ready to move on to control chart analysis.

What descriptive statistics will you use?

Measures of Central Tendency
_____ Mean
_____ Median
_____ Mode

Measures of Dispersion
_____ Minimum
_____ Maximum
_____ Range
_____ Standard deviation

10. There are five basic control charts that could be applied to your indicator. Indicate below which one you will use for this indicator and why you selected it.

Variables Charts
_____ X-bar & S chart
_____ XmR or Individuals chart

Attributes Charts
_____ c-chart
_____ u-chart
_____ p-chart

• Why did you select this chart over the other possibilities?

• What is your *subgroup?*

If you selected one of the *variables charts,* how many *observations* will be selected for each subgroup?
_____ one observation per subgroup   _____ a constant number of _____
                                                                  observations
_____ a variable subgroup size

If you selected one of the *attributes charts,* is the *area of opportunity* for a defective or defect _____ equal or _____ unequal?

▲ FIGURE 8.10 continued

11. Finally, it is important to consider who will receive this data analysis and how often it will be produced.

- Describe the *process for disseminating the control chart results.* Who will receive the output of this process? Will the results be shared with the board? The quality improvement council? Or will they be widely distributed through public postings of the control charts and/or on your organization's intranet?

- How often will you update the data and distribute reports? _____ Daily _____ Weekly _____ Monthly _____ Quarterly

- Are there any confidentiality issues associated with these data that require an IRB (Institutional Review Board) review? Do HIPAA guidelines affect these data?

  IRB review?   _____ Yes   _____ No   _____ Not Sure

  HIPAA compliance?   _____ Yes   _____ No   _____ Not Sure

  Describe any issues that need to be resolved:

This exercise has been designed to help you lay the groundwork for indicator development, data analysis, and dissemination. It should also help you figure out which steps in the quality measurement journey seem easy and which ones will require more work. Just as a dancer must practice both the easy and difficult steps over and over in order to become skilled, you, too, must practice the various steps in the measurement process in order to improve. As you practice these steps you will become more skilled at the practice of measurement.

▲ FIGURE 8.10 continued

- To operationalize our value of "Excellence" and our CQI philosophy
- To focus the organization on quantitative quality and service improvement
- To foster an environment where cross-department dialogue regarding improvement projects is strongly encouraged
- To recognize and celebrate achievements and positive results
- To provide presenters with an opportunity to learn and improve their presentation and CQI skills

Staff from the quality management department provide technical support for the teams while I serve as facilitator and coach. We have set up just-in-time (JIT) workshops on indicator development (using the Indicator Development Form© described in Chapter 3), the laying the groundwork form (Figure 8.10), control chart theory and construction, and how to make presentations. A standardized template for summarizing each team's work is used to create consistency in the presentations. Each team is asked to describe:

- The quality opportunity
- The indicator being covered (only one indicator is presented by each team)
- The operational definition of the indicator
- The data collection plan
- The results (usually shown in control chart format)
- The action plan

Frontline staff members as well as managers make the presentations. Each presentation takes approximately 10 minutes. For me, this is a highlight of each month. The PI Showcase is part education, part celebration, and total inspiration. It provides a wonderful example of how an organization can engage in both personal and organizational transformation.[6]

Societal Transformation

In Chapter 1 the history of healthcare reform from 1965 to the present was discussed. Specific social as well as economic pressures affecting the delivery of healthcare services were reviewed. What was not discussed, however, was a very fundamental question—what do we want our healthcare system to achieve? Several key issues stem from this question.

The Cost/Quality Debate

It is not uncommon to see the following title (or some variation of it) listed as either the theme of a healthcare conference or at least a breakout session during the conference: "Low Cost/High Quality: A Tradeoff or a Possibility?" When healthcare became a concern of the business and manufacturing communities back in the late 1970s, the debate was strictly over cost and quality. During those days the debate was couched as alternatives along a continuum. In the 1980s the debate became a little more sophisticated, and 2 × 2 matrices became a popular way to show four alternatives (Figure 8.11). The desired state of affairs was to have providers fall into the lower left cell (high quality and low cost). But was this a reasonable assumption? Do other industries offer products and services that fall into this cell? World-class automobiles, designer clothing, and even glamorous vacations do not fall in the high quality/low cost category. Is it possible to have low cost and high quality healthcare services?

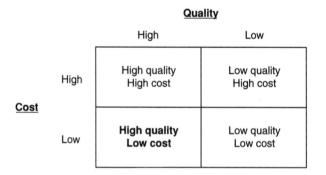

▲ FIGURE 8.11   The quality/cost matrix

Who Gets What?

The second issue has to do with access. I do not think I will surprise anyone by stating that the U.S. healthcare system is a multitiered system. People with insurance have greater access to services than do those with no insurance. The most recent estimates indicate that roughly 41 million people in this country have no health insurance or inadequate coverage. The majority of these people are not homeless people living on the street but rather the working poor. We also know that some people overuse healthcare services and others (e.g., most males) are healthcare avoiders. What this means in terms of healthcare policy is that the equation has changed. No longer are we dealing with two variables (cost and quality). At a minimum, the equation now consists of three variables: cost, quality, and access. Is it possible to maximize all three? Most healthcare economists say that it is not. In some instances it might be possible to optimize one or two of these variables, but simultaneously maximizing all three, especially at the national level, is next to impossible. From a statistical perspective, these three variables form a highly interactive simultaneous equation (Hu 1973; Namboodiri *et al.* 1975) in which all the direct and indirect effects of these three variables on the dependent variable (in this case the general health of the nation's population) must be considered together. Such a system is depicted in Figure 8.12. Each of the three variables has a direct effect on the health of the nation's population. Each variable also has a direct effect on the other two and a combined effect. For example, there is a direct effect of cost on access and a combined effect of the two of these together on the health of the nation. Some of these effects are directly measurable (e.g., dollars spent on healthcare). Others, however, are more elusive (e.g., the impact on society of the death of a small child because her family did not have the money to obtain needed medical treatments). These losses are what Deming (1992) called the "heavy losses."

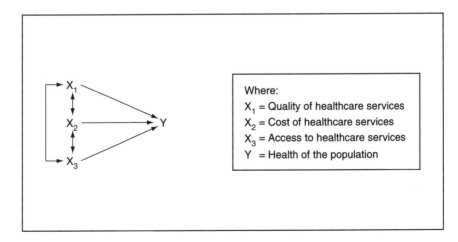

▲ FIGURE 8.12 The interaction of quality, cost, and access

A Right or a Privilege?

This issue is one of the more serious questions our nation needs to answer. Unfortunately, it is one that remains elusive. Is healthcare a right or a privilege? Stated in economic terms, is healthcare a public or a private good? Most people think that healthcare is a right rather than a privilege. They also believe that there should be unlimited access to healthcare services. Yet the way in which our healthcare system is structured, financed, and delivered makes it more of a privilege than a right. From an economic perspective healthcare is more of a private good (i.e., one that is based on the purchaser's ability to pay, like buying a car) than a public good (i.e., services that are available to all, like access to a public park). Our nation seems to be very ambivalent about the very nature of healthcare. The government pays for a sizable portion of the nation's healthcare bill, yet we have not been able to craft a consistent healthcare policy for the nation. Cuts are made in the Medicare and Medicaid programs while the politicians continue to argue that the elderly and the poor need to have greater access to healthcare services. We need to encourage a healthy debate on what we want this nation's healthcare system to accomplish. Do we want it to make sick people well, prevent people from becoming ill, or increase the quality of life for people who are already in good health? There is no doubt that this country has a very good healthcare system. The key question is how can we make it even better and simultaneously deal with the interaction of cost, quality, and access?

In this chapter I have tried to outline three key factors that I believe are critical to the expansion of quality thinking and practice in healthcare: personal transformation, organizational transformation, and societal transformation. Organizations that are successful in charting their quality journey will be ones that understand the high-level policy issues that are transforming our industry, the technical details surrounding performance measurement, and the importance of human behavior. They will have succeeded in connecting the dots.

Notes

1. In 1982 Paul Starr's classic work *The Social Transformation of American Medicine* outlined the challenges facing the U.S. healthcare industry. Michael Millenson (1999) and the two Institute of Medicine (IOM) reports published in 1999 and 2001, respectively, continued

this historical review. If you have not read these works, I would strongly recommend that you do so. Not only will these books help you understand the forces that have brought us to this point in time but they will also reinforce the simple fact that our healthcare industry is in the midst of rapid and profound change and that the forces influencing our industry will continue into the foreseeable future.

2. It has been argued by many that we really do not have a healthcare system in this country but rather a sickness system. The system is very good at treating people once they become ill is but not as efficient when it comes to preventing illness (Horowitz 1988; Inlander 1988; Millenson 1999). The way in which financial incentives have been structured in this nation has also contributed to this situation (i.e., the highest reimbursements are provided when people are placed in the hospital).

3. It is interesting to note that the Baldrige criteria, Six Sigma, and ISO all can be mapped directly to the four components of Deming's profound knowledge concepts. This is certainly not an accident. There has been a direct and intentional effort over time to establish all quality systems around the teachings of Shewhart, Deming, and Juran. Not only has the American evolution of quality been grounded in the work of these three scholars but the Japanese advancements in this field can also be traced back to their teachings, especially those of Deming and Juran. Ishikawa, Taguchi, and Kano, for example, all credit their understanding of the "new quality" to the basic teachings of Deming, Juran, and their contemporaries. Readers interested in learning more about both American and Japanese leaders of quality should read *Profiles in Quality* by L. Schultz (1994).

4. I want to thank my friend and colleague M. K. Key, Ph.D., for the ideas that led to me making this exercise. Each month Dr. Key posts on her Web site a publication called *KEYZINE,* which is an e-zine for "Leaders: About the People Part of Business." In the July 2003 issues (volume 28), she addresses issues related to pride in work. One of the tips she offers is a list of 11 potential motivators for workers. I used her basic list and then added to it to produce the exercise shown in Figure 8.1. I would suggest registering for this practical resource. Dr. Key's Web site is *www.mkkey.com.*

5. Several books that I have enjoyed on the subject of organizational change include Wheatley (1992), Lundin and Lundin (1993), Bellman (1996), Rosenbluth and Peters (1998), Tichy (1990), Hock (1999), Pritchett (1999), and Knox (2000).

6. Although everyone at Advocate Good Samaritan Hospital deserves credit for the success of the Showcase, I want to recognize several individuals who have played central roles in its creation and support. Bill Santulli was the chief executive (CE) of the hospital when the PI Showcase was first conceived. Bill was recently promoted to be the COO of the Advocate Health Care. The new CE, David Fox, continues to support and lead the showcase. Without their leadership and vision the PI Showcase would never have been initiated and sustained. On the support side, Marlene Bober, manager of quality and utilization review, and her staff in the quality management department and Sandy Churchill, director of clinical excellence, have been central to the process. They not only provide technical support but also serve as motivational leaders for the frontline staff, managers, and directors. Congratulations to all of you for sponsoring Excellence.

References

Bellman, G. *Your Signature Path: Gaining New Perspectives on Life and Work.* San Francisco: Berrett-Koehler, 1996.

Briskin, A. *The Stirring of the Soul in the Workplace.* San Francisco: Berrett-Koehler, 1998.

Covey, S. *The Seven Habits of Highly Effective People.* New York: Simon & Schuster, 1989.

Deming, E. "Quality, Productivity and Competitive Position." A four-day seminar presented by Dr. Deming. Indianapolis: Quality Enhancement Seminars, Inc., August 11–14, 1992.

Hertzberg, F. "One More Time: How Do You Motivate Employees?" *Harvard Business Review* (September/October 1987): 109–120.

Hock, D. *Birth of the Chaordic Age.* San Francisco: Berrett-Koehler, 1999.

Horowitz, L. *Taking Charge of Your Medical Fate.* New York: Random House, 1988.

Hu, T. *Econometrics: An Introductory Analysis.* Baltimore: University Park Press, 1973.

Inlander, C., L. Levin, and E. Weiner. *Medicine on Trial.* New York: Prentice Hall, 1988.

Institute of Medicine. *To Err Is Human.* Washington, D.C.: National Academy Press, 1999.

———. *Crossing the Quality Chasm.* Washington, D.C.: National Academy Press, 2001.

Key, M. K. "On Pride in Work." *KEYZINE* 28 (July 2003): *www.mkkey.com.*

Kohn, A. *No Contest: The Case Against Competition.* Boston: Houghton Mifflin Co., 1986.

———. A. *Punished by Rewards: The Trouble with Gold Stars, Incentive Plans, A's, Praise, and Other Bribes.* Boston: Houghton Mifflin Co., 1993.

Knox, P. *The Business of Healthcare.* Appleton, Wis.: PrintSource Plus, 2000.

Langley, G., K. Nolan, T. Nolan, C. Norman, and L. Provost. *The Improvement Guide.* San Francisco: Jossey-Bass, 1996.

Lundin, W., and K. Lundin. *The Healing Manager: How to Build Quality Relationships and Productive Cultures at Work.* San Francisco: Berrett-Koehler, 1993.

Millenson, M. *Demanding Medical Excellence: Doctors and Accountability in the Information Age.* Chicago: University of Chicago Press, 1999.

Mosteller, F. "Classroom and Platform Performance." *The American Statistician* 34, 1 (1980):11–17.

Namboodiri, N., L. Carter, and H. Blalock. *Applied Multivariate Analysis and Experimental Designs.* New York: McGraw-Hill, 1975.

Peter, L., and R. Hull. *The Peter Principle.* New York: Bantam Books, 1970.

Pritchett, P. *New Work Habits for a Radically Changing World.* Plano, Tex.: Pritchett Rummler-Brache, 1999.

Roberts, H., and B. Sergesketter. *Quality Is Personal.* New York: The Free Press, 1993.

Rosenbluth H., and D. Peters. *Good Company.* Reading, Mass.: Addison-Wesley, 1998.

Scherkenbach, W. *The Deming Route to Quality and Productivity.* Washington, D.C.: CEEPress Books, 1990.

———. *Deming's Road to Continual Improvement.* Knoxville, Tenn.: SPC Press, 1991.

Schultz, L. *Profiles in Quality.* New York: Quality Resources, 1994.

Senge, P. *The Fifth Discipline.* New York: Doubleday/Currency, 1990.

Senge, P., R. Ross, B. Smith, C. Roberts, and A. Kleiner. *The Fifth Discipline Fieldbook: Strategies and Tools for Building a Learning Organization.* New York: Doubleday/Currency, 1994.

Starr, P. *The Social Transformation of American Medicine.* New York: Basic Books, 1982.

Tichy, N., and M. A. Devanna, *The Transformational Leader.* New York: Wiley, 1990.

Tufte, E. *The Visual Display of Quantitative Information.* Cheshire, Conn.: Graphics Press, 1983.

———. *Envisioning Information.* Cheshire, Conn.: Graphics Press, 1990.

———. *Visual Explanations.* Cheshire, Conn.: Graphics Press, 2000.

Wheatley, M. *Leadership and the New Science: Learning About Organization from an Orderly Universe.* San Francisco: Berrett-Koehler, 1992.

Index

Entries marked in **bold** identify key terms and concepts used in this book.